"Sometimes problems are disagreeable, and it is impossible to do as one would wish. But law should offer an opportunity to decide, to act responsibly with the best intention. Speaking of the supreme command, Adams makes this case clearly."

Vice Admiral Tim Barrett, *AO, CSC, Royal Australian Navy (ret'd)*
Chief of Navy 2014–2018

Politics and the General in Supreme Command

This book argues for reform of the convention that, when politicians decide on a course of action, the general in supreme command obeys without question.

The entire spread-out chain of command is unified in the general, who offers the only connection between the military and politics. Offering the sole connection between the military and politics, only the general can turn political directions into military command and capacitate war. Thus, the general has unique opportunity to resist unconscionable direction to launch an unjust war or to conduct or expand war unjustly. This book argues for reform, so the general has the right in law to refuse direction which is lawful, but awful. The legal capacity to refuse would mean the general would be expected to act responsibly, not merely as the unresisting pawn of politics. Such reform, creating legal opportunity for the supreme command to refuse lawful but unconscionable directives, might avert unjust war.

This book will be of much interest to students of the ethics of war, civil-military relations, and international relations.

Richard Adams is a commander in the Royal Australian Navy. He has doctorates from the University of Western Australia and the University of New South Wales. He was an Australian Fulbright scholar to Yale University and a visiting research fellow to the Changing Character of War programme at the University of Oxford.

War, Conflict and Ethics
Series Editors:
Michael L. Gross
University of Haifa
and
James Pattison
University of Manchester

Ethical judgments are relevant to all phases of protracted violent conflict and inter-state war. Before, during, and after the tumult, martial forces are guided, in part, by their sense of morality for assessing whether an action is (morally) right or wrong, an event has good and/or bad consequences, and an individual (or group) is inherently virtuous or evil. This new book series focuses on the morality of decisions by military and political leaders to engage in violence and the normative underpinnings of military strategy and tactics in the prosecution of the war.

Law, Ethics and Emerging Military Technologies
Confronting Disruptive Innovation
George Lucas

Ethics at War
How Should Military Personnel Make Ethical Decisions?
Deane-Peter Baker, Rufus Black, Roger Herbert and Iain King

Military Necessity and Just War Statecraft
The Principle of National Security Stewardship
Edited by Eric Patterson and Marc LiVecche

Warfare Ethics in Comparative Perspective
China and the West
Edited by Sumner B. Twiss, Ping-cheung Lo, and Benedict S. B. Chan

Just War Thinkers Revisited
Heretics, Humanists and Radicals
Edited by Daniel R. Brunstetter and Cian O'Driscoll

Politics and the General in Supreme Command
Law Reform and Averting Unjust War
Richard Adams

For more information about this series, please visit: https://www.routledge.com/War-Conflict-and-Ethics/book-series/WCE

Politics and the General in Supreme Command

Law Reform and Averting Unjust War

Richard Adams

Routledge
Taylor & Francis Group
LONDON AND NEW YORK

First published 2025
by Routledge
4 Park Square, Milton Park, Abingdon, Oxon OX14 4RN

and by Routledge
605 Third Avenue, New York, NY 10158

Routledge is an imprint of the Taylor & Francis Group, an informa business

British Library Cataloguing-in-Publication Data
A catalogue record for this book is available from the British Library

ISBN: 9781032865096 (hbk)
ISBN: 9781032865232 (pbk)
ISBN: 9781003527886 (ebk)

DOI: 10.4324/9781003527886

Typeset in Times New Roman
by codeMantra

Contents

Acknowledgements

Over the course of this project, I have benefitted from the kindness, encouragement, and advice of many people. Sometimes support was significant and sustained. On other occasions a chance remark or a brief exchange was constructive. I am deeply grateful to everyone who helped.

I owe a special debt to my beautiful wife and my wonderful children. I cannot express my appreciation for their love, patience, unflagging support, and inspirational example.

I offer warm thanks to Geoff Morris, a scholar and a gentleman, who read the proof and improved an unattractive manuscript.

I thank Vice Admiral Tim Barrett and Commodore Tim Brown. These officers placed their confidence in me, and I owe them a debt of gratitude.

Finally, Deane-Peter Baker and Rob McLaughlin have been attentive, insightful, and professionally critical. I thank them warmly.

Richard Adams

Preface

This book comes from my concern that, after decades of unjust war, not a single reformist voice is heard. Just as *fin de siècle* politics failed, so modern statecraft falls short. Military power is understood imperfectly and used too readily. Behind the scenes, the heedless rush to avoidable, unwinnable war is aided and abetted by illiberal laws. These laws devitalise the supreme command and force the general to comply. This book argues for reform of those laws.

Richard Adams

1 Introduction

It is normal for law to insist soldiers fight when they are ordered to by legitimate authority. Some soldiers might feel strongly the war they are ordered to fight is morally impermissible. These soldiers are in a tight corner. Should they abide by the deep registers of conscience and refuse service in war they believe to be morally impermissible – in a word, unconscionable – or should they follow a legal order?

By and large, there are two established arguments. The first is by Vitoria. In his 1539 meditation "On the Laws of War," Vitoria said:

> If the war seems patently unjust to the subject, he must not fight, even if he is ordered to do so by the prince. This is obvious, since one may not lawfully kill an innocent man on any authority, and in the case we are speaking of the enemy must be innocent. Therefore it is unlawful to kill them.[1]

Accepting individuals are accountable for their deeds and unable to transfer the burdens of responsibility to others, where the justice of a conflict is dubious and the likelihood of unjust commands sufficiently great, one may have a right and a duty to refuse.[2] In broad terms the conventional and opposing view maintains that soldiers should follow legal commands from a proper authority. By conventional lights, soldiers do no wrong so far as they abide by *in bello* conditions, since they are not liable for *ad bellum* injustice.

But whilst there has been debate concerning soldiers confronted with war they find unconscionable, insufficient attention has been given to the special case of the supreme commander – the general – but also the admiral or the air chief marshal serving as Chief of the Defence Force.

In a dictionary, "supreme" is defined in terms of "the highest in rank or authority," "paramount, sovereign, chief," or "of the highest quality, degree character or importance." Only one officer can be in supreme command, at the top of the heap. In supreme command the general serves in ways soldiers do not. The general is trusted in ways soldiers are not. The general bears responsibilities ordinary soldiers never bear. The general serving in supreme command offers the only connection between the military and politics. Only the general might turn political direction into military command and thus initiate the acts of war or expand a war in an unjust

DOI: 10.4324/9781003527886-1

way. And only the general might resist political transgression and forestall unjust war. For ordinary soldiers, remote from politics and much less influential than the general, the decision to fight can be made only *after* the decision to go to war, *after* the mechanisms of war have begun to act. But the general might act in the calm before the storm.

Removed from the tumult and convulsion of the fight, the general has the time and space to reflect, to deliberate, to take advice. Thus, the citizens might trust the general in distinctive ways. Some citizens serve as soldiers; they are junior to the general and trust their lives will not be wasted in political folly. Other citizens are civilians; they trust the general to safeguard the blood and treasure of the nation and to avoid unconscionable wars.[3]

In this book I argue for reform of the convention, made explicit in section 8 (2) of the Australian *Defence Act*, which says: "the Chief of the Defence Force must comply with any directions of the Minister." I dispute that law and the conventions, routines, and assumptions collateral to law might insist on unquestioning obedience and force the general's conscience. Taking from the Martens forms, I propose law recognise the general bears an obligation to comply with direction of the Minister "except when direction is unconscionable, infringing the laws of humanity or the dictates of public conscience." The word "except" gestures to a legal exception or exemption. An exception is the first and normal way for law to accommodate individual moral sense and judgement.[4] It is by means of an exception that human conscience and judgement are integrated within the law. Thus, asking for an exception I ask that law should allow the general to exercise conscientious decision *inside* the terms of the law. To put this another way, I ask law to release the general from the burden of conscientious objection, which is a breach of law for the reason that moral scruple or conscience prohibits observance of a legal condition.[5]

I offer the Australian *Defence Act* as an explicit example. Redrafted in July 2016,[6] section 8 (2) of the *Defence Act* stipulates: "the Chief of the Defence Force *must* comply with *any* directions of the Minister [emphasis added]." But beyond the specifics of Australian law, the extended relevance of this book is conspicuous in any democracy: what does the general do when politics directs some legal but unconscionable act? The record of the Second World War demonstrates how important it is for law to offer the general a way to navigate political direction which is lawful but awful. Following Article 8 of the *Charter of the International Military Tribunal*: "the fact that the Defendant acted pursuant to [the legal] order of his Government or of a superior shall not free him from responsibility [for unconscionable conduct]" *Ceteris paribus*, the general should not do what he believes to be unconscionable, and law should not force him to infringe the deep registers of conscience.

I do not contend for open-ended reform. I propose only that the general have the right in law to *refuse* unconscionable direction. I do not dispute that those who fight should have the moral authorisation of the community[7] – an authorisation which is furnished by formal, legitimising, political authorities. I do not claim generals ought to be able to begin military action on their own initiative, and I do not claim the general should be immune from consequences or, in some way, above the law. I recognise that when a general believes he cannot be relieved, the quality of the civil-military discourse suffers, and with it the effectiveness of strategic decision-making,[8] and I recognise that the general who refuses unconscionable political direction would likely be relieved.[9] I accept the civil power must hold the reins, and I propose only that law should offer the general the right to refuse unconscionable direction.

My proposal then, is not dramatic, but I go further than orthodox doctrine made explicit in the *Defence Act*, that soldiers should refuse "manifestly illegal" direction.[10] And I go further than the Australian common law, so far as it was observed by Gibbs CJ in *A v. Hayden* (1984)[11] that

> it is fundamental to our legal system that the Executive has no power to authorise a *breach of the law* and that it is no excuse for an offender that he acted [illegally] under the orders of a superior officer.[12]

Similarly, and in the same case, Murphy J held:

> in Australia it is no defence to the commission of a *criminal* act or omission that it was done in obedience to the orders of a superior *or the government*. Military and civilians have a duty to obey *lawful* orders, and a duty to disobey *unlawful* orders.[13]

My proposal asks law to offer the general space to refuse direction which is unconscionable – lawful but awful.

If my proposal is not dramatic, neither is it a panacea. My proposal does not mean states will never use force unjustly. When the general and the government share an unethical position, my proposal will have no impact at all. My proposal has a practical bearing only when the general's conscience, being attuned to right, serves as an alarm to injustice.

Soldiers and Generals

Political theory, like theories of value, theories of ethics, theories of art, theories of language, and theories of religion depends upon assumptions about *people*.[14] I assume the citizens who serve in the armed forces are – or should be – conscientious, or morally concerned. I suppose these people want to behave responsibly in an all-things-considered sense. And I presume that a reasonably good society – which I suppose takes the form of a liberal democracy – wants people in the armed services to behave responsibly. But for soldiers and generals, the idea of responsibility connotes quite different things.

Very often, modern philosophy asks us to consider a soldier fighting an unjust war. Supposing he is not under threat, so that firing his weapon is not self-defence, he is killing soldiers on the opposing side, who have done nothing wrong, as a means of achieving unjust aims. *Prima facie*, killing in an unjust war is morally problematic.[15] But it is easy to see how a soldier might fight and be excused, even if the cause is unjust.[16] Normally, soldiers fighting a technically unjust cause believe their war is morally permissible.[17] Soldiers are often young; they are trained – coercively – to unquestioning obedience. They are acculturated so as they *feel*, when they are obedient, that they do the right thing.[18]

Reasonably, we might suppose soldiers do not think too deeply about the statutory lawfulness or the objective *ad bellum* rightness of war. And even if soldiers contemplated war's rightness, there is little they might be able to do; they cannot, for example, dispute with the minister. Perhaps a soldier who held conscientious concerns might express moral unease and disinclination to fight to a commanding officer. In this case it is possible the conscientious soldier would be relieved from duty or discharged – or worse. Flight Lieutenant Malcolm Kendall-Smith offers an example. A conscientious objector to war in Iraq, Kendall-Smith, a doctor in the Royal Air Force, was court-martialled. Making Kendall-Smith's conscience his crime, the court-martial imposed a sentence of imprisonment.[19]

In short, we might accept as Augustine has it, that the soldier owes a duty of obedience and is merely an instrument of politics.[20] We might accept, as David Estlund says, that:

> When the political and institutional process producing the commands is duly looking after the question whether the war is just, the soldier would be wrong to substitute his own private verdict and thwart the state's will. [Of course, we must remember that] these preconditions are substantial, and the soldier will need to think for himself about whether they are met. The soldier is not exonerated simply because he was following orders. [However] when the state and its procedures are of the right kind the soldier's participation in an unjust war is sanitized precisely because he was following orders.[21]

Estlund has the soldier, like the jailer, low down the pecking order, required to imprison a person whom he knows to be innocent. Estlund says, the jailer can be permitted and required to leave the job of judging and sentencing to others, such as the judge and jury, and simply be the jailer.[22]

But where Estlund is right to observe the positional obligation of soldiers to obedience,[23] and right to imply that political institutions *tend* to get things right – even if they do not *always* get things right,[24] he is mistaken to assume the plausibility of a soldier determining if or not the conditions necessary for objectively just war are met.[25] The jailer can rely upon the processes of open justice: hearings in public court, the open presentation of evidence, and the rights of defendants to appeal. This is why jailers are not permitted to follow their private judgement and let prisoners go free. The outcome of a democratic procedure – an independent judiciary, an open trial, an appeal process – has a certain irreproachable authority and acceptability.[26]

Soldiers are less advantaged than jailers. As to the *jus ad bellum*, soldiers will not know much more or less than the public who read newspapers and watch television news. Soldiers cannot know all the complex and secret political factors which inform the justice of the cause. The general in supreme command is different.

For the general, duty demands more than obedience. For the general, responsibility involves more than compliance with the law. Accepting that responsibility in the basic sense is an ability to offer justifications and excuses, to explain oneself, to give a realistic account of oneself as a rational being,[27] it seems implausible the general might be responsible, conscientious, or morally attentive and say: "I obeyed the law, though I knew obedience was morally wrong."

Thinking of the general in supreme command, I am contemplating the intersection of politics and the military. I do not contemplate the confusion of a battlefield. I contemplate the general receiving unconscionable direction from politics by telephone, text, e-mail or verbally in a comfortable meeting room or office.[28] I contemplate the general removed from face-to-face conflict like Eichmann, described at his trial by the Israeli Attorney General Gideon Hausner, killing when he lifts the telephone or by his signature.[29] But bureaucratic routine and physical distancing from conflict do not diminish responsibility. Eichmann was responsible:

> As if it was he who with his own hands knotted the hangman's noose, who lashed the victims into the gas-chambers, who shot in the back and pushed into the open pit every single one of the millions who were slaughtered. Such is his responsibility in the eyes of the law, and such is his responsibility according to every standard of conscience and morality. His accomplices in the crime were neither gangsters nor men of the underworld, but the leaders of a nation....[30]

Very senior and widely experienced, generals are typically educated highly. They are graduates of universities and military colleges. Generals are well placed, as ordinary soldiers are not, to see a war might be strictly legal, "just" in a technical statutory sense, and yet unconscionable. And generals are well placed to act, as ordinary soldiers cannot, to occlude unjust war proposed by politics. On my account, a reasonably good society will facilitate the general's moral withstanding. Thus, I ask us to reconsider the relation of politics and the general in supreme command.

Politics and Generals

The relationship between soldiers and states is an important feature of Western philosophy and politics, because the military enjoys tremendous coercive power. This is a power which might be misused; turned against the host society, or misapplied in some other way.[31] Since the military has power sufficient to overthrow the government, and since the state depends upon the military to an exceptional degree, the usual position has been that the military must be obedient without question. Offering the Ford lectures at Oxford in 1943, Admiral Sir Herbert Richmond said, "generals with their armies and admirals with their fleets are mere weapons to be wielded by the hand of the statesman."[32]

Richmond offers an overture to argument made notable by Samuel Huntington who said, "when the statesman decides on a course of action the soldier [general or not] does not question but obeys instantly."[33] Since Huntington made this claim, thinking around civil-military relations has not progressed dramatically.[34] According to Eliot Cohen, Huntington defines the theoretical standard, the "normal" theory of civil-military relations. For James Dubik, Huntington enjoys a dominant influence and defines the conventional paradigm of civil-military relations.[35]

The presumption of unquestioning obedience is overt in Australian legislation and underlined in the Australian case law where, following the case of *Coutts* (1985),[36] politics enjoys an unquestioned and total power over the military. Beyond the law, belief that the general in supreme command will be obedient without demurral resonates in the conventions, practices, etiquettes, and assumptions concerning the relation of the military to society.

Made express in the Australian legislation, convention holds the general must obey politics, even when consequences seem flagrantly heinous, appalling beyond description. So long as direction from the civil power is legal, the soldier has an unqualified obligation to obey.[37] The commonplace view holds that the civil power trumps the military view. Following durable orthodox argument, politics must be obeyed even at the risk of national security.[38] Elected politicians have a right to be wrong, and the general is bound by executive direction even when this direction is "dumb" or "foolhardy."[39] We are provoked to recall the soldiers in Shakespeare's *Henry V* [IV: i]:

> KING HENRY V [In disguise and going amongst the troops in camp at Agincourt, in order to size up the army's morale before battle]: [M]ethinks I could not die any where so contented as in the king's company: his cause being just and his quarrel honourable.
>
> MICHAEL WILLIAMS [a soldier]: That's more than we know.
>
> JOHN BATES [a soldier]: Ay; or more than we should seek after; for we know enough if we know that we are the king's subjects: if his cause is wrong our obedience to the king wipes the crime of it out of us.[40]

In this book, I reject the claim that politics and the military are utterly separate and fundamentally apart and that strategy begins where politics ends. I do not think that when politics decides on a course of action the general should obey without question.[41]

I argue that politics and the military share a co-operative partnership. Yet, whilst I accept that the civil power enjoys primacy, I dispute Peter Feaver's argument that the primary function of the civil power is in oversight of the military; monitoring, auditing, and punishing waywardness.[42] On my view, Feaver is insufficiently sympathetic to the moral commitment of the citizens who offer military service. Following Seth Lazar, I recognise the special moral status of people, which is grounded in our rational capacity to make our own choices for our own reasons, and I argue that people – even generals – are not mere tools for the realisation of value.[43]

Sensitive to the political gravity and moral onus immanent to war, Eliot Cohen described the sometimes uncomfortable, contentious, collaborative relationship between the military and politics, in which politics has the upper hand.[44] On Cohen's account it is unrealistic to expect politics, which launched a war, to remain disinterested in war[45] and naïve to expect the military to remain unconcerned by or disinterested in politics. We can't just wish away all the problems of civil-military relations by claiming that the military will obey politics no matter what.[46] In Cohen we are reminded of Clausewitz's dictum: war is a political instrument, a continuation of political intercourse, carried on with other means. What remains peculiar to war is simply the peculiar nature of its means.[47] For Clausewitz, war and politics are not separate and unconnected. For Clausewitz, war and politics are inseparable: political objectives determine military objectives and the requisite effort.[48] Likewise, Marshal Foch argued that there is nothing more absurd than the notion that the general works on one side of a barrier whilst the politicians and diplomats work the other.[49]

This is not to deny the subordination of the military to politics, but rather to assert the need for relationship, deliberation, and wrangling. Citing Clausewitz, Foch says war is not routine, strictly according to doctrine without inconsistency and paradox.[50] Usually, though not always, political considerations will over-ride the claims of the military. Normally, we accept military sacrifices in the name of larger goals, and we expect the military to be obedient to the civil power. But we must allow for exceptions. When we say the military should be obedient to the civil power, we must mean responsible obedience, sensible partnership, working together, joint effort, and a common goal.[51]

Rightly, the military has a subordinate place to the civil power. But subordination does not come without limits. Subordination does not rise to the level of unequivocal servility, or irresponsible moral docility. It does not seem sensible that legislation compels the general to follow political direction which is "foolhardy;" the sort of reckless venturesome direction, which would imperil the nation's security, occasion unjust war, expand an extant war in unjust ways, waste lives in a needless squander, or lead to some other grievously bad outcome.

Inevitable Dilemma

On occasion law might force the general to command a war which, by the general's lights, is morally impermissible. Since institutional seniority shrinks moral discretion, the general is in a tight corner.[52] The general's duty to be obedient to the executive is in plain, inflexible legal terms. Since this duty is of the utmost stringency, the regrettable outcomes of legal compliance are not normally thought to be the personal responsibility of the general, but rather the impersonal responsibility of the state.

The tension between private conscience and public duty is obvious and challenging. Public institutions and public order would be endangered were people to disregard prescribed duties. Yet, the constraints people accept in positions cannot be absolute, the unconditional disallowance of moral choosing. Reasonably, people might not duck moral responsibility by claiming they were merely obedient to the laws. On occasion, morally right action will contravene the terms of official duty.

By my lights, on occasion a person must have the courage to obey the dictates of conscience. On my account, the collective does not inoculate the individual against moral responsibility. As Kimberly Brownlee has it, terms like "the law," "the state," and "the government," downplay the extent to which the formal institutions of society are run by people who are subject to morality, and whose actions call for moral justification.[53]

Positional obligations are not irrelevant and cannot just be cast off. Most of the time, positional obligations should intern private moral preference, but not all the time. Individual moral obligation is not ended by the imperatives of politics or law, and no formal role might reasonably require people to forebear from first-order moral reasoning. *In extremis*, since democracy depends upon people prepared to resist institutional injustice, law should make moral withstanding feasible. For states, and for the general, the stakes are high.

Structure of the Book

In Chapter 2 (*What's Been Said*) I overview literature which addresses "combatants," or "soldiers," or "the military." Making these terms orthodox, scholarship makes all soldiers the same, and anonymous. But the general in supreme command is obviously and emphatically a singular figure, charged with particular responsibilities and, unlike all the other "military men," not face to face with the adversary.

The general, and the character of important supporting legal structures have escaped the attention of scholarship which tends to debate the particular *in bello* rightness of actions in the confusion of a gunfight, or the general *ad bellum* justice of war. In Chapter 3 (*War and Law*) I explain that where most analysis of law, war, and morality concerns provisions of the law of armed conflict – or perhaps international human rights law – my emphasis is on domestic law.[54] Notably, the trials at Nuremberg, made the connection between domestic and international law personal in the general. At Nuremberg, generals who complied with domestic law to abet political leaders in the enactment of unconscionable war were found responsible as the perpetrators of international crimes, not as minor accomplices.[55] Rawls sees connection between the international and the domestic law, since just institutions underpin just societies, which in turn contribute to global justice.[56] Serving as Secretary of State, General George Marshall made this point before the General Assembly of the United Nations in 1948. Marshall said: governments which "disregarded the rights of their own people were not likely to respect the rights of other nations and other people and were likely to seek their objectives by coercion and force in the international field."[57]

The international law of armed conflict (known also as the law of war or the international humanitarian law) aims to limit the harms of conflict, especially the suffering of innocents caught in hostilities.[58] Boiled down to shorthand expression in rules of engagement, the law of armed conflict aims to offer soldiers down-to-earth guidance (rules of engagement are printed on cards carried by soldiers). For Adil Haque: *in the midst of conflict* when time is short and calculations are complicated, when the consequences of getting things wrong are ghastly, the law of armed conflict provides combatants with guidance, so they might better meet their moral obligations.[59] But I am not concerned with the *in-bello* acts or practices *of* war. My concern is with decisions which put war into effect. I am concerned with moments before the fighting, with the calm before the storm, and with the domestic law that governs these moments.

Following Joseph Raz, law is the only human institution claiming unlimited authority. The legitimacy of law is categorical.[60] But without a moral accommodation law will find itself at odds with the citizens. In Chapter 4 (*Liberalism and Law*) I recognise foundational ideas of liberalism and law, and the balance point which defines the relationship of citizens to the state. On one side is power the citizens rightly reserve to themselves, on the other side there is sovereign power claimed by the state.

I explain the relationship of citizens and states by reference to the foundational theories of Hobbes and Locke. Where Hobbes emphasised the dependent and politically subordinate status of citizens, and the unchallengeable power of law, Locke acknowledged the inalienable rights inherent in citizens as people. Locke declined to accept the Hobbesian conclusion that people might be unreservedly subject to sovereign power. For Locke, government did not have unfettered authority. In the twentieth century, Lockean ideas fundamental to liberal democracy, received fresh impetus from John Rawls, who numbered an independent conscience among freedoms elemental to justice in society, and the natural right of every person.

In Chapter 5 (*Conscience*) I recognise the constitutional power and duty of the executive to safeguard Australian national interests and to uphold the laws of the Commonwealth,[61] and I set store by remarks of Wilson and Dawson JJ in *Alister v R* (1984)[62] where their Honours said, "very considerable weight must attach to the view of what national security requires as is expressed by the responsible Minister."[63] Even so, it is unreasonable for law to force the general's conscience, and I follow Rawls to acknowledge the importance in liberal society of an independent conscience. When I say, "independent conscience," I mean a person is able to exercise self-governing moral choice, able to act autonomously, not as the upshot of social pressure, they are free from coercion and able to choose knowingly and intelligently from a range of options.[64] Saying these things I distance myself from theorists who say conscientious reasons are spontaneous, intuitive, beyond rational reflective deliberation. On my account, conscience references deliberate and serious moral commitments, determining moral ideas, considered choices and decisions, aims, and aspirations, and regrets.

As conscience rises above preference, so unconscionable is more demanding than dislike. Not everything unlikable will be unconscionable. Occasionally people will feel they *must* over-ride deep moral commitments, they will feel that there is no alternative. But in the term unconscionable there is a limit, the bitter end, and the farthest reach of our moral concept. The term "unconscionable" describes action so unjust, excessive, or unreasonable it exceeds our moral range of view. Something unconscionable is morally impermissible *for us*, notwithstanding the outcome.

Chapters 6 and 7 work together to make a pair. In Chapter 6 (*For All of Us – As One of Us*) I consider the general as a citizen and argue that even though the citizen has chosen to serve in the military, the state cannot infringe inalienable rights, which attach to citizenship. In Chapter 7 (*More Than a Postman*) I explain that the general bears specific and special role responsibilities; these are responsibilities which call for the exercise of autonomous moral decision.

In Chapter 6 I say that by voluntary enlistment and by their acceptance of high command, citizens who join the military have chosen to accept the burdens of service to the state. Choosing to serve, the citizen consents, explicitly by taking an oath and tacitly by acceptance of a public salary and promotion, to abide by laws and conventions.[65] The commitment is very large and very onerous. Yet the citizen who serves does not make an infinite commitment.

In Chapter 6 I argue against the view that the "unlimited liability"[66] entails, as Colm McKeogh puts it, that soldiers might be considered to have a purely instrumental value, and that they might be treated as non-persons, not as human but as things.[67] I am concerned that the democracy might fail to recognise generals as equal citizens and moral beings. Following Mason CJ, Wilson and Dawson JJ in *Re Tracey: ex parte Ryan* (1989)[68] I claim generals do not sign away the rights of citizenship. And, following Atkin LJ in *Liversidge v. Anderson* (1942),[69] I claim the executive cannot rightly deny generals the rights of citizenship.

I acknowledge that society depends upon authorities, and institutions, and the imposed systems and routines of public administration. But political institutions must respect citizens as autonomous responsible individuals. Liberal pluralism is undermined when the integrity of the individual conscience is violated. As Michael Walzer says: democracy suffers when the citizens are coerced.[70] No just society can tolerate the idea of a person holding merely instrumental value. Yet, this is exactly the effect of the Australian legislation.

Legislation takes it for granted that by volunteering, citizens consent to everything – that they consent to do *anything* the minister directs. But consent is not like this. Consent is not given once, for all time and for all things. Consent is iterative, given – or withdrawn – over time, as instances requiring consent arise, and as the nature and the scope of circumstances change. And consent is intentional. Consent must be my own, freely carried through, not imposed or coerced.[71]

Beyond the elemental values of citizenship and the relation of the citizen to society, the general has assumed special role responsibilities which call for autonomous moral decision. In Chapter 7 (*More Than a Postman*) I make clear that the general has not sworn an oath to be a mechanism. The general has not promised to be a coward in the face of injustice; not promised to follow direction *merely* because it is executive direction. The general has promised to serve right – or should have. This is a generalised pledge, a promise not written in any formal oath or specified in any commission.[72] The general has promised to bear larger obligations than those avowed by an oath, stipulated by law, or detailed in military instructions. The general has promised to serve high principles. These ideals are not explicit. They are not itemised and particular. But neither are they unknown or dubious.[73] This is to recall the *Gorgias* where Plato makes an argument against

Callicles for right and justice[74] against power[75]; and where Plato claims society depends upon ideals and expectations that, though tacit and inconclusive, inform the shared human experience.[76]

Lessons from the trials at Nuremberg resonate throughout Chapter 7. At Nuremberg, despite different legal traditions and dissimilar political approaches, four nations were united in the need to prosecute crimes that escaped legal prescription. Generals were hanged at Nuremberg not for crimes set out on any statute book, but for iniquity. From Nuremberg we learn that, when they are confronted by unconscionable executive direction – even direction consistent with law – generals should refuse. Article 8 of the *Charter of the International Military Tribunal* at Nuremberg read: "The fact that the Defendant acted pursuant to the order of his Government or of a superior shall not free him from responsibility [for unconscionable conduct]."

Trade-offs are part and parcel of political life, and military life. The discipline of the state must be imposed, and generals must be obedient. Even so, there is a moral boundary. In Chapter 7 I argue against James Dubik who says senior military leaders must execute the decisions of politics or resign.[77] I argue that in a reasonably good society, law should offer the general a right to refuse unconscionable direction so resignation or non-conformity with law are not the only morally acceptable courses of action. Thus, I go further than the former British Major General Christopher Elliott, who says it should be "a constitutional duty for the Chiefs to satisfy themselves that the correct or essential planning prerequisites [and political commitments] are in place, at least in outline," before going to war.[78] For Major General Elliott, the anonymous "Chiefs" must satisfy themselves of nothing more than that planning and strategy line up.

In Chapter 8 (*Let the General Say No*) I set out the case for law reform so the general in supreme command might occlude injustice and so we might have fewer unjust wars. The reform for which I ask is an exception or exclusion *within* the law so generals might (legally) refuse executive direction. I argue for morally better law. I argue for reform so the general in supreme command might have the right in law to refuse executive direction, which even if it is legal and logistically well-planned, is unconscionable.

I do not stipulate what will be unconscionable. I recognise that it is for the general to determine circumstantial reasonableness, to make judgements of fact and value, to weigh concepts that are beyond capture in law. And I recognise limits to my asking. Granting an exception does not mean the general might refuse executive direction without consequence. Granting an exception means the general might refuse unconscionable direction without punishment, a word which has a condemnatory significance beyond penalty or consequence.[79]

Asking for reform, I look to the standard set down in the case law. In *Ansett Transport Industries (Operations) Pty. Ltd. v. Commonwealth*[80] Mason J said, of a decision maker, if he is bound by law to "accept a direction from his Minister it cannot be said that the decision is his decision; (rather, the decision) becomes the decision of the Minister."[81] Gesturing to ideas of responsible independence, I observe the decision in In *R v. Anderson ex parte Ipec Air Pty. Ltd*,[82] where the

High Court found proper independent decision to be according to the rules of reason and justice, not according to private opinion. I further observe where, in *Minister for Immigration and Citizenship v. Li*,[83] French CJ found reasonable minds may reach different conclusions.[84]

Citing these decisions, I point to the way law might offer discretionary space for independent decision and for refusal. The asking is for reform of relations between the general and the executive, not for freedom from legal control. The asking is for discretionary space in the law; so the general might act with reasonable independence, carefully and with a mind to principles which find their best expression in the Martens Clause. In the terms of Scanlon's formula, the Martens forms recognise people establish their moral identity in community and offer generals a basis to decide what they might "reasonably reject."[85] To emphasise this point, the officers convicted at Nuremberg were found to have acted *unreasonably*, *contra* the chivalrous ideals of arms and the dictates of the public conscience – but not illegally, not against specific statutory laws of the Nazi state.[86]

Conclusion

Recognising the best approach to practical morality is casuistic,[87] I write in a casuist style and relate general principles to the law and the general in supreme command.

Speaking of the law, my explicit reference is to the Australian *Defence Act,* but I address an issue of pervasive importance. Ubiquitously, law has confused duty with conformity, and conformity has come to be everything. Thus, in practice, it is inevitable the general will be confronted by the dilemma of political direction which is lawful but awful; legal yet morally unconscionable.

I hope for real-world law reform. I ask law to relax the claim it makes for unconditional obedience so that the general might *legally* refuse unconscionable direction from politics. I do not offer escapist fancy or ideal theory. I do not expect full compliance – no mistakes or missteps or falling short.[88] I see the value of philosophy in practical application,[89] and I ask law to enable the general to refuse political injustice. When law says the general *must* comply with *any* of the Minister's directions, law makes it infeasible for the general to act morally, which, to my mind, means "autonomously."[90] Better law would account for moral obligation and the material claims of conscience.

Notes

1 Anthony Pagden and Jeremy Lawrence, "On the Law of War," in Francisco de Vitoria (ed.), *Political Writings* (Cambridge: Cambridge University Press, 2010), p. 307.
2 John Rawls, *A Theory of Justice* (Cambridge, MA: The Belknap Press of Harvard University Press, 1999), pp. 341, 334, 335.
3 H.R. McMaster, *Dereliction of Duty: Lyndon Johnson, Robert McNamara, the Joint Chiefs of Staff, and the Lies that Led to Vietnam* (New York: HarperPerennial, 1998), p. 135. McMaster describes how General Wheeler, Chairman of the Joint Chiefs of Staff – thus equivalent to "the general" serving as Chief of the Australian Defence Force – offered an undeniable credibility to political decisions to go to war.

James Dubik, *Just War Reconsidered: Strategy, Ethics and Theory* (Kentucky: University Press of Kentucky, 2018), pp. 83, 92. Speaking of anonymous "military leaders" confronted by political idiocy, Dubik says the citizens do not expect blind obedience.

4 Jeremy Horder, *Excusing Crime* (Oxford: Oxford University Press, 2004), p. 200.

5 Joseph Raz, *The Authority of Law: Essays on Law and Morality* (Oxford: Clarendon Press, 1979), p. 263. At p. 262, Raz says such a conscientious refusal appears much like an ordinary violation of the law.
Jeremy Horder, *Excusing Crime* (Oxford: Oxford University Press, 2004), pp. 224–225. Conscientious objection then, is a private act – meaning that it is not a political act. The conscientious objector does not challenge the rule-making system, or even seek to change any specific legal rule. Conscientious objection does nothing but eschew a legal demand to which the objector cannot conscientiously accede.

6 Angeline Lewis, "History of the ADF Military Law System," in Robin Creyke, Dale Stephens and Peter Sutherland (eds.), *Military Law in Australia* (Sydney: Federation Press, 2019), p. 21. "In the *Defence Legislation Amendment (First Principles) Act* 2015 (Cth) the command of the Chief of the Defence Force and the role of the Vice Chief of the Defence Force were formally established in the *Defence Act*, entering into force on 1 July 2016."

7 Seth Lazar, "Authorization and the Morality of War," in *Australasian Journal of Philosophy*, (2016) 94:2, pp. 211–226.

8 Thomas Ricks, *The Generals: American Military Command from World War II to Today* (New York: Penguin, 2012), p. 96.

9 Cameron Moore, *Crown and Sword: Executive Power and the Use of Force by the Australian Defence Force* (Australia: Australian National University Press, 2017), pp. 93–94, 95–96.

10 ss. 46 (6) (c), 51 (z) (2) (c).

11 156 CLR 532.

12 156 CLR 532, 540 per Gibbs CJ [My emphasis].

13 156 CLR 532, 562 per Murphy J [My emphasis].

14 Philip Rhinelander, *Is Man Incomprehensible to Man?* (San Francisco: W.H. Freeman and Company, 1974), p. 1.

15 Jeff McMahan, Foreword to Ellner, Andrea, Robinson, Paul and Whetham, David. (eds.) *When Soldiers Say No: Selective Conscientious Objection in the Modern Military* (England: Ashgate, 2014), p. xi.

16 Seth Lazar, "Responsibility, Risk, and Killing in Self-Defense," in *Ethics*, (2009) 119:4, pp. 699–728, 707. "Many combatants on the unjustified side may well be excused for their part in the war, on grounds either of nonculpable ignorance or of duress." Seth Lazar, "Evaluating the Revisionist Critique of Just War Theory," in *Dædalus, the Journal of the American Academy of Arts & Sciences*, (2017) 146:1, pp. 113–124, 120, 121–122, 116. Lazar notes Walzer says combatants on both sides of most conflicts have very similar experiences. They tend to believe they are justified in fighting, and indeed fight for good reasons: loyalty, a belief that their country is under threat, and trust in their leaders, to name a few. Where these reasons are absent, combatants often fight under duress. In either case, they fight because they think they must. When they share so many similar motivations, it would be hypocritical of either side's soldiers to blame the other side for fighting.

17 Jeff McMahan, *Killing in War* (Oxford: Clarendon Press, 2009), p. 31. At p. 61 McMahan says it is entirely reasonable for soldiers to trust their political leaders. But McMahan considers soldiers – not the general. Unlike soldiers, the general engages with politics at the level of strategy – or should.

18 Jeff McMahan, *Killing in War* (Oxford: Clarendon Press, 2009), pp. 119, 120.
Hilary Putnam, *Pragmatism and Realism* (London and New York: Routledge, 2006), p. 20.

19 Owen Dyer, "Air Force Doctor Imprisoned for Refusing Third Tour in Iraq," in *British Medical Journal*, (2006) 332:7547, p. 931.
20 Augustine, (tr.) Henry Bettenson *Concerning the City of God Against the Pagans* (England: Penguin, 1984), Book 1, Ch. 21, p. 32.
21 David Estlund, "On Following Orders in an Unjust War," in *The Journal of Political Philosophy*, (2007) 15:2, pp. 213–234, 213.
22 David Estlund, "On Following Orders in an Unjust War," in *The Journal of Political Philosophy*, (2007) 15:2, pp. 213–234, 220. Though, says Estlund – unrealistically – (p. 213), the soldier will need to determine if the proper institutional conditions are met.
23 Massimo Renzo, "Democratic Authority and the Duty to Fight Unjust Wars," in *Analysis*, (2013) 73:4, pp. 668–676, 670.
24 Massimo Renzo, "Democratic Authority and the Duty to Fight Unjust Wars," in *Analysis*, (2013) 73:4, pp. 668–676, 671.
25 David Estlund, "On Following Orders in an Unjust War," in *The Journal of Political Philosophy*, (2007) 15:2, pp. 213–234, 213.
26 Massimo Renzo, "Democratic Authority and the Duty to Fight Unjust Wars," in *Analysis*, (2013) 73:4, pp. 668–676, 671.
27 John Gardner, "The Mark of Responsibility," in *Oxford Journal of Legal Studies*, (2003) 23:21, pp. 157–171, 161.
28 Michael Pezzullo (Deputy Secretary, the Department of Defence), Senate Legal and Constitutional Legislation Committee, Report on Defence Legislation Amendment (Aid to Civilian Authorities) Bill 2005 *Committee Hansard*, 31 January 2006, para 2.136, p. 35: "…members of the executive, who are so much better connected these days than they have ever been with secure communications, can quickly give effect to a call-out by doing something as simple as making a secure telephone call which can be properly and duly recorded later." Mr. Pezzullo presumes (Astoundingly? Naively?) that the general will obey ANY direction – even when this direction is not offered in any official form or logged or detailed in any official record.
29 *Attorney General of the Government of Israel v. Eichmann*, Unreported Minutes of the opening address, Chapter 1, Attorney General's Opening Address, "Introduction," by Mr. Gideon Hausner, p. 1.
30 *Attorney General of the Government of Israel v. Eichmann*, Unreported Minutes of the opening address, Chapter 1, Attorney General's Opening Address, "Introduction," by Mr. Gideon Hausner, p. 2.
31 Peter D. Feaver, *Armed Servants: Agency, Oversight, and Civil-Military Relations* (Cambridge, MA: Harvard University Press, 2005), p. 5.
32 Herbert Richmond, *Statesmen and Sea Power* (Oxford: Clarendon Press, 1946), pp. vii, ix.
33 Samuel P. Huntington, *The Soldier and the State: The Theory and Politics of Civil-Military Relations* (Cambridge, MA: Belknap Press of the Harvard University Press, 1981), p. 73.
General Sir John Winthrop Hackett, "The Military in the Service of the State," in Malham M. Wakin (ed.), *War, Morality, and the Military Profession* (Boulder, Colorado: Westview Press, 1986), pp. 115–117.
34 Peter D. Feaver, *Armed Servants: Agency, Oversight, and Civil-Military Relations* (Cambridge, MA: Harvard University Press, 2005), p. 2.
35 James Dubik, *Just War Reconsidered: Strategy, Ethics and Theory* (Kentucky: University Press of Kentucky, 2018), pp. 60, 66.
36 (1985) 157 CLR 91.
37 Samuel P. Huntington, *The Soldier and the State: The Theory and Politics of Civil-Military Relations* (Cambridge, MA: Belknap Press of the Harvard University Press, 1981), pp. 76–77.
Peter D. Feaver, *Armed Servants: Agency, Oversight, and Civil-Military Relations* (Cambridge, MA: Harvard University Press, 2005), p. 172.

Risa Brooks, "Paradoxes of Professionalism: Rethinking Civil-Military Relations in the United States," in *International Security*, (2020) 44:4, pp. 7–44, 10.

38 Peter D. Feaver, *Armed Servants: Agency, Oversight, and Civil-Military Relations* (Cambridge, MA: Harvard University Press, 2005), p. 298.
Herbert Richmond, *Statesmen and Sea Power* (Oxford: Clarendon Press, 1946), p. vii. Richmond cites Mahan to say: "If the statesman misinterprets the nature of national defence or the ultimate object of a war…[he] may pave the way to defeat [and] render useless all the skill and courage of the fighting men at sea, on land and in the air."

39 Peter D. Feaver, *Armed Servants: Agency, Oversight, and Civil-Military Relations* (Cambridge, MA: Harvard University Press, 2005), p. 172.

40 William Shakespeare, "King Henry V," in William G. Clark and William A. Wright (eds.), *The Works of William Shakespeare* (London: MacMillian and Co, 1866), (IV: i), p. 456.

41 Samuel P. Huntington, *The Soldier and the State: The Theory and Politics of Civil-Military Relations* (Cambridge, MA: Belknap Press of the Harvard University Press, 1981), pp. 73, 308. Huntington cites a General Staff School publication and goes on to say: "Strategy begins where politics ends. All that soldiers ask is that once the policy is settled, strategy and command shall be regarded as being in a sphere apart from politics…. The line of demarcation must be drawn between politics and strategy, supply and operations. Having found this line, all sides must abstain from trespassing."
General Sir John Winthrop Hackett, "The Military in the Service of the State," in Malham M. Wakin (ed.), *War, Morality, and the Military Profession* (Boulder, CO: Westview Press, 1986), pp. 115–117.

42 Peter D. Feaver, *Armed Servants: Agency, Oversight, and Civil-Military Relations* (Cambridge, MA: Harvard University Press, 2005), pp. 83–86, 87.

43 Seth Lazar, "Evaluating the Revisionist Critique of Just War Theory," in *Dædalus, the Journal of the American Academy of Arts & Sciences*, (2017) 146:1, pp. 113–124, 119.

44 Eliot A. Cohen, *Supreme Command, Soldiers Statesmen and Leadership in Wartime* (New York: Anchor Books, 2003), p. 10.

45 Eliot A. Cohen, *Supreme Command, Soldiers Statesmen and Leadership in Wartime* (New York: Anchor Books, 2003), pp. 13, 14. And, (p. 5) the example of Lincoln, Clemenceau, Churchill and Ben Gurion demonstrates the constructive contribution politics can make to warfighting.

46 Risa Brooks, "Paradoxes of Professionalism: Rethinking Civil-Military Relations in the United States," in *International Security*, (2020) 44:4, pp. 7–44, 16–17. A reviewer of *The Soldier and the State* said Huntington wishes away all the problems of civil-military relations.

47 Carl von Clausewitz, *On War*, (ed. and tr.) Michael Howard and Peter Paret (London: Folio: 2011), § I. i, p. 32.

48 Carl von Clausewitz, *On War*, (ed. and tr.) Michael Howard and Peter Paret (London: Folio, 2011), § I.i, pp. 24–25.

49 Raymond Recouly (tr.) Joyce Davis, *Foch: My Conversations with the Marshal* (New York: D. Appleton and Company, 1929), p. 45.

50 Ferdinand Foch, *Principes de la Guerre: Conferences a L'Ecole Superieure de Guerre* (Nancy-Paris: Berger-Levrault, 1919), p. 15. "Comme l'a dit Clausewitz: 'La guerre n'est pas une systeme, une doctrine ferme. Tout systeme, toute doctrine, a la nature limitative d'une synthese. Il y'a necessairement contradiction entre une pareille theorie et la guerre, car la pratique de la guerre s'etend jusqu'a des limites indeterminees dans presque toutes les directions.'"

51 S.L.A. Marshall, *Men Against Fire: The Problem of Battle Command* (Norman: University of Oklahoma Press, 2000), p. 165.
Alex Danchev and Daniel Todman (ed.) *The War Diaries of Field Marshal Lord Alanbrooke* (London: Weidenfeld & Nicholson, 2001), p. 170. Alanbrooke said: "The more I see of politicians, the less I think of them!"

52 Joel Feinberg, *Problems at the Root of Law* (Oxford: Oxford University Press, 2003), p. 17.

53 Kimberley Brownlee, *Conscience and Conviction: The Case for Civil Disobedience* (Oxford: Oxford University Press, 2015), p. 109.
54 The relationship between the laws of armed conflict and the human rights law is addressed with authority by Naz K. Modirzadeh, "The Dark Sides of Convergence: A Pro-civilian Critique of the Extraterritorial Application of Human Rights Law in Armed Conflict" in *United States Naval War College International Law Studies*, (2010) 86, pp. 349–410.
55 Philippe Sands, *East West Street* (Great Britain: Weidenfeld & Nicholson, 2016), p. 349. The fact that acts were lawful according to the German statutes offered no defence, since the acts of the German defendants were crimes against the "law of nations."
56 John Rawls, *The Law of Peoples with The Idea of Public Reason* (Revisited) (Cambridge, MA: Harvard University Press, 2000), p. 29.
57 UN GAOR, 3d Sess., 139th plen. mtg. at 36, 37 [UN Doc. A/PV.13–187] (1948). Cited in Eric Stein, "International Law in Internal Law: Toward Internationalization of Central-European Constitutions?" *The American Journal of International Law*, (1994) 88:3, pp. 427–450, 427.
58 Jeff McMahan, *Killing in War* (Oxford: Clarendon Press, 2009), p. 107.
Naz K. Modirzadeh, "The Dark Sides of Convergence: A Pro-civilian Critique of the Extraterritorial Application of Human Rights Law in Armed Conflict" in *United States Naval War College International Law Studies*, (2010) 86, pp. 349–410, 356, 357.
59 Adil A. Haque, *Law and Morality at War* (Oxford: Oxford University Press, 2017), pp. 3, 15, 21, 28, 42, 43, 44.
Seth Lazar, "Evaluating the Revisionist Critique of Just War Theory," in *Dædalus, the Journal of the American Academy of Arts & Sciences*, (2017) 146:1, pp. 113–124, 121. Lazar concurs with Haque.
60 Joseph Raz, *The Morality of Freedom* (Oxford: Clarendon Press, 2009), p. 76.
61 s 61 (also ss. 51 (vi), 119) of the *Commonwealth of Australia Constitution Act*. *Farey v. Burvett* (1916) 21 CLR 433, 452–453 per Isaacs J.
Sir Victor Windeyer, Appendix 9 to *The Protective Security Review Report*, Chairman The Hon. Justice R.M. Hope AC, CMG, QC (Australian Government Publishing Service: Canberra, 1979) (Unclassified Version), pp. 279, 280.
62 154 CLR 404.
63 154 CLR 404, 435.
64 Bernard Williams, *Ethics and the Limits of Philosophy* (Cambridge, MA: Harvard University Press, 1985), p. 7.
Joseph Raz, *The Morality of Freedom* (Oxford: Clarendon Press, 2009), pp. 407–409.
65 Michael Walzer, *Obligations: Essays on Disobedience, War and Citizenship* (Cambridge, MA: Harvard University Press, 1970), pp. xi, 100.
66 Lt. Gen Sir John Winthrop Hackett, *The Profession of Arms: The 1962 Lees Knowles Lectures Given at Trinity College Cambridge* (London: Times Publishing, 1962), p. 63.
67 Colm McKeogh, *Innocent Civilians: The Morality of Killing in War* (Great Britain: Palgrave, 2002), p. 12.
68 166 CLR 518 at 546 citing Lord Mansfield CJ in *Burdett v. Abbot* (1812) 128 ER 384.
69 (1942) AC 206.
70 Michael Walzer, *Obligations: Essays on Disobedience, War and Citizenship* (Cambridge, MA: Harvard University Press, 1970), p. 141.
71 Michael Walzer, *Obligations: Essays on Disobedience, War and Citizenship* (Cambridge, MA: Harvard University Press, 1970), p. xiii–xiv.
72 No such phrase or idea appears on the commission of the author, a serving officer in the Royal Australian Navy. The only obligation specified in the author's commission is an obligation to "observe and execute all orders and instructions."
73 Mary Follett, *Creative Experience* (New York: Peter Smith, 1951), p. 220.
74 Plato "Gorgias" 499e, 527b.
75 Plato "Gorgias" 488b, 492.
76 Plato "Gorgias" 481d.

77 James Dubik, *Just War Reconsidered: Strategy, Ethics and Theory* (Kentucky: University Press of Kentucky, 2018), pp. 63–64.
78 Christopher Elliott, *High Command: British Military Leadership in the Iraq and Afghanistan Wars* (Oxford and New York: Oxford University Press, 2015), p. 230. (Emphasis in the original.)
79 David Lefkowitz, cited by Kimberley Brownlee, *Conscience and Conviction: The Case for Civil Disobedience* (Oxford: Oxford University Press, 2015), p. 243.
80 (1977) 139 CLR 54.
81 (1977) 139 CLR 54 at 83 *per* Mason J.
82 (1965) 113 CLR 177.
83 (2014) 249 CLR 217.
84 (2014) 249 CLR 217 at 351 *per* French CJ.
85 T.M. Scanlon, *What We Owe to Each Other* (Cambridge, MA: Harvard University Press, 2000), p. 153.
86 George Finch, "The Nuremberg Trial and International Law," in *American Journal of International Law*, (1947) 41:20, pp. 20–37.
87 Michael Walzer, *Just and Unjust Wars*: *A Moral Argument* (Basic Books: New York, 2000), pp. xxii, 44–45.
88 Laura Valentini, "Ideal vs. Non-ideal Theory: A Conceptual Map," in *Philosophy Compass*, (2012) 7:9, pp. 654–664.
89 Hilary Putnam, *Pragmatism and Realism* (London and New York: Routledge, 2006), p. 19.
90 Bernard Williams, *Ethics and the Limits of Philosophy* (Cambridge, MA: Harvard University Press, 1985), p. 7.

References

Australian Cases

A v. Hayden (1984) 156 CLR 532.
Alister v. R (1984) 154 CLR 404.
Ansett Transport Industries (Operations) Pty. Ltd. v. Commonwealth (1977) 139 CLR 54.
Coutts v. The Commonwealth (1985) 157 CLR 91.
Farey v. Burvett (1916) 21 CLR 433.
Minister for Immigration and Citizenship v. Li (2014) 249 CLR 217.
R v. Anderson ex parte Ipec Air Pty. Ltd (1965) 113 CLR 177.

United Kingdom Cases

Liversidge v. Anderson (1942) AC 206.

Unreported Case Minutes

Attorney General of the Government of Israel v. Eichmann, Unreported Minutes held in the Library of St. Antony's College, the University of Oxford.

Journal Articles

Brooks, Risa. "Paradoxes of Professionalism: Rethinking Civil-Military Relations in the United States," in *International Security*, (2020) 44:4, pp. 7–44.

Dyer, Owen. "Air Force Doctor Imprisoned for Refusing Third Tour in Iraq," in *British Medical Journal*, (2006) 332:7547, p. 931.

Estlund, David. "On Following Orders in an Unjust War," in *The Journal of Political Philosophy*, (2007) 15:2, pp. 213–234.

Finch, George. "The Nuremberg Trial and International Law," in *American Journal of International Law*, (1947) 41:20, pp. 20–37.

Gardner, John. "The Mark of Responsibility," in *Oxford Journal of Legal Studies*, (2003) 23:21, pp. 157–171.

Lazar, Seth. "Responsibility, Risk, and Killing in Self-Defense," in *Ethics*, (2009) 119:4, pp. 699–728.

Lazar, Seth. "Authorization and the Morality of War," in *Australasian Journal of Philosophy*, (2016) 94:2, pp. 211–226.

Lazar, Seth. "Evaluating the Revisionist Critique of Just War Theory," in *Dædalus, the Journal of the American Academy of Arts & Sciences*, (2017) 146:1, pp. 113–124.

McMahan, Jeff. "Collectivist Defenses of the Moral Equality of Combatants," in *Journal of Military Ethics*, (2007) 6:1, pp. 50–59.

Modirzadeh, Naz K. "The Dark Sides of Convergence: A Pro-civilian Critique of the Extraterritorial Application of Human Rights Law in Armed Conflict," in *United States Naval War College International Law Studies*, (2010) 86, pp. 349–410.

Renzo, Massimo. "Democratic Authority and the Duty to Fight Unjust Wars," in *Analysis*, (2013) 73:4, pp. 668–676.

Stein, Eric. "International Law in Internal Law: Toward Internationalization of Central-European Constitutions?" in *The American Journal of International Law*, (1994) 88:3, pp. 427–450.

Valentini, Laura. "Ideal vs. Non-ideal Theory: A Conceptual Map," in *Philosophy Compass*, (2012) 7:9, pp. 654–664.

Books

Anthony Pagden and Jeremy Lawrence, "On the Law of War," in de Vitoria, Francisco (ed.), *Political Writings* (Cambridge: Cambridge University Press, 2010).

Augustine, (tr.) Henry Bettenson *Concerning the City of God Against the Pagans* (England: Penguin, 1984).

Brownlee, Kimberley. *Conscience and Conviction: The Case for Civil Disobedience* (Oxford: Oxford University Press, 2015).

von Clausewitz, Carl. *On War*, (ed. and tr.) Michael Howard and Peter Paret (London: Folio, 2011).

Cohen, Eliot A. *Supreme Command, Soldiers Statesmen and Leadership in Wartime* (New York: Anchor Books, 2003).

Danchev, Alex and Todman, Daniel. (eds.) *The War Diaries of Field Marshal Lord Alanbrooke* (London: Weidenfeld & Nicholson, 2001).

Dubik, James. *Just War Reconsidered: Strategy, Ethics and Theory* (Kentucky: University Press of Kentucky, 2018).

Elliott, Christopher. *High Command: British Military Leadership in the Iraq and Afghanistan Wars* (Oxford and New York: Oxford University Press, 2015).

Feaver, Peter D. *Armed Servants: Agency, Oversight, and Civil-Military Relations* (Cambridge, MA: Harvard University Press, 2005).

Feinberg, Joel. *Problems at the Root of Law* (Oxford: Oxford University Press, 2003).

Foch, Ferdinand. *Principes de la Guerre: Conferences a L'Ecole Superieure de Guerre* (Nancy-Paris: Berger-Levrault, 1919).

Follett, Mary. *Creative Experience* (New York: Peter Smith, 1951).

Hackett, Lt. Gen Sir John Winthrop. *The Profession of Arms: The 1962 Lees Knowles Lectures Given at Trinity College Cambridge* (London: Times Publishing, 1962).

Hackett, General Sir John Winthrop. "The Military in the Service of the State," in Malham M. Wakin (ed.), *War, Morality, and the Military Profession* (Boulder, CO: Westview Press, 1986).

Haque, Adil A. *Law and Morality at War* (Oxford: Oxford University Press, 2017).

Horder, Jeremy. *Excusing Crime* (Oxford: Oxford University Press, 2004).

Huntington, Samuel P. *The Soldier and the State: The Theory and Politics of Civil-Military Relations* (Cambridge, MA: Belknap Press of the Harvard University Press, 1981).

Lewis, Angeline. "History of the ADF Military Law System," in Robin Creyke, Dale Stephens, and Peter Sutherland (eds.), *Military Law in Australia* (Sydney: Federation Press, 2019).

Marshall, S.L.A. *Men Against Fire: The Problem of Battle Command* (Norman: University of Oklahoma Press, 2000).

McKeogh, Colm. *Innocent Civilians: The Morality of Killing in War* (Great Britain: Palgrave, 2002).

McMahan, Jeff. *Killing in War* (Oxford: Clarendon Press, 2009).

McMahan, Jeff. Foreword to Ellner, Andrea, Robinson, Paul and Whetham, David. (eds.) *When Soldiers Say No: Selective Conscientious Objection in the Modern Military* (England: Ashgate, 2014).

McMaster, H.R. *Dereliction of Duty: Lyndon Johnson, Robert McNamara, the Joint Chiefs of Staff, and the Lies that Led to Vietnam* (New York: HarperPerennial, 1998).

Moore, Cameron. *Crown and Sword: Executive Power and the Use of Force by the Australian Defence Force* (Australia: Australian National University Press, 2017).

Plato, "Gorgias," in John M. Cooper (ed.) *Plato: Complete Works* (Indianapolis and Cambridge: Hackett, 1997).

Putnam, Hilary. *Pragmatism and Realism* (London and New York: Routledge, 2006)

Rawls, John. *A Theory of Justice* (Cambridge, MA: The Belknap Press of Harvard University Press, 1999).

Rawls, John. *The Law of Peoples with The Idea of Public Reason* (Revisited) (Cambridge, MA: Harvard University Press, 2000).

Raz, Joseph. *The Authority of Law: Essays on Law and Morality* (Oxford: Clarendon Press, 1979).

Raz, Joseph. *The Morality of Freedom* (Oxford: Clarendon Press, 2009).

Recouly, Raymond. (tr.) Joyce Davis, *Foch: My Conversations with the Marshal* (New York: D. Appleton and Company, 1929).

Rhinelander, Philip. *Is Man Incomprehensible to Man?* (San Francisco: W.H. Freeman and Company, 1974).

Richmond, Herbert. *Statesmen and Sea Power* (Oxford: Clarendon Press, 1946).

Ricks, Thomas. *The Generals: American Military Command from World War II to Today* (New York: Penguin, 2012).

Sands, Philippe. *East West Street* (Great Britain: Weidenfeld & Nicholson, 2016).

Scanlon, T.M. *What We Owe to Each Other* (Cambridge, MA: Harvard University Press, 2000).

Shakespeare, William. "King Henry V," in William G. Clark and William A. Wright (eds.), *The Works of William Shakespeare* (MacMillian and Co: London, 1866).

Walzer, Michael. *Obligations: Essays on Disobedience, War and Citizenship* (Cambridge, MA: Harvard University Press, 1970).
Walzer, Michael. *Just and Unjust Wars: A Moral Argument* (New York: Basic Books, 2000).
Williams, Bernard. *Ethics and the Limits of Philosophy* (Cambridge, MA: Harvard University Press, 1985).

Commonwealth of Australia Committee Hansard

Senate Legal and Constitutional Legislation Committee, Report on Defence Legislation Amendment (Aid to Civilian Authorities) Bill 2005 *Committee Hansard*, 31 January 2006.

Australian Government Documents

Hope, Justice the Hon. R.M., AC, CMG, QC. *The Protective Security Review Report*, Chairman (Australian Government Publishing Service: Canberra, 1979) (Unclassified Version).

2 What's Been Said – Scholarship has Paid Insufficient Attention to the General

The general in supreme command is different from the anonymous "combatants," "soldiers," and "military men." Positioned at the intersection of law, politics and public interest, and central to the exercise of national power, the general bears a singular burden. Only the general might turn political direction into military command and set the armed forces in motion to war. But scholarship has paid insufficient attention to the general, and to the relationship between the general and the state.

In this book I am concerned with law and the general in supreme command. I am concerned with law's proper reach. I dispute law might force the general in supreme command to obey politics without question. I do not dispute that the military should be subordinate to the civil power. I argue against law which denies the general in supreme command the privilege to resist direction from politics which is lawful but unconscionable – "lawful, but awful."

The General

The general in supreme command does not command forces in the field. The general oversights war: offering the only connection between the military and politics, turning political direction into the military command which is war's first step.[1] The general is removed from the imminence, horror, shock, consternation, and dismay of fighting; removed from the hair trigger fright of imminent peril. For the general, the situation is not dubious and uncertain, as it might be for the soldier imagined by Seth Lazar; confronted by high stakes and disputable facts, or deliberately obscured and inaccessible facts, and with little time to think or deliberate.[2]

The general has access to facts and the chance to weigh options. When the general receives direction from politics by telephone, text, e-mail, or in person,[3] perhaps years in advance of war, the general is not eyeball to eyeball with an adversary. For the general, "military necessity" is different from the *in bello* urgency or the *in extremis* moral crossroad which might confront soldiers in battle. For the general in supreme command, military necessity is enmeshed with political *ad bellum* decisions.

Michael Walzer hints at this point when he says generals might sometimes "straddle the line" between *ad bellum* political decisions and *in bello* military

DOI: 10.4324/9781003527886-2

judgements.[4] But Walzer does not pursue the point, and he does not make the distinction between general officers commanding in the field and *the* general commanding the military from the political centre stage. Failing to address the special case of the general in supreme command, Walzer is not alone. For Stephen Shalom, "the generals bear more responsibility for launching unjust war than do the privates, and the political leaders who ordered the generals into action bear greater responsibility than the generals."[5] But Shalom – who speaks of "generals" in general – says nothing more. James Dubik speaks in collective terms of "senior political and military leaders" and "senior officials" who variously set war aims, identify strategies and policies, approve the military and non-military campaigns necessary to achieve those war aims, and establish bureaucratic "coordinative bodies."[6] But the special, singular, and attributable case of the general in supreme command remains unmapped.

Speaking of generals in general, the literature is unmindful of *the* general, the one officer in supreme command. Speaking of generals, the literature offers a predictable unanalytic account of character, tactics, and strategies.[7] But the literature does not speak to the relation of the general to politics, or to problems which obtain from inapt law.

In *The Mask of Command*, John Keegan offers a survey of military command across the span of 2000 years. In a complement to *The Face of Battle*, Keegan offers a clear and wide-ranging consideration of how generals command: that is, how they persuade soldiers to fight. Keegan's text reflects a deep understanding of military history. But it is not an analysis of the relationship between generals and the state, nor a study of the way law affects *the* general.

Keegan speaks more broadly about generals, and in particular about the "mask," the persona adopted by generals in command. On Keegan's account, this mask offers authority a practical voice. It will be epochal, different as society and technology develop. Illustrating his point, Keegan offers studies of Alexander the Great; the Duke of Wellington; Ulysses S. Grant, and Hitler.

Describing Hitler, a "false hero,"[8] Keegan gestures obliquely to law which suffocates moral discretion. But Keegan does not contemplate the relationship of generals to the law. Keegan's focus is historical and biographical, the personality of generals, their strengths and failings.

On Keegan's account, Hitler gave the Army "strength and pride, but he took from it in compensation, though in scarcely perceptible instalments, its independence and autonomy and so eventually its dignity and conscience."[9] However, Keegan does not ponder the seeming unremarkable steps by which Hitler came to prevail over the Army. Extorted by force and fear, these instalments were formalised in law and made constitutional by the rubber-stamp Reichstag. William Shirer cites a Reichstag order:

> In his capacity as Leader of the Nation, Supreme Commander of the Armed Forces, Head of Government and supreme executive chief, as Supreme Justice and Leader of the Party – the Fuehrer must be in a position to force with all means at his disposal every German, if necessary, whether he be common

> soldier or officer… to fulfill his duties. In case of violation of these duties, the Fuehrer is entitled after conscientious examination, regardless of so-called well-deserved rights, to mete out due punishment.[10]

Hiding behind law and unwilling to face justice before the Tribunal at Nuremberg, Goering argued: "we had orders to obey from the head of state. We weren't a band of criminals meeting in the woods in the dead of night."[11] General Jodl spoke of the inevasible duty to follow orders.[12] General Ohlendorf, formerly leader of the *Einsatzkommandos*, confessed calmly to the murder of 90,000 people and said: "it was inconceivable that a subordinate leader should not carry out orders given by the leaders of the State."[13] Field Marshal Keitel, formerly the most senior officer in the German Army and Chief of the Armed Forces, put his rank and authority behind political direction he recognised as unconscionable.[14] Keitel drove his subordinates to obedience. He withdrew from personal responsibility attached to his high rank and behaved as though the office of Field Marshal was trivial. "What could I do?" he asked.[15]

Disavowing that they were eager votaries willing to abet Hitlerian crimes,[16] the generals claimed to have had no option but to obey Hitler's evil plan. Their argument was dismissed. At Nuremberg, recognising that the international law is – to some extent – binding on individuals,[17] the Tribunal recognised the obligation of generals to do more than merely pass on political direction without a moral second thought. However, the Tribunal did not consider the responsibility of the legislature to enact law which makes it practicable for the general to refuse political injustice.

In *Dereliction of Duty*, H.R. McMaster offers a study of why and how the United States came to war in Vietnam. The Vietnam war is remembered for its tremendous consequence; for the deaths of 58,000 American servicemen, for ruining the American economy, and for dividing American society.[18] McMaster shows the war should also be remembered for poor decisions made by America's generals. He criticises the generals for pusillanimity,[19] but he does not contemplate, even in passing, the way in which the generals were inhibited by law from resolute, autonomous moral decision.

Where McMaster's canvas was Vietnam, in *The Generals*, Ricks contemplates American military command from World War Two to the present. Like McMaster, Ricks does not muse upon the law and conventions which obtain. Ricks does not consider the way law might best serve the general who serves in supreme command. Ricks offers a study of:

> A remarkable group of men, the Army general officers of the past three quarters of a century, and the wars they fought [and the way in which the Army promoted them, and relieved them]. Each of these men was given powers we accord to few: responsibilities for saving lives and for taking lives, power over promotion and demotion; the responsibility to advise presidents on our most fundamental national issues; and – perhaps most valued by these Army general officers – the responsibility and the privilege of shaping their own institution.[20]

How could it be, wonders Ricks, that in the contemporary United States Army, generals seem unable to speak truth to power, unwilling to hold themselves or their friends accountable. How could it be that relief from command has become so rare that the private who loses a rifle suffers more than the general who loses a war.[21] Ricks asks,

> how did we go from a tough-minded thinker like George Marshall, who made his reputation in part by speaking truth to power, to eminently pliable chairmen of the Joint Chiefs of Staff such as Air Force General Richard Meyers … and his successor, Marine General Peter Pace?[22]

Gesturing to an answer, Ricks describes a culture ridden with the unpleasing habits of bureaucracy: junior officers in thrall to senior officers, generals in bonds to the politicians who control their careers, no-one accountable for anything.[23] But Ricks does not speak directly to the law, or to the way law and conventions allied with law privilege obedience above moral responsibility.

In *British Generals in Blair's Wars*, Jonathan Bailey, Richard Iron, and Hew Strachan discuss generals in general. They acknowledge "generals are a varied and eclectic bunch, they defy simple categorisation, despite attempts to typecast them, or to ascribe to them a singular fixed view."[24] The focus of the work is on campaigning and inexact ideas of "generalship." The authors review the challenges faced by the commanding general in Northern Ireland, Kosovo, Sierra Leone, Iraq, and Afghanistan. But the general in supreme command is unnoticed. And the obligation of generals to refuse injustice is unperceived. Jonathan Baily says:

> Politicians provide constitutional authority for the conduct of campaigns, muster the particular support to make them domestically viable, assure their legal justification and secure sufficient international support to share risk and avoid disabling sanction. They provide the means, commensurate with the demands of a campaign, based on their understanding of its nature: and they will be heavily reliant on senior officers of the Armed Forces for professional advice in all of this.[25]

By these lights, generals are made the mere masterminds of preparation and undertaking. They are cut away from the most important decision of all – the *ad bellum* decision to go to war in the first place. In the conclusion Hew Strachan gestures to deceits uncovered by the Chilcot Inquiry and says:

> The failure to develop grand strategy and to consider Britain's needs independently of the United States has been seen as a failing on the part of politicians, and has meant that the disappointment and setbacks of the wars in Iraq and Afghanistan have been laid at the feet the Labour Government in general and of Tony Blair in particular.[26]

But Strachan dissembles. He mentions the "disappointment and setback of war" but not the obvious injustice of war. Strachan implicates political deceit, but not law which entraps the general in political madness. And Strachan does not consider the need for law reform, a precondition to strategic discourse between politics and the general. Without co-equal strategic conversation, the general will be a slave to politics, and thus unable to resist misdirection which prefigures unjust war.

The recounting of campaigns and the way generals and politics were variously at odds with each other and with common sense, is a feature of texts dealing with high command. In *The Sleepwalkers: How Europe Went to War in 1914* Christopher Clark describes the foolishness of politics and the blind following of generals. The same can be said of Barbara Tuchman's *The Guns of August*. These are accounts of war, politics, and high command; typical in that they do not consider the way reform of the law might have averted conflict. Similarly, Christopher Elliott – *High Command: British Military Leadership in the Iraq and Afghanistan Wars* – describes generals at odds with politics, but he does not contemplate the place of law in this friction, or the possibility of law reform.

The Chiefs, a text published by the Australian Defence College and sponsored (whatever that means) by the Chief of the Defence Force, represents itself as "a study of strategic leadership" and claims: "an unusual focus: namely, how we work together as a team in the nation's capital, close to the Government we serve, and operating in a complex mix of competing interests, bureaucracy and politics."[27] Yet, this text does not mention law once. Neither does the text consider the tight corner of the general directed by politics to prosecute some unconscionable course.

The text is assuming, theoretically barren, and concerned to tell how "getting things done within a complex bureaucracy requires the ability to influence in the absence of formal authority, through coalition building, networking, negotiating and the exercise of 'small p' political skills."[28] "Organisational politics,"[29] the pamphlet's main feature, is brought to an underwhelming culmination by Air Chief Marshal Houston – a former Chief of the Defence Force: "at the end of the day, strategic leadership is not a program or a sequence but the ability to present 'your plan' in ways that will be acceptable to other stakeholders, especially political ones."[30] The word "ethical" is used to describe the sort of image the Chief of the Defence Force should project,[31] or to describe regulatory standards or codes. The text does not mention conscience, integrity or moral obligation, or the obligation of the legislature to make space for these ideas in the law's shadow.

In a Sandhurst Occasional Paper, Patrick Mileham offers a plain, careful, engaging analysis of commissioned rank. Speaking to the moral obligation immanent to a commission, Mileham mentions "a hard to explain universal moral truth,"[32] an unlimited moral liability, *jus in bello* ethical principles,[33] "the laws of humanity and the dictates of the public conscience."[34] Mileham grasps the moral onus of commissioned rank expertly. But he does not speak to the special burdens of the general, and he does not speak to the dilemma of the general given unconscionable yet legal political direction. Doubtless, Mileham would have the general refuse political injustice. But, on its face, the Australian legislation, obstructs such refusal, no matter how principled or constructive the refusal might be.

War Waging, War Fighting, and Strategy

The literature has recognised that strategy is formed in dialogue between politics and the military. But the literature has not considered the obligation of the legislature to enable constructive exchange.

In *Modern Strategy,* Colin Gray contends "there is an essential unity to strategic experience in all periods of history because nothing vital to the nature and function of war and strategy changes."[35] Gray asks us to recall the Clausewitzian idea that war and politics are inseparable.[36] This is not a new idea. In 1911 Julian Corbett claimed good strategy depended upon a dialogue between politicians and leading military officers. Corbett observed disaster follows routinely when "officers dumbly acquiesce in ill-advised operations simply for lack of the mental power and verbal apparatus to convince an impatient Minister where the errors of his plan lay."[37] To underline his point, Corbett says: "Conference is always necessary," But for conference to succeed Corbett understood there must be a "a common vehicle of expression and a common plane of thought."[38]

In his analysis of *Supreme Command,* Eliot Cohen observes the need for conference or collaboration, which he describes as unequal. On Cohen's account, there is little debate about the subordination of the soldier to civilian control but there is a pervasive tension. The military is a political community; soldiers and statesmen share an uneasy, unequal, collaborative relationship, in which politics has the upper hand.[39] Summarising the tension and collaboration between politics and the military, Cohen cites Dr. Strangelove:

> Do you recall what Clemenceau said about war? He said war was too important to be left to the generals. When he said that, fifty years ago, he might have been right. But today, war is too important to be left to politicians. They have neither the time, the training, or the inclination for strategic thought.[40]

Retired lieutenant general, James Dubik, follows Cohen. Dubik says war is neither solely military nor solely political. Speaking of the *jus in bello*, Dubik says the responsibilities of soldiers and the political figures who enmesh nations in war are braided together. and he recognises the need for plans to be formed and thought-through in a political-military dialogue.[41] The significance of dialogue is explained by Hew Strachan, who describes the failure of Iraq and Afghanistan where "strategy was driven out by the wishful thinking of [politics]."[42] Strachan says:

> In the ideal model of civil-military relations, the democratic head of state sets out his or her policy, and armed forces coordinate the means to enable its achievement. The reality is that this process – a process called strategy – is iterative, a dialogue where ends also reflect means, and where the result – also called strategy – is a compromise between the ends of policy and the military means available to implement it.[43]

Strachan speaks of the contemporary neglect of diplomacy and the collateral readiness to militarise foreign policy. He describes the linguistic fusion of "war" with "terror," and "strategy" with "policy," and the calamity of misused military power which follows in the wake of lexical incoherence.[44] Strachan attributes fault to politicians who, since they have failed to grasp the difference of political policy from military strategy, have used soldiers and perverted military power.[45] But Strachan does not speak to reform of the political-military dialogue, which is the seed corn of strategy.

I open the aperture to a practical correction. On my account, political-military dialogue is unfeasible when law makes politics unsurpassably powerful. I argue for law reform so the general might refuse unconscionable political direction in plain sight. James Dubik gestures to the need for amendment when he describes Donald Rumsfeld: abrasive, assertive, exceptionally self-confident, abrupt, unafraid of imposing his view on professional officers, and keen to dominate the military. Rumsfeld broke the civil-military dialogue, thus undermining the planning for and the execution of the Iraq war.[46] But Rumsfeld did not act alone. The unseen despoiler of the political-military dialogue was law which gives politics transcendent power and denies the general a right to refuse.

Justice and War

Thinking about just war reflects a constantly advancing tradition; an intellectual convention which has never contemplated the special obligations of law in relation to the general in supreme command.

In *Just and Unjust* Wars Michael Walzer sets out the modern orthodoxy. But Walzer does not describe an established, unchanging just war "theory." Rather he describes the "norms, customs, professional codes, legal precepts, religious and philosophical principles and reciprocal arrangements that shape our judgments of military conduct."[47] Similarly, James Turner Johnson describes an inherited body of belief "including many individual doctrines from various sources within the culture and various periods of historical development and representing variations in content."[48]

The deep provenance of western thinking about just war is Greek. Greek wars reflected the need of a *polis* to protect its land.[49] The notion was *aporthetos* – the belief ancestral land should remain inviolate.[50] Beyond the pragmatic need of physical security, the Greek wars were infused with a sense of honour, justice, and chivalry. Honour and land were indivisible.[51] The idea that land should be inviolate *was* attached to the practical needs of subsistence. But the more powerful, pervasive thinking was attached to intangible ideas of civic duty and just cause. Pritchett recalls Onasander who observed in his *Strategikos*, (4.1–3) that:

> It should be evident to all that one fights on the side of justice. For then the gods also, kindly disposed, become comrades in arms to the soldiers, and men are more eager to take their stand against the foe. For with the knowledge that they are not fighting an aggressive but defensive war, with

> conscience free from evil designs, they contribute a courage that is complete; while those who believe an unjust war is displeasing to heaven.[52]

Infused with a sense of civic obligation and confident in the rightness of their cause, hoplites marched not only in defence of ground, but in defence of the position, prestige and fame of their native city.[53] In *Hellenika*, Xenophon records soldiers, standing together in the phalanx, seeking pitched battle as the honourable way to preserve "country, homes, freedom and honours," recognising that no amount of money could precure so fine a moment as death in the fight for a just cause.[54]

These ideas resonate in the Western canon. Like their classical precursors, modern cenotaphs lionise war dead as literal and figurative monuments to the greatness and glory of the state.[55] And, like the hoplite, the modern citizen soldier is a volunteer fighting not merely in defence of geographic territory, but in defence of right and a just cause. The rationale is in United States Army and Marine Corps doctrine which claims, without "moral legitimacy" or just cause, the war is lost.[56]

The hoplite stands as the rhetorical cornerstone of the civic militarism, pivotal to western armies which, like hoplites, fight in the service of the state. The hoplite exemplifies the western soldier who fights, not because he is forced or threatened, but because he is committed to a common cause.[57] These ideas make clear why cowardice was the most serious offence in the phalanx.[58] And they are ideas which resonate with Aristotle's argument that fighting in the phalanx was consistent with the *telos* of human life.[59] Following Plato,[60] Aristotle contended, in a phrase which sounds familiar to modern ears, that a just war will be fought for the sake of peace.[61] But not all the *telee* cited by Aristotle as justification for war are attractive. Aristotle also saw justifications for war in the acquisition of property,[62] the establishment of proper leadership over those who are incapable of proper government,[63] and the enslavement of those who are servile by nature.[64] For Aristotle, political hierarchy was a natural phenomenon, and war the natural means to realise justice.[65] For Aristotle, it was natural and just that some people were enslaved.[66] Uneager for war, Cicero offers a more careful account.

For Cicero, the Roman statesman, lawyer, philosopher, writer, and sceptic; war might be waged only as a last resort, and only for justice. In *On Obligations* (*De Officiis*) Cicero said famously: "even the most unjust peace is preferable to the justest of wars."[67] On Cicero's account, Rome must fight honourably and show mercy to the conquered, even though Roman law permitted the seizure of property and enslavement. Cicero also introduced the idea of proper authority, saying no war is considered just unless it has been declared.[68]

Fragmented, too large to govern effectively, and under constant attack by Barbarian invaders, the Roman Empire collapsed in Europe in 400 AD. In the West, the only institution to survive collapse was the Catholic church. Through the Dark Ages, it was Catholic thinkers who carried on the Greek and Roman contribution to just war thinking. Ambrose (AD 340–397) added to Cicero's *jus in bello*; stressing that soldiers should display the classical virtues, and adding the ideas of just cause, proper authority, public declaration, and last resort to the Graeco-Roman *jus ad bellum*. Augustine followed Ambrose in this regard.[69]

In the fifth century, Augustine was the first Christian thinker to consider the problem of Christians and violence.[70] Augustine argued that the wise man will wage just war to safeguard the state.[71] He acknowledged exemptions to the law against killing and reasoned that when a soldier owes a duty of obedience, he does not kill, but serves merely as an instrument in the hands of a legitimate authority.[72]

Nine hundred years later, in the *Summa Theologica,* Thomas Aquinas built upon this argument.[73] For Aquinas, military force was the proper means by which secular authority might claim peace. Morality was compatible with armed force used in the aim of justice and commanded by a right authority. In the *Summa,* Aquinas acknowledges war is wrong.[74] But, when he asks whether "some kind of war is lawful?"[75] and "is it always sinful to wage war?"[76] Aquinas concedes occasions may arise when war is justified.

Aquinas is most significant since he marks a transition on the idea of legitimate authority.[77] For Aquinas, it was not the Church which might wage a just war, but political authorities.[78] Aquinas believed: since political authorities are responsible for "the common weal of the city, kingdom or province subject to them ... it is lawful for them to have recourse to the material sword in defending that common weal against internal disturbances (and) against external enemies."[79] Vittoria continued this line of reasoning, arguing that since the subjects must fight the prince's wars – guilt for an unjust war must rightly fall on the prince, and not on the soldiers. Vittoria reasoned: "a prince is not able, and ought not always to render reasons for the war to his subjects, and if the subjects cannot serve in the war except they are first satisfied of its justice, the state would fall into grave peril."[80] In the seventeenth century, Grotius followed Vittoria to bestride the gap between morality and law,[81] and to establish the roots of the law of armed conflict in European politics.[82] In 1648, three years after Grotius' death, the Peace of Westphalia saw an end to the Thirty Years War. Formalising principles of religious tolerance, Westphalia also formalised principles of inviolable political sovereignty, and thus, the principle of non-intervention was generated.

Just war thinking remained largely neglected and fallow until the United States Civil War. In this conflict the Union issued a *jus in bello* code; formulated by Dr. Francis Lieber in 1863, on the command of President Abraham Lincoln as *General Order 100 for the Government of United States Armies in the Field.*[83] The Lieber Code speaks *inter alia* of "principles of justice, honor and humanity – virtues adorning a soldier even more than other men, for the very reason that he possesses the power of his arms."[84] These ideas culminated in the Hague Conventions of 1899 and 1907 wherein *jus in bello* rules, which remain alive in the international law, were detailed for the first time.

After the First World War, the 1928 Kellogg-Briand Pact renounced war as an instrument of national policy[85] and sought to secure the settlement of all disputes by pacific means.[86] But the record of history shows the Pact to have been idealistic. The Second World War and its aftermath propagated more substantial practical effect.

The 1945 Charter of the United Nations, which came out of the 1941 Atlantic Charter, addressed the *jus ad bellum,* placing more emphasis on collective security and international authorisation for war than the League of Nations.[87] Notably, the Nuremberg Tribunals followed the Second World War to punish generals who had commanded unjust war. The moral basis for the Tribunal is resonant in the 1948 Universal Declaration of Human Rights. Drafted by representatives from different legal and cultural traditions from all over the world, the Universal Declaration offers emphatic, belletristic commitment to the equal inalienable rights of all people.[88]

The Universal Declaration is not a component of the just war tradition, but no just war theorist might reasonably be insensible to the Universal Declaration or to the other great conventions and declarations. These are the constitutive articles of the international system. They harmonise with the norms, customs, codes, precepts, and philosophical principles which shape our judgements of military conduct and echo throughout international law.[89] The great covenants and treaties which have shaped the world since the end of the Second War, make it evident that the general in supreme command bears an *erga omnes* onus to avoid unjust war. Likewise, in a reasonably good society, legislatures bear coexistent duties to allow the general to refuse political direction which prefaces unjust war. But modern just war thinking is insensitive to the special obligations of the general, and collateral obligations of the law.

The Modern Debate

The mileposts of modern debate are set down by Michael Walzer on one side and, on the other side, by so-called revisionist philosophers.[90] The revisionists oppose the weight Walzer awards to the state. For the revisionist, moral responsibility for killing in war is wholly a matter for individuals. Arguing against Walzer, the revisionist claims rules which regulate killing in war are the same as those outside of war; whether in war or peace, one set of moral principles applies all the time.[91]

Following Walzer, the modern orthodoxy,[92] codified in the Laws of Armed Conflict, assumes a type of moral equivalence or likeness between soldiers who, no matter which side they serve, are trapped in a war they did not contrive.[93] Walzer imagines soldiers forced to fight by the coercive instruments of the state. He depicts soldiers as victims, irrespective of the side for which they fight.[94] For Walzer, soldiers are detached from the political root causes of war. So long as they abide by *in bello* rules, soldiers are morally blameless.[95] The crucial point is that there are *rules* of war. When soldiers abide by these rules, regardless of the cause for which they fight, we treat them as if they believe themselves to be in the right.[96] By Walzer's lights, soldiers have a "war right," a licence to do things which are conventionally prohibited.[97] In exercise of a "war right," and so long as they abide by the laws and conventions, soldiers are entitled to kill the soldiers who oppose them.[98] Seth Lazar calls this the "symmetry thesis."[99]

For the critic, symmetry between soldiers is merely presumed. For the critic, there is no moral equality or symmetry.[100] Thus, in *Killing in War*, Jeff McMahan argues in contradiction of Walzer that soldiers fighting unjustly – mounting an aggressive war against an innocent state – are not morally equal to soldiers who fight in the cause of national self-defence. McMahan argues that since only one side in a war might claim a just cause, soldiers might not share moral equality. Rather, says McMahan, soldiers share a legal equality.[101] Nigel Biggar says likewise; an unjust war should not be fought, and those who fight unjustly do not share moral equality with their adversaries. But moral difference does not preclude the recognition of a legal correspondence which is at once practical and moral: namely to stop the conduct of war from spinning out of all moral control, and so to limit its evils. This does not imply the logical impossibility that the same belligerency can be both just and unjust at the same time.[102]

Saba Bazargan agrees that combatants do not share a moral equivalence. But Bazargan rejects McMahan's reasons. McMahan argues that liability to be attacked should be grounded in moral responsibility for posing an unjust threat. Bazargan calls this a liability-based account of war. Since combatants fighting for a just cause – we might imagine a war in the defence of their country – do not contribute to unjust threats, they are not morally liable to be killed. Thus, it is an error to claim that combatants fighting in a just cause share a moral equivalence with combatants fighting an unjust cause. For Bazargan, the problem is that many so-called unjust combatants contribute very little to the war in which they participate; in fact, many civilians contribute more consequentially and, because of this contribution, seem more liable to be killed. Thus, if we agree with McMahan we seem to be forced to choose between a version of pacifism and total war.[103] Seth Lazar has called this the "Responsibility Dilemma."[104] Bazargan gets around the responsibility dilemma by arguing that the moral liability of unjust combatants lies – beyond individual liability – in collusion or collective complicity. On Bazargan's view, unjust combatants, regardless of the degree to which they contribute to an unjust war, are complicitously liable to be killed, since it is by their collusion that the unjust war is made possible.[105]

Adil Haque rejects McMahan's argument that "the legal equality of combatants consists in symmetrical legal permissions to fight irrespective of one's aims."[106] For Haque, the equality of combatants stems from "symmetrical legal immunities from criminal persecution for acts that are not prohibited by the law of war."[107] By this argument, Haque also disputes Walzer's claim that "combatants who kill in an unjust war have committed no crime." For Haque, unjust combatants have committed a crime; but a crime for which they might not be punished.[108]

Like Walzer, Thomas Hurka claims soldiers share a moral equality. But for Hurka, the moral equality of soldiers obtains from voluntarism not, as Walzer has it, since they have been forced to fight by the coercive instruments of the state. For Hurka, the two sides are not morally equal, but insofar as they target each other, soldiers act permissibly regardless of the side for which they fight. On Hurka's account, soldiers volunteer. Soldiers take on the status of soldiers voluntarily, freely accepting that they may be permissibly killed during a war. Permissible killing describes killing in accordance with the laws and conventions by enemy soldiers who have made a reciprocal surrender of rights. By volunteering, soldiers surrender their right not to be killed in certain circumstances and so their killing in these circumstances is not unjust.[109]

Hurka describes enlistment in the military as an unconditional, global surrender of rights.[110] In this regard, Hurka reminds us that combatants act as members of a political body, which has important implications. Political rights and duties make a difference as to whether soldiers can fight permissibly,[111] and a difference to the perception of soldiers who are acculturated to reckon on the moral rightness of obedience.

Specifically, political rights and duties find practical expression in military culture and training. As Jessica Wolfendale has it, coercive military training "works by deliberately reinforcing pre-existing dispositions towards unreflective obedience … eradicating the moral and emotional distress associated with obedience to destructive authority."[112] I have personal experience of this type of training. At the Australian Defence Force Academy – where I have been posted as a Navy officer – midshipmen and officer cadets spend the first two months of their enlistment shouting. They march around chanting; "left, right, left, right." When a path curves, a command is bawled; "follow the path around." It is as though the ordinary capacity for following paths has evaporated. Mark Osiel puts things in a nutshell when he says the redundant addictions of military life, the starched uniforms, the close order drill, and the rigid discipline-and-obedience hierarchy reinforce habits of compliance and incuriosity, and acculturate the etiquettes of consensus and inattentive repetition.[113] Nothing is done unless it is commanded, or unless permission is granted. Marching and shouting and all the other rigmarole is the seed corn of a culture which, in the words of Australian military doctrine, takes for granted that soldiers "have had little say in the Government's decision to go to war," and argues that soldiers are required to "subjugate [their] will to that of the Government."[114]

Reflected in section 8 (2) of the Australian *Defence Act*, which stipulates "the Chief of the Defence Force *must* comply with *any* directions of the Minister [emphasis added]," the word "subjugation" is a categorical term which implies something more than orderliness or dutifulness. In subjugation there is the allusion to non-resistance, to unassertive tractability, to servility. In subjugation there is the implication that by enlistment, soldiers promise to be out-and-out obedient; that they waive their claim to independent decision, to moral autonomy. The connotation is Walzerian; soldiers are victims, compelled to fight by the coercive instruments of their own state.

A Different Course

I dispute that law might rightly force the general's conscience and compel obedience. I am concerned with law's proper reach. I claim, *ceteris paribus*, that generals should obey the minister, refusing only when they find ministerial direction unconscionable. Generals should not do what they believe to be unconscionable, and law should not force them to infringe the deep registers of their conscience. Offering this argument, I shape an uncharted course. I am focused on *the* one general in supreme command as Chief of the Defence Force. I am not talking about "combatants," or "warriors" or "soldiers" – to cite terms commonly used to describe men and women in uniform.

The general is the only officer who has capacity to turn political direction into military command: who can initiate the movement of ships, soldiers, and aircraft to war. The dilemma which confronts the general will not be that which meets the soldier in a firefight. The general will have time to deliberate over the justice of ministerial direction to launch an unjust war or to prosecute a war in an unjust way. For the general, ideas of "necessity" implicate ideas of national grand strategy and beliefs which have come from the Second World War to find paradigmatic expression in the conventions, declarations, and great charters which define the general's *erga omnes* duty. Law should enable this officer to act well and rightly.

Notes

1 Politicians do not command service personnel, and service personnel do not obey political direction. The Minister gives political direction to the general, who in turn offers military command to service personnel.
2 Seth Lazar, "In Dubious Battle: Uncertainty and the Ethics of Killing," in *Philosophical Studies*, (2018) 175, pp. 859–883, 859.
3 Michael Pezzullo (Deputy Secretary, the Department of Defence), Senate Legal and Constitutional Legislation Committee, Report on Defence Legislation Amendment (Aid to Civilian Authorities) Bill 2005 *Committee Hansard*, 31 January 2006, para 2.136, p. 35.
4 Michael Walzer, *Just and Unjust Wars*: *A Moral Argument* (New York: Basic Books, 2000), p. 39.
5 Stephen R. Shalom, "Killing in War and Moral Equality," in *Journal of Moral Philosophy*, (2011) 8, pp 495–512, 497.
6 James Dubik, *Just War Reconsidered: Strategy, Ethics and Theory* (Kentucky: University Press of Kentucky, 2018), pp. 3, 7, 13, 18, 89.
7 Archibald P. Wavell, *Generals and Generalship: The Lees Knowles Lectures Delivered at Trinity College, Cambridge in 1939* (London: Times Publishing, 1941).
Julian Thompson, *Masters of the Battlefield: The World's Greatest Military Commanders and their Battles, from Alexander the Great to Schwarzkopf* (Rowville: Five Mile Press, 2007).
Francis Dodd, *Generals of the British Army* (London: Country Life,1917).
Barrett Parker (ed.), *Famous British Generals* (London: Nicholson & Watson, 1951).
Aimee Fox, "Learning to Command," in *Wartime – Official Magazine of the Australian War Memorial*, (2021) 94, pp. 26–30.
8 John Keegan, *The Mask of Command* (New York: Penguin, 1987), p. 235.
9 John Keegan, *The Mask of Command* (New York: Penguin, 1987), pp. 267, 268.
10 William Shirer, *The Rise and Fall of the Third Reich* (New York: Simon & Schuster, 2011), p. 867.
11 G.M. Gilbert, *Nuremberg Diary* (United States: Da Capo, 1995), p. 106.
12 G.M. Gilbert, *Nuremberg Diary* (United States: Da Capo, 1995), pp. 28, 252.
13 Michael Berenbaum, *Witness to the Holocaust* (New York: HarperCollins, 1997), p. 135.
Telford Taylor, *The Anatomy of the Nuremberg Trials: A Personal Memoir* (New York: Skyhorse, 2013), p. 248.
William Shirer, *The Rise and Fall of the Third Reich* (New York: Simon & Schuster, 2011), p. 959.
14 Telford Taylor, *The Anatomy of the Nuremberg Trials: A Personal Memoir* (New York: Skyhorse, 2013), pp. 354, 355.
15 G.M. Gilbert, *Nuremberg Diary* (United States: Da Capo, 1995), p. 245. Gilbert reports that Keitel said (p. 27): "How can an officer object?" and (p. 327) that: "[he] felt he had

no choice as an officer but to obey…'I have been a soldier for forty years and that is the only code I know.'"

Telford Taylor, *The Anatomy of the Nuremberg Trials: A Personal Memoir* (New York: Skyhorse, 2013), p. 356.

Walter Gorlitz, "Keitel, Jodl and Warlimont," in Correlli Barnett (ed.), *Hitler's Generals* (New York: Grove Press, 1989), p. 153. "In Keitel's view … one had to stand by one's master … honour, as he knew it, demanded this."

Albert Speer, *Inside the Third Reich* (New York: Simon & Schuster, 1970), p. 421. Offering an account of General Heinz Guderian, Speer shows what might have been done when he says: "Guderian opposed Hitler with an [unprecedented] openness."

16 Chester Wilmot, *The Struggle for Europe* (London: Collins, 1967), p. 160.

17 James T. Johnson, *Just War and the Restraint of War* (Princeton, NJ: Princeton University Press, 1984), p. 64.

18 H.R. McMaster, *Dereliction of Duty: Lyndon Johnson, Robert McNamara, the Joint Chiefs of Staff and the Lies that Led to Vietnam* (New York: HarperPerennial, 1998), p. xiii.

19 Harry G. Summers, Jr, (*Historical Atlas of the Vietnam War* (Houghton Mifflin: Boston and New York, 1995), p. 86.) also criticises the generals who served as the Joint Chiefs of Staff.

20 Thomas Ricks, *The Generals: American Military Command from World War II to Today* (New York: Penguin, 2012), p. 8.

21 Thomas Ricks, *The Generals: American Military Command from World War II to Today* (New York: Penguin, 2012), p. 8.

22 Thomas Ricks, *The Generals: American Military Command from World War II to Today* (New York: Penguin, 2012), p. 12.

23 Thomas Ricks, *The Generals: American Military Command from World War II to Today* (New York: Penguin, 2012), pp. 388–446.

Richard Adams, "A Lot of Bureaucracy, Not Enough Leadership," in *The Naval Review*, (2021) 109:1, pp. 65–69.

24 Jonathan Bailey, Richard Iron and Hew Strachan, (eds.) *British Generals in Blair's Wars* (London: Ashgate, 2013), p. 1.

25 Jonathan Baily, "The Political Context: Why We Went to War and the Mismatch of Ends, Ways and Means," in Jonathan Bailey, Richard Iron and Hew Strachan (eds.), *British Generals in Blair's Wars*, (London: Ashgate, 2013), pp. 5, 14.

26 Hew Strachan, "Conclusion," in Jonathan Bailey, Richard Iron and Hew Strachan (eds.), *British Generals in Blair's Wars* (London: Ashgate, 2013), p. 332.

27 General David Hurley, Chief of the Defence Force, "Foreword," to Nicholas Jans, Stephen Mugford, Jamie Cullens and Judy Frazer-Jans, *The Chiefs: A Study of Strategic Leadership* (Canberra: Australian Defence College, 2013).

28 Executive Summary to Nicholas Jans, Stephen Mugford, Jamie Cullens and Judy Frazer-Jans, *The Chiefs: A Study of Strategic Leadership* (Canberra: Australian Defence College, 2013).

29 Nicholas Jans, Stephen Mugford, Jamie Cullens and Judy Frazer-Jans, *The Chiefs: A Study of Strategic Leadership* (Canberra: Australian Defence College, 2013), p. 26.

30 Nicholas Jans, Stephen Mugford, Jamie Cullens and Judy Frazer-Jans, *The Chiefs: A Study of Strategic Leadership* (Canberra: Australian Defence College, 2013), p. 19.

31 Nicholas Jans, Stephen Mugford, Jamie Cullens and Judy Frazer-Jans, *The Chiefs: A Study of Strategic Leadership* (Canberra: Australian Defence College, 2013), p. 98.

32 Patrick Mileham, *Fit and Proper Persons: Officership Revisited*, Sandhurst Occasional Paper Number 10 (Sandhurst: Central Library – Royal Military Academy, 2012), p. 5.

33 Patrick Mileham, *Fit and Proper Persons: Officership Revisited*, Sandhurst Occasional Paper Number 10 (Sandhurst: Central Library – Royal Military Academy, 2012), pp. 6, 7.

34 Patrick Mileham, *Fit and Proper Persons: Officership Revisited*, Sandhurst Occasional Paper Number 10 (Sandhurst: Central Library – Royal Military Academy, 2012), p. 16.

35 Colin S. Gray, *Modern Strategy* (Oxford: Oxford University Press, 1999), p. 1.
36 Carl von Clausewitz, *On War*, (ed. and tr.) Michael Howard and Peter Paret (London: Folio, 2011), § I. i, pp. 24–25.
37 Julian Corbett, (ed.) Eric Grove, *Some Principles of Maritime Strategy* (Annapolis, MD: Naval Institute Press, 1988), p. 5.
38 Julian Corbett, (ed.) Eric Grove, *Some Principles of Maritime Strategy* (Annapolis, MD: Naval Institute Press, 1988), p. 8.
39 Eliot A. Cohen, *Supreme Command, Soldiers Statesmen and Leadership in Wartime* (New York: Anchor Books, 2003), p. 10.
James Dubik, *Just War Reconsidered: Strategy, Ethics and Theory* (Kentucky: University Press of Kentucky, 2018), pp. 90, 91.
40 Eliot A. Cohen, *Supreme Command, Soldiers Statesmen and Leadership in Wartime* (New York: Anchor Books, 2003), pp. 12–13.
41 James Dubik, *Just War Reconsidered: Strategy, Ethics and Theory* (Kentucky: University Press of Kentucky, 2018), pp. 21, 22, 23, 26, 33, 34, 35, 36, 37, 38, 39, 40, 48, 49, 132, 145.
42 Hew Strachan "The Lost Meaning of Strategy," in *Survival*, (2005) 47:3, pp. 35–54, 51.
43 Hew Strachan, "The Lost Meaning of Strategy," in *Survival*, (2005) 47:3, pp. 35–54, 52.
44 Hew Strachan "The Lost Meaning of Strategy," in *Survival*, (2005) 47:3, p. 52.
45 Hew Strachan "The Lost Meaning of Strategy," in *Survival*, (2005) 47:3, p. 52.
46 James Dubik, *Just War Reconsidered: Strategy, Ethics and Theory* (Kentucky: University Press of Kentucky, 2018), p. 72.
47 Michael Walzer, *Just and Unjust Wars: A Moral Argument* (New York: Basic Books, 2000), p. 44.
48 James T. Johnson, *Can Modern War be Just?* (New Haven and London: Yale University Press, 1984), p. 12.
49 Doyne Dawson, *The Origins of Western Warfare: Militarism and Morality in the Ancient World* (Colorado and Oxford: Westview Press, 1996), p. 52.
Frank E. Adcock, *The Greek and Macedonian Art of War* (Berkeley and Los Angeles: University of California Press, 1957), p. 6.
50 Victor Davis Hanson, *The Western Way of War: Infantry Battle in Classical Greece* (Berkeley, Los Angeles and London: University of California Press, 2000), p. 4.
John Keegan, *A History of Warfare* (New York: Vantage, 1994), pp. 244, 245, 246. Keegan accepts the logic of the *aporthetos* idea, and the likelihood of highly ritualised, brutal and decisive battles.
51 Doyne Dawson, *The Origins of Western Warfare: Militarism and Morality in the Ancient World* (Colorado and Oxford: Westview Press, 1996), pp. 52, 55.
52 W. Kendrick Pritchett, *The Greek State at War* (Part III) (Berkeley, Los Angeles, and London: University of California Press, 1979), p. 323.
53 Frank E. Adcock, *The Greek and Macedonian Art of War* (Berkeley and Los Angeles: University of California Press, 1957), p. 9.
54 Xenophon, *Hellenika*, 2.4.17.
55 Pamela Vaughn, "The Identification and Retrieval of the Hoplite Battle-Dead," in Victor Davis Hanson (ed.), *The Western Way of War: Infantry Battle in Classical Greece* (Berkeley, Los Angeles and London: University of California Press, 2000), p. 58.
56 United States Army and Marine Corps Counterinsurgency Doctrine FM 3–24: MCWP 3–33.5, para. 7.1, 7.2, 7.9, 7.10, 7.11, 7.21, 7.44.
57 Victor D. Hanson, *Why the West Has Won* (London: Faber and Faber, 2002), p. 21.
Michael Walzer, *Just and Unjust Wars: A Moral Argument* (New York: Basic Books, 2000), p. 27.
58 W. Kendrick Pritchett, *The Greek State at War* (Part II) (Berkeley, Los Angeles, and London: University of California Press, 1974), pp. 239–241.

59 John MacCunn, "The Ethical Doctrine of Aristotle," in *International Journal of Ethics*, (1906) 16:3, pp. 288–311, 309.
Nancy Sherman, *The Fabric of Character: Aristotle's Theory of Virtue* (Oxford: Clarendon Press, 2004), p. 51.
60 Plato, "Laws," Bk. 1, 628d: a true statesman "designs his legislation about war as a tool for peace, rather than his legislation for peace as an instrument of war."
61 Aristotle, "Politics," Bk. 7, Ch. 14, 1333a, 35.
62 Aristotle, "Politics," Bk. 7, Ch. 14, 1333b, 16–17.
63 Aristotle, "Politics," Bk. 7, Ch. 14, 1333b, 43.
64 Aristotle, "Politics," Bk. 1, Ch. 6, 1255a, 6., "Politics," Bk. 7, Ch. 14, 1334a, 43.
65 Aristotle offers a general treatment of justice in book 5 of the "Nichomachean Ethics."
66 Aristotle, "Politics," Bk. 1, Ch. 6, 1255b, 6–9.
67 Cicero, *On Obligations* (Oxford: Oxford University Press, 2008), note 35, p. 133. Also: Bk. I, 34–35, pp. 13–14.
68 Cicero. (tr.) Clinton W. Keyes, *De Re Publica* (Cambridge, MA: Harvard University Press, Loeb, 1928), III, xxiii.
Cicero, *On Obligations* (Oxford: Oxford University Press, 2008), I, 36, p. 14.
Brian Orend, *The Morality of War* (Canada: Broadview Press, 2006), p. 11
69 Brian Orend, *The Morality of War* (Canada: Broadview Press, 2006), p. 12.
70 James T. Johnson, *Just War and the Restraint of War* (Princeton, NJ: Princeton University Press, 1984), p. xxiv.
71 St. Augustine, *Concerning the City of God Against the Pagans* (England: Penguin, 1984), Bk. XIX, Ch. 7, p. 861.
72 St. Augustine, *Concerning the City of God Against the Pagans* (England: Penguin, 1984), Bk. 1, Ch. 21, p. 32
73 St. Thomas Aquinas, *The Summa Theologica*, Translated by Fathers of the English Dominican Province, revised by Daniel J. Sullivan (Chicago, London, Toronto and Geneva: William Benton, Encyclopaedia Britannica and the University of Chicago, 1952) Pt. II, Second Part Q. 40, Art. 1, *Reply to Objection* 1, pp. 578–579.
74 St. Thomas Aquinas, *The Summa Theologica*, Translated by Fathers of the English Dominican Province, Revised by Daniel J. Sullivan (Chicago, London, Toronto and Geneva: William Benton, Encyclopaedia Britannica and the University of Chicago, 1952) Pt. II, Second Part, Q. 40, Art. 1, p. 578.
75 St. Thomas Aquinas, *The Summa Theologica*, Translated by Fathers of the English Dominican Province, Revised by Daniel J. Sullivan (Chicago, London, Toronto and Geneva: William Benton, Encyclopaedia Britannica and the University of Chicago, 1952) Pt. II, Second Part, Q. 40, Art. 1, p. 577.
76 St. Thomas Aquinas, *The Summa Theologica*, Translated by Fathers of the English Dominican Province, Revised by Daniel J. Sullivan (Chicago, London, Toronto and Geneva: William Benton, Encyclopaedia Britannica and the University of Chicago, 1952) Pt. II, Second Part, Q. 40, Art. 1, p. 578.
77 Brian Orend, *The Morality of War* (Canada: Broadview Press, 2006), pp. 15–16.
Gregory M. Reichberg, "The Moral Equality of Combatants – A Doctrine in Classical Just War Theory? A Response to Graham Parsons," in *Journal of Military Ethics*, (2013) 12:2, pp. 181–194.
Seth Lazar, "Authorization and the Morality of War," in *Australasian Journal of Philosophy*, (2016) 94:2, pp. 211–226. Lazar draws a distinction between the ideas of moral authorisation and formal political legitimation. This distinction is beyond the scope of my argument here. Suffice it to say I agree with Lazar that those who fight must fight with the moral authorisation or support of a larger community.
78 Hague Convention III mandates in Article One that contracting parties [being signatory governments, and thus manifestly proper authorities] must not commence war without public declaration.

79 St. Thomas Aquinas, *The Summa Theologica*, Translated by Fathers of the English Dominican Province, revised by Daniel J. Sullivan (Chicago, London, Toronto and Geneva: William Benton, Encyclopaedia Britannica and the University of Chicago, 1952), Pt. II, Second Part, Q. 40, Art. 1, *On the Contrary*, p. 578. Aquinas cites Augustine: "the natural order conducive to peace among mortals demands that the power to declare and counsel war should be in the hands of those who hold the supreme authority."

80 Cited in Michael Walzer, *Just and Unjust Wars*: *A Moral Argument* (New York: Basic Books, 2000), p. 39.

81 W.S.M. Knight, "Introduction," to Hugonis Grotii (Grotius), *De Jure Belli ac Pacis* (London: Sweet and Maxwell Ltd., 1922), pp. 9–12.

82 Christian N. Braun, "The Historical Approach and the 'War of Ethics within the Ethics of War'," in *Journal of International Political Theory*, (2018) 14:3, pp. 349–366, 359.

83 James T. Johnson, *Just War and the Restraint of War* (Princeton, NJ: Princeton University Press, 1984), p. xii.

84 Francis Lieber, *General Order 100, Instructions for the Government of Armies of the United States in the Field* (New York: D. van Nostrand, 1863), paragraph 4, p. 4.
Telford Taylor, *The Anatomy of the Nuremberg Trials: A Personal Memoir* (New York: Skyhorse, 2013), pp. 8, 9.

85 Article One.

86 Article Two.

87 Brian Orend, *The Morality of War* (Canada: Broadview Press, 2006), p. 22.

88 Preamble to the Declaration.

89 Michael Walzer, *Just and Unjust Wars: A Moral Argument* (New York: Basic Books, 2000), p. 44.

90 Massimo Renzo, "Democratic Authority and the Duty to Fight Unjust Wars," in *Analysis*, (2013) 73:4, pp. 668–676, 668–669.
Christian N. Braun, "The Historical Approach and the 'War of Ethics within the Ethics of War'," in *Journal of International Political Theory*, (2018) 14:3, pp. 349–366.

91 Christian N. Braun, "The Historical Approach and the 'War of Ethics within the Ethics of War'," in *Journal of International Political Theory*, (2018) 14:3, pp. 349–366, 353–354. Braun cites Helen Frowe and Seth Lazar.

92 Uwe Steinhoff ("Rights, Liabilities and the Moral Equality of Combatants," in *Ethics*, (2012) 16, pp. 339–366, 339–346) notes the irony that Walzer "explicitly stated (in a passage that seems to have been widely overlooked by those who take him to represent "the tradition") that his far-reaching thesis of the moral equality of combatants is not shared by traditional authors: [Walzer says] Catholic writers have long argued that [men] ought not to volunteer, ought not to serve at all, if they know the war to be unjust." Accepting Steinhoff's clarifications, I acknowledge that authorities for millennia have asserted the moral inequality of combatants as the norm; and that it is Walzer and not McMahan who is the "revisionist." But modern convention describes Walzer's "moral equality" thesis as "orthodox," and that is what I have done in this section. Gregory M. Reichberg, ("The Moral Equality of Combatants – A Doctrine in Classical Just War Theory? A Response to Graham Parsons," in *Journal of Military Ethics*, (2013) 12:2, pp. 181–194) also makes this point.

93 Michael Walzer, *Just and Unjust Wars: A Moral Argument* (New York: Basic Books, 2000), pp. 34, 36, 145.
David Rodin and Henry Shue (eds.) *Just and Unjust Warriors: The Moral and Legal Status of Soldiers* (Oxford: Oxford University Press, 2013), p. 1.

94 Michael Walzer, *Just and Unjust Wars: A Moral Argument* (New York: Basic Books, 2000), p. 37.
David Rodin and Henry Shue (eds.) *Just and Unjust Warriors: The Moral and Legal Status of Soldiers* (Oxford: Oxford University Press, 2013), p. 2.

95 Michael Walzer, *Just and Unjust Wars: A Moral Argument* (New York: Basic Books, 2000), p. 136.

Graham Parsons, "Public War and the Moral Equality of Combatants," in *Journal of Military Ethics*, (2012) 11:4, pp. 299–317.

96 Michael Walzer, *Just and Unjust Wars: A Moral Argument* (New York: Basic Books, 2000), p. 128.

97 Michael Walzer, *Just and Unjust Wars: A Moral Argument* (New York: Basic Books, 2000), p. 36.

98 Michael Walzer, *Just and Unjust Wars: A Moral Argument* (New York: Basic Books, 2000), p. 36.

99 Seth Lazar, "Responsibility, Risk, and Killing in Self-Defense," in *Ethics*, (2009) pp. 699–728, 700.
Seth Lazar, "Necessity and Non-combatant Immunity" in *Review of International Studies*, (2014) 40, pp. 53–76, 54.
Seth Lazar, "Evaluating the Revisionist Critique of Just War Theory," in *Dædalus, the Journal of the American Academy of Arts & Sciences*, (2017) 146:1, pp. 113–124, 115.

100 Massimo Renzo, "Democratic Authority and the Duty to Fight Unjust Wars," in *Analysis*, (2013) 73:4, pp. 668–676, 669.

101 Jeff McMahan, "*The Sources and Status of Just War Principles*," in *Journal of Military Ethics*, (2007b) 6:2, pp. 91–106, 99.
Jeff McMahan, "Duty, Obedience, Desert, and Proportionality in War: A Response," in *Ethics*, (2011) 122, pp. 135–167.
Morten H. Jensen, "Complicity and the Responsibility Dilemma," in *Philosophical Studies*, (2020) 177, pp. 109–127, 110.

102 Nigel Biggar, *In Defence of War* (Oxford: Oxford University Press, 2014), p. 196.

103 Saba Bazargan, "Complicitous Liability in War," in *Philosophical Studies*, (2013) 165, pp. 177–195.
Morten H. Jensen, "Complicity and the Responsibility Dilemma," in *Philosophical Studies*, (2020) 177, pp. 109–127.

104 Seth Lazar, "The Responsibility Dilemma for Killing in War: A Review Essay," in *Philosophy and Public Affairs*, (2010) 38:2, pp. 180–213, 181, 189.
Seth Lazar, "Responsibility, Risk, and Killing in Self-Defense," in *Ethics*, (2009) pp. 699–728, 701, 710.
Seth Lazar, "Evaluating the Revisionist Critique of Just War Theory," in *Dædalus, the Journal of the American Academy of Arts & Sciences*, (2017) 146:1, pp. 113–124, 117, 118.

105 Saba Bazargan, "Complicitous Liability in War," in *Philosophical Studies*, (2013) 165, pp. 177–195.
Seth Lazar, "Evaluating the Revisionist Critique of Just War Theory," in *Dædalus, the Journal of the American Academy of Arts & Sciences*, (2017) 146:1, pp. 113–124, 116.
Morten H. Jensen, "Complicity and the Responsibility Dilemma," in *Philosophical Studies*, (2020) 177, pp. 109–127, 110–111. For Jensen, the prime condition for moral liability is not mere participation, but causal responsibility.

106 Adil A. Haque, *Law and Morality at War* (Oxford: Oxford University Press, 2017), p. 23. Also p. 29, n. 38.

107 Adil A. Haque, *Law and Morality at War* (Oxford: Oxford University Press, 2017), p. 15.

108 Adil A. Haque, *Law and Morality at War* (Oxford: Oxford University Press, 2017), p. 29. Haque says, "often [unjust combatants] have committed a crime, albeit crimes for which they may not be prosecuted."

109 Thomas Hurka, "Liability and Just Cause," in *Ethics and International Affairs*, (2010) 21:2, pp. 199–218, 210.

110 Thomas Hurka, "Liability and Just Cause," in *Ethics and International Affairs*, (2010) 21:2, pp. 199–218, 211.

111 Massimo Renzo, "Democratic Authority and the Duty to Fight Unjust Wars," in *Analysis*, (2013) 73:4, pp. 668–676.
112 Jessica Wolfendale, *Torture and the Military Profession* (Hampshire: Palgrave MacMillan, 2007), p. 128.
113 Mark Osiel, *Obeying Orders: Atrocity, Military Discipline and the Law of War* (New Brunswick and London: Transaction, 2002), p. 21.
114 *Leadership in the Australian Defence Force* (Australian Defence Doctrine Publication 00.6), (Commonwealth of Australia, 2007), para 2.7.

References

Journal Articles

Adams, Richard. "A Lot of Bureaucracy, Not Enough Leadership," in *The Naval Review*, (2021) 109:1, pp. 65–69.

Bazargan, Saba. "Complicitous Liability in War," in *Philosophical Studies*, (2013) 165, pp. 177–195.

Braun, Christian N. "The Historical Approach and the 'War of Ethics within the Ethics of War'," in *Journal of International Political Theory*, (2018) 14:3, pp. 349–366.

Fox, Aimee. "Learning to Command," in *Wartime – Official Magazine of the Australian War Memorial*, (2021) 94, pp. 26–30.

Hurka, Thomas. "Liability and Just Cause," in *Ethics and International Affairs* (2010) 21:2, pp. 199–218.

Jensen, Morten H. "Complicity and the Responsibility Dilemma," in *Philosophical Studies*, (2020) 177, pp. 109–127.

Lazar, Seth. "Responsibility, Risk, and Killing in Self-Defense," in *Ethics*, (2009) pp. 699–728.

Lazar, Seth. "The Responsibility Dilemma for Killing in War: A Review Essay," in *Philosophy and Public Affairs*, (2010) 38:2, pp. 180–213.

Lazar, Seth. "Necessity and Non-combatant Immunity" in *Review of International Studies*, (2014) 40, pp. 53–76, 54.

Lazar, Seth. "Authorization and the Morality of War," in *Australasian Journal of Philosophy*, (2016) 94:2, pp. 211–226.

Lazar, Seth. "Evaluating the Revisionist Critique of Just War Theory," in *Dædalus, the Journal of the American Academy of Arts & Sciences*, (2017) 146:1, pp. 113–124.

Lazar, Seth. "In Dubious Battle: Uncertainty and the Ethics of Killing," in *Philosophical Studies*, (2018) 175, pp. 859–883.

MacCunn, John. "The Ethical Doctrine of Aristotle," in *International Journal of Ethics*, (1906) 16:3, pp. 288–311, 309.

McMahan, Jeff. "The Sources and Status of Just War Principles," in *Journal of Military Ethics*, (2007b) 6:2, pp. 91–106.

McMahan, Jeff. "Duty, Obedience, Desert, and Proportionality in War: A Response," in *Ethics*, (2011) 122, pp. 135–167.

Parsons, Graham. "Public War and the Moral Equality of Combatants," in *Journal of Military Ethics*, (2012) 11:4, pp. 299–317.

Reichberg, Gregory M. "The Moral Equality of Combatants – A Doctrine in Classical Just War Theory? A Response to Graham Parsons," in *Journal of Military Ethics*, (2013) 12:2, pp. 181–194.

Renzo, Massimo. "Democratic Authority and the Duty to Fight Unjust Wars," in *Analysis*, (2013) 73:4, pp. 668–676.
Shalom, Stephen R. "Killing in War and Moral Equality," in *Journal of Moral Philosophy*, (2011) 8, pp. 495–512.
Strachan, Hew. "The Lost Meaning of Strategy," in *Survival* (2005) 47:3, pp. 35–54.

Books

Adcock, Frank E. *The Greek and Macedonian Art of War* (Berkeley and Los Angeles: University of California Press, 1957).
Aquinas, *The Summa Theologica*, Translated by Fathers of the English Dominican Province, Revised by Daniel J. Sullivan (Chicago, London, Toronto and Geneva: William Benton, Encyclopaedia Britannica and the University of Chicago, 1952).
Aristotle, "Nichomachean Ethics," Jonathan Barnes (ed.), in *The Complete Works of Aristotle* (Princeton, NJ: Princeton University Press, 1995).
Augustine, (tr.) Henry Bettenson *Concerning the City of God Against the Pagans* (England: Penguin, 1984).
Bailey, Jonathan, Iron, Richard and Strachan, Hew (eds.) *British Generals in Blair's Wars* (London: Ashgate, 2013).
Barnett, Correlli. (ed.) *Hitler's Generals* (New York: Grove Press, 1989).
Berenbaum, Michael. *Witness to the Holocaust* (New York: HarperCollins, 1997).
Biggar, Nigel. *In Defence of War* (Oxford: Oxford University Press, 2014).
Cicero. (tr.) Clinton W. Keyes, *De Re Publica* (Cambridge, MA: Harvard University Press, Loeb, 1928).
Cicero. *On Obligations*, (tr.) P.G. Walsh (Oxford: Oxford University Press, 2008).
Clausewitz, Carl von. *On War*, (ed. and tr.) Michael Howard and Peter Paret (London: Folio, 2011).
Cohen, Eliot. *Supreme Command, Soldiers Statesmen and Leadership in Wartime* (New York: Anchor Books, 2003).
Corbett, Julian. (ed.) Eric Grove, *Some Principles of Maritime Strategy* (Annapolis, MD: Naval Institute Press, 1988).
Dawson, Doyne. *The Origins of Western Warfare: Militarism and Morality in the Ancient World* (Colorado and Oxford: Westview Press, 1996)
Dodd, Francis. *Generals of the British Army* (London: Country Life,1917).
Dubik, James. *Just War Reconsidered: Strategy, Ethics and Theory* (Kentucky: University Press of Kentucky, 2018).
Gilbert, G.M. *Nuremberg Diary* (United States: Da Capo, 1995).
Gray, Colin S. *Modern Strategy* (Oxford: Oxford University Press, 1999).
Grotii, Hugonis. (tr.) W.S.M. Knight *De Jure Belli ac Pacis* (London: Sweet and Maxwell Ltd., 1922).
Hanson, Victor D. *The Western Way of War: Infantry Battle in Classical Greece* (Berkeley, Los Angeles and London: University of California Press, 2000).
Hanson, Victor D. *Why the West Has Won* (London: Faber and Faber, 2002).
Haque, Adil A. *Law and Morality at War* (Oxford: Oxford University Press, 2017).
Johnson, James T. *Can Modern War be Just?* (New Haven and London: Yale University Press, 1984).
Johnson, James T. *Just War and the Restraint of War* (Princeton, NJ: Princeton University Press, 1984).
Keegan, John. *The Mask of Command* (New York: Penguin, 1987).

Keegan, John. *A History of Warfare* (New York: Vantage, 1994).
Lieber, Francis. *General Order 100, Instructions for the Government of Armies of the United States in the Field* (New York: D. van Nostrand, 1863).
McMaster, H.R. *Dereliction of Duty: Lyndon Johnson, Robert McNamara, the Joint Chiefs of Staff and the Lies that Led to Vietnam* (New York: HarperPerennial, 1998).
Orend, Brian. *The Morality of War* (Canada: Broadview Press, 2006).
Osiel, Mark. *Obeying Orders: Atrocity, Military Discipline and the Law of War* (New Brunswick and London: Transaction, 2002).
Parker, Barrett. (ed.) *Famous British Generals* (London: Nicholson & Watson, 1951).
Plato, "Laws," in John M. Cooper (ed.), *Plato: Complete Works* (Indianapolis and Cambridge: Hackett, 1997).
Pritchett, W. Kendrick. *The Greek State at War* (Part II) (Berkeley, Los Angeles, and London: University of California Press, 1974).
Pritchett, W. Kendrick. *The Greek State at War* (Part III) (Berkeley, Los Angeles, and London: University of California Press, 1979).
Ricks, Thomas. *The Generals: American Military Command from World War II to Today* (New York: Penguin, 2012).
Rodin, David and Shue, Henry (eds.). *Just and Unjust Warriors: The Moral and Legal Status of Soldiers* (Oxford: Oxford University Press, 2013).
Sherman, Nancy. *The Fabric of Character: Aristotle's Theory of Virtue* (Oxford: Clarendon Press, 2004).
Shirer, William. *The Rise and Fall of the Third Reich* (New York: Simon & Schuster, 2011).
Speer, Albert. *Inside the Third Reich* (New York: Simon & Schuster, 1970).
Summers, Harry G., Jr, (*Historical Atlas of the Vietnam War* (Boston and New York: Houghton Mifflin, 1995).
Taylor, Telford. *The Anatomy of the Nuremberg Trials: A Personal Memoir* (New York: Skyhorse, 2013).
Thompson, Julian. *Masters of the Battlefield: The World's Greatest Military Commanders and their Battles, from Alexander the Great to Schwarzkopf* (Rowville: Five Mile Press, 2007).
Walzer, Michael. *Just and Unjust Wars: A Moral Argument* (New York: Basic Books, 2000).
Wavell, Archibald P. *Generals and Generalship: The Lees Knowles Lectures Delivered at Trinity College, Cambridge in 1939* (London: Times Publishing, 1941)
Wilmot, Chester. *The Struggle for Europe* (London: Collins, 1967).
Wolfendale, Jessica. *Torture and the Military Profession* (Hampshire: Palgrave MacMillan, 2007).
Xenophon. *The Landmark Xenophon Hellenika*, Robert B. Strassler (ed.) (New York, London, Toronto, and Sydney: Free Press, 2009).

Commonwealth of Australia Committee Hansard

Senate Legal and Constitutional Legislation Committee, Report on Defence Legislation Amendment (Aid to Civilian Authorities) Bill 2005 *Committee Hansard*, 31 January 2006.

Australian Government Documents

Anonymous. *Leadership in the Australian Defence Force* (Australian Defence Doctrine Publication 00.6), (Commonwealth of Australia, 2007).

Jans, Nicholas, Mugford, Stephen, Cullens, Jamie and Frazer-Jans, Judy. *The Chiefs: A Study of Strategic Leadership* (Canberra: Australian Defence College, 2013).

United Kingdom Government Documents

Mileham, Patrick. *Fit and Proper Persons: Officership Revisited*, Sandhurst Occasional Paper Number 10, (Sandhurst: Central Library – Royal Military Academy, 2012).

United States Government Documents

United States Army and Marine Corps Counterinsurgency Doctrine FM 3–24: MCWP 3–33.5 (Washington, DC: Department of the Army, and Department of the Navy, Marine Corps Combat Development Command, 2006).

3 Law and War – Law Cannot Capture War's Moral Complexity

A liberal democracy takes the moral convictions of citizens seriously and enables individuals to examine and act upon deeply held beliefs. This claim is additionally important in the case of the supreme command, where the citizen who serves bears a positional onus to exercise especially careful moral judgement.[1] But Australian law denies the general a right to conscientious refusal. On the terms of Australian legislation, when the general is confronted by morally repugnant direction from politics; non-conformity with law (in the form of conscientious refusal), or resignation are the only morally feasible courses of action.

If we are going to take the moral claims of military service seriously, if we are going to expect the general to act at anything except a modest administrative level of responsibility, and if we want to pull the plug on seeming endless unjust war, then we must reform laws that make the general the unresisting pawns of politics. We must reform law which fails to see the general is different from the soldier, and different from all other officers. In supreme command, the general is alone at the junction between politics and the military; the only person who might translate political direction into military command and initiate the action of war or avert unjust war.

In this chapter I consider limitations immanent to law. I offer the exception as a means by which domestic law might accommodate moral obligations which are part and parcel of the supreme command. I define these obligations along lines set out in the Martens Clause.

The Exaggeration of Law

In this book, I ask us to reform law which might inhibit the general from being morally good. We can acknowledge that there are occasions when, following a rule, we will better meet moral obligations. But rules do not supersede the need for independent moral decision. We must *decide* to follow a rule. We fall short in our moral obligations when we *merely* follow. Limitless confidence in law is the Enlightenment mistake.

For Hannah Arendt, the Enlightenment inaugurated liberalism and an excessive confidence in impersonal rules. Arendt says, at the end of the eighteenth century The Declaration of the Rights of Man was an historical turning point.

DOI: 10.4324/9781003527886-3

The Declaration meant that, from then on Man, not God or the customs of history, should be the source of law.[2] The Finnish diplomat and lawyer Martii Koskenniemi explains the Enlightenment as the seed corn of three liberal principles: freedom, equality, and the Rule of Law. A free people has magistrates not masters; and obeys the laws, not men.[3] Iterating these ideas, Clement Fatovic says liberalism has become so closely identified with the "rule of law" that any conclusion not explicitly sanctioned by law is viewed with intense scepticism.[4] Following Paul Kahn, law has come to be seen as the sign and instrument of progress. More law has come to mean more reform, and better reasons.[5] But the liberal fascination or preoccupation with law blinkers other important perspectives.

In what Max Weber called the "rational" liberal state, law has come to displace practical reasonableness, lawyers have come to dominate politics,[6] and law has come to offer a cover for turpitude. The claim that "we don't torture" comes with lawyerly provisos as we cavil over the meaning of "torture."[7] So it was that a small group of Bush administration lawyers, working in secrecy, made certain that inquisitors authorised by the president were immune from criminal laws against torture.[8] Immoral violence was made legal and, made legal, was done.[9] But infinite confidence in law is a mistake. As Koskenniemi says, unchangeable prefabricated rules do not always resolve contextual injustice.[10] When law is hyperbolised and over-worked, our moral perceptiveness and our sense of moral obligation waste away. Modernity is subverted by the collaborative avoidance of responsibility, and the decay of leadership. In this sense, the idea of law in war gestures to the delusional evasion of accountability.[11] A habituated moral inattention obtains from the overemphasis of legal structures. Responsibility is understood as a legal term, a feature of bureaucratic office, but not a moral trait of people. People come to be accountable merely for following rules. There is an ensuing moral palsy, a lack of moral sensitivity and insight. When the law and compliance with law are over-emphasised, there is the subdual of analytical criticism and the fear of difference, which Umberto Eco described as veering to fascism and dangerous for democracy.[12]

Something Measly about the Law

War is different. In the idea of war, we insinuate the discontinuation of peacetime routine, and the jettison of peacetime aspirations.[13] War – the prospect of war and the conduct of war – demands careful decision by those who bear responsibility for its violence. War's nature demands those responsible for its proceeding evaluate moral reasons. But in the liberal democracies, it seems reasons are overwhelmingly legal. In the liberal democracies it seems war's moral character is disremembered. Law has a cardinal, crucial significance. Yet by itself, the law's paper world fails to cope with war's tormenting moral complexity.[14] Compliance with law is unable to meet responsibility for war's evil. There is something measly about using law to confront the unspeakable horror of mass killing. Killing a person is almost unthinkable. Even the most benevolent form of killing – voluntary assisted euthanasia – is controlled exactingly if it is not prohibited. Yet, invocation of the word "war" conjures up a convoluted set of legal rules and dissolves moral scruple, so killing no longer seems a horrifying crime but instead, an achievement.[15]

Gerry Simpson says: "something other than law [is] at stake here, and to address it in legal terms [is] a mistake."[16] Simpson's remarks supervene upon the international law's post-1945 determination to prevent mass atrocity crime. But since the holocaust, as the language of law has come to be ubiquitous, so war's immanent evil has come to be redacted and bowdlerised by the forceless lawyerly nomenclature of the bureaucracy.[17]

The law seeks to categorise and specify. But the fetish for exactitude weakens law's capacity to deal with the moral ideas which are axial to war. For example, "atrocity," a morally expressive term, but not a legal term of art, does not occupy any place within the language of international military law. Rather than "atrocity," we speak of "manifest illegality," or "war crimes," or "grave breaches" of the Geneva Conventions. These are terms which call for lawyerly precision, not spontaneous, emotional, common sense moral perceptivity.[18]

Infatuated with qualification and fine points, law is gulled by the myth that the costs, benefits, and moral proportions of war can be measured and defined.[19] But law's certitude is entirely made-up. Law is a social creation which cannot capture the moral implication of circumstances, or the nuance of individual judgement.[20]

Law and War

As domestic law has come to be all-pervading in peacetime society, so international law has come to partition war's landscape.[21] The institutional corridors to war are defined by the law, and politics exhausts the vocabulary of law to assort, to justify, and to excuse violence.[22] Terms of engagement are legal. Means and consequences are construed in legal language which gives the impression that by legal compliance one will have taken account of all the relevant considerations.[23] But the law's determinate words and phrases do not capture the moral texture and onus of war. Beyond law's exacting terms war is an atrocity, an outrage. Taking from David Kennedy, violence and injury have lost their author and their judge as modernity has come to be captivated by a morally detached, legalistic, and bureaucratic vernacular.[24]

Failing to see the moral consequence of war, the *Defence Act* falls afoul of the false belief that there is no difference between law and ethics.[25] Of course, for soldiers in wartime, legally compliant behaviour and ethical behaviour bear a close correlation. Adil Haque makes this point. He says combatants who comply strictly with legal stipulations are more likely to meet moral obligations, which can be difficult to weigh out in the confusion of battle.[26] Perhaps we might be prepared to accept that Haque's analysis applies to soldiers engaged in a fight. But Haque's account does not pertain to the general.

The general is not like ordinary soldiers engaged in a firefight and confronting death at hand. The general is removed from the immediacy of fighting. The general does not need to respond to ministers unthinkingly, reflexively, or spontaneously. The general has the chance to deliberate – and should. Directed by the minister to follow unconscionable venturesome direction, generals will better meet moral obligations when they evaluate circumstances. For the general confronted by political direction which would imperil the nation's security, occasion unjust war, expand extant war in unjust ways, waste lives in a needless squander, or lead to some other grievously bad outcome; it will be wrong to comply merely since law prescribes compliance. The general must think things through. The general must act morally, with moral purpose and a mind to circumstances. Saying this I assert that moral decision is deliberate, not the result of coercion, and not the result of automatic conformance with the rule or convention.

War is Hell

On the battlefield, and beyond it, war is hell; an atrocity, made war and not mass murder on account of moral justifications named for its prosecution. Noting the substratal consequence of moral justification, and noting the unfettered, immeasurable catastrophe of war, the absence of moral perception in the Australian legislation is grotesque. In the *Defence Act* there is a lawyerly narrow-mindedness, there is no gesture to the moral reasons which offer palliation and reason for conflict. The *Defence Act* does not account for the moral character and significance of war, for the tragic resonance of war across cultures and lifetimes. Aeschylus captures war's moral gravity and compass in *Agamemnon* (458 BC) when he has the Chorus of City Elders say:

> Even in our sleep, pain which cannot forget
> Falls drop by drop from the heart,
> Until, in our own despair,
> Against our will,
> Comes wisdom
> Through the awful grace of God.[27]

Describing the return of Agamemnon from the Trojan War, Aeschylus sees the resonance of conflict span the whole of society. Public life is united with domestic households in shared calamity. Even victory comes at the cost of unutterable distress. Aeschylus lets us see that to be wholly responsible and well-founded, decisions about war must account for moral ideas that eclipse the law of armed conflict. In *The Trojan Women* (415 BC), Euripides gestures similarly to the moral perspective which should inform decisions about war. Following the capitulation and slaughter of Melos, and the barbarism at Plataea, Scione, Hysiae, and – almost – Mytilene (where a decree to murder the populace was rescinded at the last minute), Euripides was heartsick at "simple barbarity"[28] justified by realist politics. When he has Hecuba exclaim: "Achaeans! All your strength is in your spears, not in the mind,"[29] Euripides illustrates the ethical perspective which should distinguish soldiers from murderers. When he has Poseidon curse the victorious Greeks: "That mortal who sacks fallen cities is a fool, / Who gives the temples and the tombs and hallowed places / Of the dead to desolation. His own turn must come;"[30] Euripides shows us that war demands more than a morally insensible readiness to kill and devastate. War demands the sort of moral perspective to which the Australian domestic law is oblivious.

War, in Sherman's famous phrase, is "hell" – rich with meaning, which transcends the capacity of politics or law to depict. In the *New York Times* Bob Herbert argued war is always about sorrow and suffering. Despite half-baked legal rationalisations, the reality is always wanton bloodshed, and lifelong trauma.[31] Beyond the legalistic, bureaucratic monotone, which seems inevitable in the modern state,[32] the meaning of war is moral and rooted in the cultural inheritance of western society. Telling us how Hephaestus forged the shield of Achilles, Homer lets us see the deep roots of the western understanding:

> First of all Hephaestus forged a shield that was huge and heavy …/ On it he wrought in all their beauty two cities of mortal men …/ But around the city were two forces of armed men shining in their war gear. For one side counsel was divided / whether to storm and sack, or share between both sides the property / and all the possessions the lovely citadel held hard within it. / But the city's people were not giving way, and armed for an ambush / Their beloved wives and their little children stood on the rampart.[33]

Among other scenes wrought on the shield are a wedding, feasts, a market, dancing, a law court, and a battle. Homer shows us that war is a forge of cultures – and a product of cultures. To speak of war only in the language of law is to undermine our grasp of a diabolical, grievous, inexpressibly complex moral endeavour. Fortunately, a constellation of inexplicit, indispensable moral ideas finds legal recognition in the Martens Clause.

The Martens Clause

In a time of moral perplexity or urgency, the general must act deliberately, decidedly, autonomously for "right." The claim of "right" is unspecified and rhetorical, but it is not puzzling. We understand Jeff McMahan when he says, "some types of acts are so seriously objectionable that they cannot become permissible even if they are demanded by institutions that are both just and important."[34] We understand the legal theorist Gerry Simpson when he says, "certain acts are offences against the whole of humanity or, indeed, the very idea of humanity. They shock the conscience of mankind."[35] We understand critical ideas of honour, virtue, and chivalry.[36] These are moral notions, Bernard Williams describes them as "thick concepts," a union of fact and value.[37]

R.M. Hare sees thick concepts as "value words" which combine "descriptive" and "evaluative" elements.[38] Thick concepts are not objective and categorical. They are not captured in law. Their meaning and relevance do not derive from codification, but from context, incidence, and utility.[39] These are complex ideas. They are difficult to express. But they are known, they permeate the lived experience of western democracy, and they exert a profound shaping effect upon the western approach to war. Even though war is a world apart, where life itself is at stake, where human nature is reduced to self-interest, where necessity prevails, we speak about war in a language rich with moral meaning.[40] We understand moral ideas, and it is unreasonable to dismiss them as a fig leaf to hypocrisy.[41] We understand the best prospects for minimising atrocity derive from the virtues of chivalry and martial honour.[42]

The constellation of innominate virtues crowded in the idea of chivalry finds formal expression in the Martens Clause. Named for F. F. de Martens, a jurist, and a Russian delegate to the first and second Hague Peace Conferences in 1899, the Martens Clause obtains from a rich provenance in natural law and chivalry.[43] Set out in the Hague Conventions, reaffirmed in the Geneva Conventions, and cited with approval in the international jurisprudence, the Martens Clause asserts "the laws of humanity and the dictates of public conscience." The Clause provides authority for acknowledging moral ideas in the international law. On my account, the Martens Clause gestures to moral ideas which should be incorporated in the domestic law by means of an exception.

As Commander in Chief of the Continental Army, George Washington prefigured the Martens forms when he agreed with his British adversary that the Revolutionary War would be "carried on agreeable to the rules which humanity formed."[44] Similarly, the celebrated and significant Lieber Code speaks to general and unspecified principles of humanity. Formulated by Dr. Francis Lieber in 1863, on the command of President Abraham Lincoln as *General Order 100 for the Government of United States Armies in the Field*, the Lieber Code speaks *inter alia* of "principles of justice, honor and humanity – virtues adorning a soldier even more than other men, for the very reason that he possesses the power of his arms."[45]

F. F. de Martens acknowledged the influence of these ideas[46] upon the code he formulated in 1899 to acknowledge "the laws of humanity, and the requirements of the public conscience."[47] Resonant throughout the international humanitarian law,[48] the Martens Clause has been replicated in the Preamble to the Hague Conventions, relied upon in the Nuremberg jurisprudence and reiterated in many humanitarian law treaties. The Martens Clause was restated in the 1949 Geneva Conventions, the 1977 Additional Protocols to those Conventions, and the Preamble to the Convention on Prohibitions or Restrictions on the Use of Certain Conventional Weapons. The Clause was paraphrased in Resolution XXIII of the 1968 Tehran Conference on Human Rights, and it is cited or referred to in several national military manuals, including those of the United States, the United Kingdom, and Germany.[49]

In the case of *Krupp*[50] heard before the United States Military Tribunal III-A between 17 November 1947 and 31 July 1948, Wilkins J described the Martens clause as "much more than a pious declaration. It is a general clause, making the usages established among civilized nations, the laws of humanity, and the dictates of public conscience into the legal yardstick."[51] In his Foreword to Volume 15 of the *Law Reports of the Trials of War Criminals*, Lord Wright observed similarly:

> The governing effect of that sovereign clause [the Martens Clause] … does really in a few words state the whole animating and motivating principle

> of the law of war, and indeed of all law, because the object of all law is to secure as far as possible in the mutual relation of the human beings concerned, the rule of law, and of justice and of humanity. [The Martens Clause] aims, however imperfectly, at giving effect to the sense of justice and of right and wrong which is naturally inherent in all human beings except only the abandoned and vicious.[52]

In the International Court of Justice *Nuclear Weapons Advisory Opinion*, Shahabuddeen J said generalised moral principles are infixed in law through the Martens Clause. His Honour observed, "the Martens Clause provide[s] authority for treating the principles of humanity and the dictates of the public conscience as principles of international law."[53] His Honour noted that the standard implied by these principles is not to settled and established, but rather to be ascertained in the light of changing conditions.

Perhaps there are better concepts than moral concepts but, in the words of James Turner Johnson, "that is like saying there may be life in the fifth dimension; we simply cannot know because our knowledge is limited by the circumstance of our existence."[54]

The Exception

Law seeks to be stable and, if not fixed, at least constant and predictable. But the unruliness of the world makes invariance a practical impossibility. Eventually, the predictability sought by law runs up against the instability and irregularity of the world. Events disrupt and destabilise the order of law's paper world.[55] An exception allows law to accommodate moral judgement, to be practically realistic, workable, and fit for situations.

Famously – perhaps notoriously – in an echo of Plato[56] and Hobbes[57] and Locke,[58] Carl Schmitt claimed the sovereign decides on the exception.[59] Schmitt spoke to the terms of political power and the personalism of political authority. For Schmitt, the capacity to determine the exception was the conclusive expression of political prerogative.[60] Schmitt's argument was straightforward: when preservation of the state demands, prerogative power must overmaster the written law.

Since the military must be subordinate to the civil power, I do not imagine offering the general conclusive sovereign power. My concern is with the illiberal personality of the law. My argument is that an exception might offer the general nothing more than legal space to refuse political injustice.

I follow Jeremy Horder, who argues the first and normal way law might accommodate circumstantial reasonableness and moral sense is by the creation of an exception.[61] Law regularly anticipates "exceptions" to the rule. Raz observes the doctrines of self-defence and necessity.[62] By its nature, an exception cannot be specified. But an exception can be foretold. In the *Second Treatise*, John Locke argues, the law must make some reasonable accommodation for the commonplace uncertainty and variableness of human affairs.[63] Similarly, Thomas Jefferson, the third President of the United States, saw how law's fixed terms could be "inadequate" to the circumstances, a "manacle"[64] to right and a detriment to justice.[65]

The point is, in some situations the conventional practice, the familiar usages, and the commonplace operation of law will not apply. There are moments when the right thing to do would normally be morally objectionable.[66] Sometimes, as Adil Haque says the public welfare will be better served by disregarding the terms of pre-formed law. In exceptional cases, generally reliable rules will prohibit an act that is morally required or require an act that is morally prohibited. In such moments, individuals should abide by their conscience or moral judgement.[67]

In exceptional cases, where law is unfit to the circumstances, we find a "borderline," law's "outermost sphere," the limit of law's capacity to define and specify.[68] In these moments, we place our confidence in human virtue which, recalling Locke: "in a great measure every-where corresponds with the unchangeable Rule of Right and Wrong … there being nothing that so directly and visibly secures, and advances the general Good of Mankind in this World."[69] Shakespeare illuminates the aperture between explicit law and circumstantial moral reason when, in *The Merchant of Venice,* he has Portia say to Shylock:

> The sceptre shows the force of temporal power, / But mercy is above this sceptre sway; / It is enthroned in the hearts of kings, / It is an attribute to God himself, / And earthly power doth then show likest God's. [4:1][70]

By his word "mercy" Shakespeare gestures to the demands of justice beyond indifferent rules. To be properly functional, law needs to offer space for circumstantial reasonableness, for human judgement.[71] The exception allows law to fit the situation. This does not mean the abandonment of legal compliance.

When the state is confronted by war and imperilled, when time is short and the calculations are complicated, when the consequences of getting things wrong are ghastly beyond description; then the Chief of the Defence Force *must* comply with ministerial direction (probably). In an argument from Hobbes: "When the defence of the Common-wealth requireth at once the help of all that are able to bear Arms, everyone is obliged."[72] But we can imagine circumstances where circumspection should be the order of the day, where the best thing would be for the general to refuse. War presents a special case where the routine operation of law as it is in the *Defence Act* is not fitting. It will not always be reasonable for the general to do everything the minister wants. Law cannot capture the complexity of moral obligations, which are circumferential and immanent to war. Absolute rules lead us to fancy we can define right and wrong, always and for everyone. But justice is not like that. Justice must be imagined and re-imagined and redefined in new ways to suit the circumstances.[73]

Aristotle spoke to this view when he reasoned there is no one ideal, quintessential, irrefutable definition of "good."[74] G. E. Moore described "good" (and other ideas like "justice") as "thin" or "simple" concepts. In *Principia Ethica* Moore explains how thin concepts escape explicit definition and how, when we try to define them, we commit what he calls the naturalistic fallacy.[75] Moore argued the term "good" denotes an indefinable quality. On Moore's view, goodness is a special kind of property – a non-naturalistic property. "Good," as an adjective, requires to be complemented by a noun, which, says Philippa Foot, "plays an essential role in determining whether we are able to speak of goodness rather than badness, or indeed of goodness or badness at all."[76] Foot explains this point by reference to Peter Greach, who puts good in a class of adjectives called attributive adjectives. Attributive adjectives are not like predicative adjectives – words such as "red" – which make sense independent of the nouns to which they refer. In contrast, an attributive adjective like "good" depends upon the noun to which it refers. For example, "bad" may change to "good" when we consider a book of philosophy first as a book of philosophy and then as a soporific.[77]

Stipulating the general "must" comply with executive direction, Australian law supposes the inevitable, undeniable goodness of compliance. Australian law presumes compliance will be right, always and for everyone. But the legal "must" is quite different from the moral "ought." Generals ought to act well, for goodness and rightness against the forces of chaos and evil. Sometimes, even mostly, moral ideas of good and right will coincide with the legal stipulation "must" – but not always. Sometimes, morally right action will be inconsistent with the law. Saying this, I do not suggest that law's categorical demands are immaterial. My claim is rather for conscience and principle as existential cornerstones of law, and for law to be interpreted and applied as circumstances demand. Law is a complete system but not an exclusive system. Legal ideas are tied to other forms of meaning. This is to say, the connotations and conclusions adjacent to explicit legal forms might involve political and moral ideas. The one account does not eclipse the other.[78]

Asking for an exception I ask law to discern a larger, more practically viable, circumstantially reasonable, idea of justice. I ask the categorical, clear-cut idea of law articulated by Locke, to welcome the human insight and the personal judgement articulated by Hobbes. Without the boundary of definite and inelastic law, Locke was concerned the citizens would not know their duty, and the government would not remain within just bounds.[79] But Locke is not alert to the abstractly valid human conscience, which recognises justice beyond static law.[80] In contrast, Hobbes captures the power and significance of human decision when he argues level-headed human judgement is the basis of law.[81] Hobbes speaks to an idea of "personalism," which he calls the law of nature – natural law. For Hobbes, natural law and positivist or made law balance each other in society. Hobbes says: "the [civil, positivist or made] law [which] can never be against Reason [*viz*: natural law]"[82] operates to restrain the "natural liberty of man" so as people "might not hurt, but assist one another, and join together against a common enemy."[83] The definitive point is in the Hobbesian claim that people are ultimately subject to the natural law. Hobbes says: "Temporall, or Civill Power is subject to the Spirituall." He says: "Subjection, Command, Right and Power are accidents, not of Powers but of Persons."[84]

Recognising the essential application of the natural law, Hobbes contrasts with John Rawls who follows Locke to locate the true expression of liberalism in the Supreme Court[85] and the constitution.[86] For Rawls, justice depends upon an all-encompassing background framework, a point of view which is not distorted by the features of circumstances.[87] On the Rawlsian account, ultimate power is in law, set out on the cornerstone of a constitution.[88] Without a constitution and without the administration of fixed principles, Rawls imagines the people to be critically deprived. Rawls places his faith in rationality and in unalterable, pre-ordained principles, which he believes will defend against the arbitrary opinion of transient majorities.[89]

Rawls places his emphasis on unfluctuating, impartial, emphatic law – no exceptions.[90] He is indifferent to the particularities of people and circumstance. Rawls says the real task is to formulate the deep conception of justice in law, so as people might have a common point upon which to base their interactions.[91] I take a different tack. Allowing an exception, I would stretch a point on the circumference, without dislocating the centre. Rawls would want laws and institutions to be equally fair for everyone. He says, "the task is to articulate a public conception of justice that all can live with,"[92] and he seeks legal and institutional reform in cases of injustice.[93] But I argue pre-formed law will, at some point, inevitably be at odds with the circumstances.

Arguing for an exception I gesture to Carl Schmitt. In *Political Theology* Schmitt describes the exception as a jurisprudential domain *within law and, at the same time, beyond the law*; a moral space in the shadow of the law.[94] The importance of this argument is in the relation of conscience to law. I do not claim conscience should take precedence over the law. I am concerned when law and legal proceduralism operate in excess, to crowd out conscience and moral sensitivity. I claim a liberal democracy should take the moral convictions of citizens seriously and enable individuals to examine and to act upon deeply held beliefs. Thus, rather than placing conscience over law, I ask for an exception so that conscience might find space *within* the law.

I accept law is the only human institution rightly claiming unlimited authority.[95] In other words, I do not dispute the authority of law. I merely say law may not rightly force our conscience. Thus, I propose an exception so law might recognise or accommodate conscience. This asking is not unusual.

When law touches on matters likely to involve conscience, the first and usual accommodation is in the creation of an exception *within* the law.[96] The exception thus corresponds with doctrines of equity which, on the view of Meagher, Gummow and Lehane JJ: "soften[s] and modifie[s] many of the injustices in common law, and provide[s] remedies where at law they were either inadequate or non-existent."[97] But the exception does not overturn the law. Nor does the exception operate to put conscience *above* the law. Rather, the exception enables law to recognise conscience.

Thus conceived, the exception overcomes the incapacity of law to account for moral nuance and moral commitment. Moral ideas are different from unconditional laws. Where law makes a straitjacket of rules, moral ideas interblend with circumstances. Moral ideas thus counteract inflexible, legalist, bureaucratic, economic-technical thinking.[98] To be properly functional, law needs to perceive likely states of affairs and account for plausible exceptions. On my account, better law would allow an exception so generals might refuse direction which contravenes the Martens forms.

Conclusion

War is hell. War has a moral significance beyond capture in law's paper world. The lived experience of war is visceral, and desperate, and very far from quibbling over legal fine-points. Resonant over cultures and lifetimes the moral consequence of war is unconcealed and well-known. Our knowing is in our language. Discussing war, language is rich with moral meaning developed through centuries. Words like faithfulness, honour, shame, betrayal, cruelty, ruthlessness, atrocity, and massacre are filled with moral meaning.[99]

Offering an exception so law might respond reasonably to the moral tumult of war is prudent. And, since law controls the terms of the exception, the exception cannot pose a threat to law's overarching authority.

Notes

1 Seth Lazar, "Evaluating the Revisionist Critique of Just War Theory," in *Dædalus, the Journal of the American Academy of Arts & Sciences*, (2017) 146:1, pp. 113–124, 119–120. Lazar says: "One can be responsible for a threat in virtue of posing it oneself, or contributing to it, or even failing to prevent it. So liability can potentially extend not only to the soldier who pulls the trigger, but to the commander who orders him to do so, and to the politicians who give the commanders their orders."

2 Hannah Arendt, *The Origins of Totalitarianism* (Orlando, Austin, New York, San Diego, London: Harvest, 1994), p. 290.

3 Martii Koskenniemi, "The Politics of International Law," in *European Journal of International Law*, (1990) 1:4, pp. 4–32, 5.
Martii Koskenniemi, *The Politics of International Law* (Oxford: Hart Publishing, 2011), p. 36.

4 Clement Fatovic, *Outside the Law* (Baltimore: Johns Hopkins University Press, 2009), p. 253.

5 Paul Kahn, *Sacred Violence: Torture, Terror and Sovereignty* (Ann Arbor: University of Michigan Press, 2011), pp. 4, 5, 67.

6 Max Weber, "Politics as a Vocation," David Owen and Tracy Strong (eds.) and Rodney Livingstone (tr.), *The Vocation Lectures* (Indianapolis: Hackett Publishing, 2004), p. 51.

7 David Luban, *Torture, Power and Law* (Cambridge: Cambridge University Press, 2014), p. 208.

8 David Luban, *Torture, Power and Law* (Cambridge: Cambridge University Press, 2014), p. 211.

9 David Luban, *Legal Ethics and Human Dignity* (Cambridge: Cambridge University Press, 2007), p. 163.

10 Martii Koskenniemi, "The Politics of International Law," in *European Journal of International Law*, (1990) 1:4, pp. 4–32, 32.

11 David Kennedy, *Of War and Law* (Princeton and Oxford: Princeton University Press, 2006) p. 147.

12 Umberto Eco, "Ur-fascism," in *New York Review of Books*, (June 22, 1995) 42:11, 12.

13 David Kennedy, *Of War and Law* (Princeton and Oxford: Princeton University Press, 2006), pp. 2–3.

14 Michael Walzer *Just and Unjust Wars: A Moral Argument* (New York: Basic Books, 2000), p. xix.
15 Jeff McMahan, *Killing in War* (Oxford: Clarendon Press, 2009), p. vii.
16 Gerry Simpson, *Law War and Crime* (Cambridge: Polity, 2007), pp. 83, 84.
17 Gerry Simpson, *Law War and Crime* (Cambridge: Polity, 2007), p. 84.
18 Mark Osiel, "Obeying Orders: Atrocity, Military Discipline and the Law of War," in *California Law Review*, (1998) 86:5 pp. 943–1129, 951.
19 David Kennedy, *Of War and Law* (Princeton and Oxford: Princeton University Press, 2006), p. 144.
20 Bernard Williams, *Ethics and the Limits of Philosophy* (Cambridge, MA: Harvard University Press, 1985), p. 3.
21 David Kennedy, *The Dark Side of Virtue: Reassessing International Humanitarianism* (Princeton and Oxford: Princeton University Press, 2004), p. 263.
David Kennedy, *Of War and Law* (Princeton and Oxford: Princeton University Press, 2006), p. 7.
22 David Kennedy, *Of War and Law* (Princeton and Oxford: Princeton University Press, 2006), pp. 25, 32, 33
23 David Kennedy, *Of War and Law* (Princeton and Oxford: Princeton University Press, 2006), p. 143.
24 David Kennedy, *Of War and Law* (Princeton and Oxford: Princeton University Press, 2006), p. 169.
25 Hannah Arendt, *The Origins of Totalitarianism* (Orlando, Austin, New York, San Diego, London: Harvest, 1994), p. 394.
26 Adil A. Haque, *Law and Morality at War* (Oxford: Oxford University Press, 2017), pp. 3, 15, 21, 28, 42, 43, 44, 45, 46.
27 This form is from Senator Robert F. Kennedy speaking after the assassination of the Rev. Martin Luther King Jr. in William Safire, *Lend Me Your Ears: Great Speeches in History* (New York and London: W.W. Norton, 2004), p. 230.
The original form is at: Aeschylus, *Agamemnon*, Lines 176–183.
28 Euripides, *Trojan Women*, Line 764: Andromache as she kisses and relinquishes Astyanax.
29 Euripides, *Trojan Women*, Lines 1158–1159.
30 Euripides, *Trojan Women*, Lines 95–97.
31 Bob Herbert, "The Agony of War," in *New York Times*, April 25, 2005, p. 21.
32 Max Weber, "Politics as a Vocation," in *The Vocation Lectures*, David Owen and Tracy Strong (eds.) and Rodney Livingstone (tr.), (Indianapolis: Hackett Publishing, 2004), p. 37.
33 Richmond Lattimore (tr.), *The Iliad of Homer* (Chicago and London: University of Chicago Press, 1961), Lines 478–514, pp. 388–389.
34 Jeff McMahan, "The Ethics of Killing in War," in *Ethics*, (2004) 114, pp. 693–733, 705
35 Gerry Simpson, *Law War and Crime* (Cambridge: Polity, 2007), p. 46.
36 David Kennedy, *The Dark Side of Virtue: Reassessing International Humanitarianism* (Princeton and Oxford: Princeton University Press, 2004), p. 268.
37 Bernard Williams, *Ethics and the Limits of Philosophy* (Cambridge, MA: Harvard University Press, 1985), p. 129.
38 R.M. Hare, *The Language of Morals* (Oxford: Clarendon Press, 2003), p. 175.
39 Clifford Geertz, *The Interpretation of Cultures* (New York: Basic Books, 1973), pp. 6–7.
40 Michael Walzer, *Just and Unjust Wars: A Moral Argument* (New York: Basic Books, 2000), p. 3.
41 Eliot A. Cohen, *Supreme Command, Soldiers Statesmen and Leadership in Wartime* (New York: Anchor Books, 2003), pp. 263–264. "Enough of the officers' code survives, despite the allure of a materialistic culture, to make concepts like honour distinguishing characteristics of the military way."

42 Mark Osiel, "Obeying Orders: Atrocity, Military Discipline and the Law of War," in *California Law Review*, (1998) 86:5, pp. 943–1129, 955.
Mark Osiel, *Obeying Orders: Atrocity, Military Discipline and the Law of War* (New Brunswick and London: Transaction, 2002), p. 37. "Where the illegality of a superior's order is not manifest, [then a sense of] martial honour [will] help the soldier identify the proper course of action."
Kenneth Anderson, "The Rise of International Criminal Law: Intended and Unintended Consequences," in *The European Journal of International Law*, (2009) 20:2, pp. 331–358, 342. Citing John Keegan, Anderson says, "there is no substitute for honour as a medium for enforcing decency on the battlefield, never has been, and never will be."
43 Theodor Meron, "The Martens Clause, Principles of Humanity and Dictates of Public Conscience," in *American Journal of International Law*, (2000) 94:1, pp. 78–89, 79.
Telford Taylor, *The Anatomy of the Nuremberg Trials: A Personal Memoir* (New York: Skyhorse, 2013), p. 10.
44 Stephen W. Preston, General Counsel of the Department of Defense, Foreword to *Department of Defense Law of War Manual* (Office of General Counsel, Department of Defense, Pentagon, 12 June 2015), p. ii.
45 Francis Lieber, *General Order 100, Instructions for the Government of Armies of the United States in the Field* (New York: D. van Nostrand, 1863), paragraph 4, p. 4.
Telford Taylor, *The Anatomy of the Nuremberg Trials: A Personal Memoir* (New York: Skyhorse, 2013), pp. 8, 9.
46 Daniel C. Gilman, "Francis Lieber," in *Yale Law Journal*, (1901) 10:7, pp. 271–274, 274. Citing F. F. de Martens.
47 Theodor Meron, "The Martens Clause, Principles of Humanity and Dictates of Public Conscience," in *American Journal of International Law*, (2000) 94:1, pp. 78–89, 79.
48 Theodor Meron, "The Martens Clause, Principles of Humanity and Dictates of Public Conscience," in *American Journal of International Law*, (2000) 94:1, pp. 78–89, 79.
49 Theodor Meron, "The Martens Clause, Principles of Humanity and Dictates of Public Conscience," in *American Journal of International Law*, (2000) 94:1, pp. 78–89, 78.
50 *Krupp* concerned charges of war crimes and crimes against humanity resulting from economic exploitation of captured territory beyond the needs of an army of occupation.
51 *The United States of America v. Alried Felix Alwyn Krupp von Bohlen und Halbach et al.*, p. 1341 per Wilkins J.
52 L.J. Wright, "Foreword" to *Law Reports of the Trials of War Criminals: Selected and Prepared by the United Nations War Crimes Commission* (16 Volumes) Vol. XV, *Digest of Laws and Cases* (London: HMSO, 1949), p. xiii.
53 *Legality of the Threat or Use by a State of Nuclear Weapons in Armed Conflict*, International Court of Justice Advisory Opinion, International Court of Justice Reports 1996, General List No. 95, p. 226, per Shahabuddeen J at p. 406 and similarly, at p. 409.
54 James T. Johnson, *Can Modern War be Just?* (New Haven and London: Yale University Press, 1984), p. 17.
Ludwig Wittgenstein, *Tractatus Logico-Philosophicus* (New York: Dover, 1999), paragraph 5.633, 5.6331, p. 89.
55 Clement Fatovic, *Outside the Law* (Baltimore: Johns Hopkins University Press, 2009), pp. 1–2.
56 Plato, "Statesman" 294a: "…the best thing is not that laws should prevail, but rather the kingly man who possesses wisdom."
57 Thomas Hobbes, *Leviathan* (England: Penguin, 1985), Ch. 26, §1, 2, pp. 312–313.
58 John Locke, "Second Treatise," in Ian Shapiro (ed.), *Two Treatises of Government and a Letter Concerning Toleration* (New Haven: Yale University Press, 2003), Ch. XIV, "Of Prerogative," §160, p. 172. Locke says: "The power to act according to discretion for the public good, without the prescription of the law, and sometimes even against it, is that which is called the prerogative… [it is the practical] latitude left to the executive

power to do many things of choice which the laws do not prescribe." Less dramatically (§159, p. 171) Locke says: "…it is fit that the laws themselves should in some cases give way …"

59 Carl Schmitt, *Political Theology: Four Chapters on the Concept of Sovereignty*, George Schwab (tr.), (Chicago and London: University of Chicago Press, 2005), p. 5.

60 Carl Schmitt, *Political Theology: Four Chapters on the Concept of Sovereignty*, George Schwab (tr.), (Chicago and London: University of Chicago Press, 2005), p. 6.

61 Jeremy Horder, *Excusing Crime* (Oxford: Oxford University Press, 2004), p. 200.

62 Joseph Raz, *The Morality of Freedom* (Oxford: Clarendon Press, 2009), p. 77.

63 John Locke, "Second Treatise," in Ian Shapiro (ed.), *Two Treatises of Government and a Letter Concerning Toleration* (New Haven: Yale University Press, 2003), Ch. XIII, "On the Subordination of the Powers of the Commonwealth," §156 p. 169.

64 Clement Fatovic, *Outside the Law* (Baltimore: Johns Hopkins University Press, 2009), pp. 36, 204.

65 Clement Fatovic, *Outside the Law* (Baltimore: Johns Hopkins University Press, 2009), p. 205.
Jeremy D. Bailey, "Executive Prerogative and the 'Good Officer' in Thomas Jefferson's Letter to John B. Colvin," in *Presidential Studies Quarterly*, (2004) 34:4, p. 732, pp. 734–735.

66 Bernard Williams, "Politics and Moral Character," in *Moral Luck* (Cambridge: Cambridge University Press, 1999), p. 59.

67 Adil Ahmad Haque, *Law and Morality at War* (Oxford: Oxford University Press, 2017), p. 45.

68 Carl Schmitt, *Political Theology: Four Chapters on the Concept of Sovereignty,* George Schwab (tr.) (Chicago and London: University of Chicago Press, 2005), p. 5.

69 John Locke, *An Essay Concerning Human Understanding*, Pewter H. Nidditch (ed.) (Oxford: Clarendon Press, 2011), Book II, Ch. 28, "Of Other Relations," §11 p. 356.
Alan Norrie, *Crime, Reason and History* (London: Butterworths, 2001), p. 173.

70 William Shakespeare, "The Merchant of Venice," in William George Clark and William A. Wright (eds.), *The Works of William Shakespeare* (London: MacMillian and Co., 1866), pp. 198–199.

71 Lon Fuller, "The Forms and Limits of Adjudication," in *Harvard law Review*, (1978) 92:2, pp. 372, 382.
Roscoe Pound, "The Limits of Effective Legal Action," in *International Journal of Ethics*, (1917) 27:2, p. 166.

72 Thomas Hobbes, *Leviathan*, C.B. Macpherson (ed.) (England: Penguin, 1985), Ch. 21, p. 270.

73 David Kennedy, *Of War and Law* (Princeton and Oxford: Princeton University Press, 2006), p. 104.

74 Aristotle, *Nichomachean Ethics*, 1096b.

75 G.E. Moore, *Principia Ethica* (Cambridge: Cambridge University Press, 1922), §10 pp. 9–10; § 26 pp. 39–41; § 73 pp. 123–125.

76 Philippa Foot, *Natural Goodness* (Oxford: Clarendon Press, 2010), p. 2.

77 Philippa Foot, *Natural Goodness* (Oxford: Clarendon Press, 2010), pp. 2–3.

78 Paul Kahn, *Political Theology: Four New Chapters on the Concept of Sovereignty* (New York: Columbia University Press, 2011), p. 33.

79 John Locke, *Two Treatises of Government and a Letter Concerning Toleration* (New Haven: Yale University Press, 2003), Ch. XI, "On the Extent of the Legislative Power," §137, p. 161. Also: Ch. IV "Of Slavery," §22, pp. 109–110. And, Ch. VII, "Of Political or Civil Society," §87, pp. 136–137. And, Ch. XI, "On the Extent of the Legislative Power," §137, pp. 160, 161.

80 Carl Schmitt, *Political Theology: Four Chapters on the Concept of Sovereignty*, George Schwab (tr.) (Chicago and London: University of Chicago Press, 2005), pp. 32, 33.

81 Thomas Hobbes, *Leviathan*, C.B. Macpherson (ed.) (England: Penguin, 1985), Ch. 26 "Of Civill Lawes," pp. 316–335: *sed autoritas, non veritas facit legem.* (Authority not truth makes law.)
82 Thomas Hobbes, *Leviathan*, C.B. Macpherson (ed.), (England: Penguin, 1985), Ch. 26 "Of Civill Lawes," p. 316.
83 Thomas Hobbes, *Leviathan*, C.B. Macpherson (ed.) (England: Penguin, 1985), p. 316. Also p. 227.
84 Thomas Hobbes, *Leviathan*, C.B. Macpherson (ed.) (England: Penguin, 1985), Ch. 42 "Of a Christian Commonwealth," p. 601.
85 John Rawls, *Political Liberalism* (New York: Columbia University Press, 2005), p. 231.
86 John Rawls, *Political Liberalism* (New York: Columbia University Press, 2005), p. 232.
87 John Rawls, "Justice as Fairness: Political not Metaphysical," in *Philosophy and Public Affairs*, (1985) 14:3, pp. 223–251, 235.
88 John Rawls, *Political Liberalism* (New York: Columbia University Press, 2005), p. 232.
89 John Rawls, *Political Liberalism* (New York: Columbia University Press, 2005), p. 233. John Rawls, "Kantian Constructivism in Moral Theory," in *Journal of Philosophy*, (1980) 77:9, pp. 515–572, 517.
90 John Rawls, *A Theory of Justice* (Cambridge, MA: The Belknap Press of Harvard University Press, 1999), pp. 322, 389.
91 John Rawls, "Kantian Constructivism in Moral Theory," in *Journal of Philosophy*, (1980) 77:9, pp. 515–572, 518.
92 John Rawls, "Kantian Constructivism in Moral Theory," in *Journal of Philosophy*, (1980) 77:9, pp. 515–572, 519.
93 John Rawls, *A Theory of Justice* (Cambridge, MA: The Belknap Press of Harvard University Press, 1999), p. 209.
94 Carl Schmitt, *Political Theology: Four Chapters on the Concept of Sovereignty*, George Schwab (tr.), (Chicago and London: University of Chicago Press, 2005), p. 13.
95 Joseph Raz, *The Morality of Freedom* (Oxford: Clarendon Press, 2009), p. 76.
96 Jeremy Horder, *Excusing Crime* (Oxford: Oxford University Press, 2004), p. 200.
97 J.D. Heydon, M.J. Leeming and P.G. Turner, *Meagher, Gummow & Lehane's Equity: Doctrines and Remedies* (5th Edition) (Australia: LexisNexis Butterworths, 2015), p. 5.
98 Carl Schmitt, *Political Theology: Four Chapters on the Concept of Sovereignty*, George Schwab (tr.) (Chicago and London: University of Chicago Press, 2005), pp. 48, 65.
99 Michael Walzer, *Just and Unjust Wars: A Moral Argument* (New York: Basic Books, 2000), p. 3.

References

International Cases and Opinions

The United States of America v. Alfried Krupp, et al., in *Trials of War Criminals Before the Nuernberg Military Tribunals Under Control Council Law Number 10*, Nuernberg October 1946–April 1949 (Vol. IX) (United States Government Printing Office: Washington, 1950).

Law Reports of the Trials of War Criminals: Selected and Prepared by the United Nations War Crimes Commission (16 Volumes) Vol. XV, *Digest of Laws and Cases* (London: HMSO, 1949).

Legality of the Threat or Use by a State of Nuclear Weapons in Armed Conflict, International Court of Justice Advisory Opinion, International Court of Justice Reports 1996, General List No. 95.

Journal Articles

Anderson, Kenneth. "The Rise of International Criminal Law: Intended and Unintended Consequences," in *The European Journal of International Law*, (2009) 20:2, pp. 331–358.

Bailey, Jeremy D. "Executive Prerogative and the 'Good Officer' in Thomas Jefferson's Letter to John B. Colvin," in *Presidential Studies Quarterly*, (2004) 34:4, pp. 732–754, 734–735.

Eco, Umberto. "Ur-fascism," in *New York Review of Books* (22 June 1995) 42:11, p. 12. https://www.nybooks.com/articles/1995/06/22/ur-fascism/

Fuller, Lon. "The Forms and Limits of Adjudication," in *Harvard Law Review*, (1978) 92:2, pp. 353–409.

Gilman, Daniel C. "Francis Lieber," in *Yale Law Journal*, (1901) 10:7, pp. 271–274.

Koskenniemi, Martii. "The Politics of International Law," in *European Journal of International Law*, (1990) 1:4, pp. 4–32.

Lazar, Seth. "Evaluating the Revisionist Critique of Just War Theory," in *Dædalus, the Journal of the American Academy of Arts & Sciences*, (2017) 146:1, pp. 113–124.

McMahan, Jeff. "The Ethics of Killing in War," in *Ethics*, (2004) 114, pp. 693–733

Meron, Theodor. "The Martens Clause, Principles of Humanity and Dictates of Public Conscience," in *American Journal of International Law*, (2000) 94:1, pp. 78–89.

Osiel, Mark. "Obeying Orders: Atrocity, Military Discipline and the Law of War," in *California Law Review*, (1998) 86:5, pp. 943–1129.

Pound, Roscoe, "The Limits of Effective Legal Action," in *International Journal of Ethics*, (1917) 27:2, pp. 150–167.

Rawls, John. "Kantian Constructivism in Moral Theory," in *Journal of Philosophy*, (1980) 77:9, pp. 515–572.

Rawls, John. "Justice as Fairness: Political not Metaphysical," in *Philosophy and Public Affairs*, (1985) 14:3, pp. 223–251.

Books

Aeschylus, "Agamemnon," in David Grene and Richmond Lattimore (eds.), *The Complete Greek* Tragedies, Vol. 1 *Aeschylus* (Chicago and London: University of Chicago Press, 1991).

Arendt, Hannah. *The Origins of Totalitarianism* (Orlando, Austin, New York, San Diego, London: Harvest, 1994).

Aristotle, "Nichomachean Ethics," in Jonathan Barnes (ed.), *The Complete Works of Aristotle* (Princeton, NJ: Princeton University Press, 1995).

Cohen, Eliot. *Supreme Command, Soldiers Statesmen and Leadership in Wartime* (New York: Anchor Books, 2003).

Euripides, "The Trojan Women," in David Grene and Richmond Lattimore (eds.), *The Complete Greek Tragedies* (Vol. 3 of three volumes) (Chicago and London: University of Chicago Press, 1992).

Fatovic, Clement. *Outside the Law* (Baltimore: Johns Hopkins University Press, 2009).

Foot, Philippa. *Natural Goodness* (Oxford: Clarendon Press, 2010).

Geertz, Clifford. *The Interpretation of Cultures* (New York: Basic Books, 1973).

Haque, Adil A. *Law and Morality at War* (Oxford: Oxford University Press, 2017).

Hare, R.M. *The Language of Morals* (Oxford: Clarendon Press, 2003).

Heydon, J.D., Leeming, M.J. and Turner, P.G. *Meagher, Gummow & Lehane's Equity: Doctrines and Remedies* (5th Edition) (Australia: LexisNexis Butterworths, 2015).

Hobbes, Thomas. (ed.) C.B. Macpherson, *Leviathan* (England: Penguin, 1985).
Horder, Jeremy. *Excusing Crime* (Oxford: Oxford University Press, 2004).
Johnson, James T. *Can Modern War be Just?* (New Haven and London: Yale University Press, 1984).
Kahn, Paul. *Sacred Violence: Torture, Terror and Sovereignty* (Ann Arbor: University of Michigan Press, 2011).
Kennedy, David. *The Dark Side of Virtue: Reassessing International Humanitarianism* (Princeton and Oxford: Princeton University Press, 2004).
Kennedy, David. *Of War and Law* (Princeton and Oxford: Princeton University Press, 2006).
Koskenniemi, Martii. *The Politics of International Law* (Oxford: Hart Publishing, 2011).
Lattimore Richmond (tr.) *The Iliad of Homer* (Chicago and London: University of Chicago Press, 1961).
Lieber, Francis. *General Order 100, Instructions for the Government of Armies of the United States in the Field* (New York: D. van Nostrand, 1863).
Locke, John. "Second Treatise," in Ian Shapiro (ed.), *Two Treatises of Government and a Letter Concerning Toleration* (New Haven: Yale University Press, 2003).
Locke, John. *An Essay Concerning Human Understanding*, Pewter H. Nidditch (ed.) (Oxford: Clarendon Press, 2011).
Luban, David. *Legal Ethics and Human Dignity* (Cambridge: Cambridge University Press, 2007).
Luban, David. *Torture, Power and Law* (Cambridge: Cambridge University Press, 2014).
McMahan, Jeff. *Killing in War* (Oxford: Clarendon Press, 2009).
Moore, G.E. *Principia Ethica* (Cambridge: Cambridge University Press, 1922).
Norrie, Alan. *Crime, Reason and History* (London: Butterworths, 2001).
Osiel, Mark. *Obeying Orders: Atrocity, Military Discipline and the Law of War* (New Brunswick and London: Transaction, 2002).
Plato, "Statesman," in John M. Cooper (ed.), *Plato: Complete Works* (Indianapolis and Cambridge: Hackett, 1997).
Rawls, John. *A Theory of Justice* (Cambridge, MA: The Belknap Press of Harvard University Press, 1999).
Rawls, John. *Political Liberalism* (New York: Columbia University Press, 2005).
Raz, Joseph. *The Morality of Freedom* (Oxford: Clarendon Press, 2009).
Rousseau, Jean-Jacques. (ed.) Susan Dunn, *The Social Contract and The First and Second Discourses* (New Haven and London: Yale University Press, 2002).
Safire, William. *Lend Me Your Ears: Great Speeches in History* (New York and London: W.W. Norton, 2004).
Schmitt, Carl. *Political Theology: Four Chapters on the Concept of Sovereignty*, George Schwab (tr.) (Chicago and London: University of Chicago Press, 2005).
Shakespeare, William. "The Merchant of Venice," in George Clark and William A. Wright (eds.), *The Works of William Shakespeare* (London: MacMillian and Co., 1866).
Simpson, Gerry. *Law War and Crime* (Cambridge: Polity, 2007).
Taylor, Telford. *The Anatomy of the Nuremberg Trials: A Personal Memoir* (New York: Skyhorse, 2013).
Twomey, Anne. *The Veiled Sceptre: Reserve Powers and Heads of State in Westminster Systems* (Cambridge: Cambridge University Press, 2018).
Walzer, Michael. *Just and Unjust Wars: A Moral Argument* (New York: Basic Books, 2000).
Weber, Max. "Politics as a Vocation," in David Owen and Tracy Strong (eds). and Rodney Livingstone (tr.), *The Vocation Lectures* (Indianapolis: Hackett Publishing, 2004).

Williams, Bernard. *Ethics and the Limits of Philosophy* (Cambridge, MA: Harvard University Press, 1985).

Williams, Bernard. *Moral Luck* (Cambridge: Cambridge University Press, 1999).

Wittgenstein, Ludwig. (tr.) C.K. Ogden with an introduction by Bertrand Russell, *Tractatus Logico-Philosophicus* (New York: Dover, 1999).

United States Government Documents

Department of Defense Law of War Manual (Office of General Counsel, Department of Defense, Pentagon, June 12, 2015).

Newspapers

Herbert, Bob. "The Agony of War," in *New York Times*, April 25, 2005, p. 21. https://www.nytimes.com/2005/04/25/opinion/the-agony-of-war.html

4 Liberalism and Law – The Risk in Law's Overstatement

In this chapter I overview ideas of liberalism and law, and I explain how the Australian Prime Minister might mimic a tyrant king and send the nation to war on the basis of personal decision, without reference to parliament, without reference to cabinet, without judicial review, and without reference to the electorate. Confronted by unconscionable political direction, the general in supreme command has no remedy, no recourse, no way out. Unless the general chooses to resign, section 8 (2) of the *Defence Act* compels obedience.

We should be concerned. A reasonably good society – which I presume to take a liberal democratic form – should take the moral convictions of citizens seriously and enable individuals to examine and act upon conscientious beliefs. This claim is especially important in the case of the citizen who serves as the general in supreme command since the general bears a positional onus to exercise especial moral judgement. Generals are different from soldiers. Alone at the junction between law, politics and public interest, the general is the only person who might translate political direction into military command and initiate the action of war.

Liberalism

A doctrine about political morality, which revolves around ideas of personal liberty, liberalism is not the same as individualism. But liberalism is closely related to individualism, and to democracy. In his book, *The Morality of Freedom*, Joseph Raz says liberalism holds human well-being is best achieved in communities subject to political authorities. These authorities are obligated to promote and protect the freedom of the citizens. Failure by political authorities to safeguard liberal freedoms undermines the legitimacy of the authority.[1]

This argument is consistent with the Lockean account offered up by John Rawls who construes liberal freedom in the terms of a free conscience.[2] For Rawls, government should safeguard a framework of rights within which citizens might enjoy the liberty of conscience and act to realise their own values and ends.[3] This "framework of rights" is known commonly as law. The obvious risk is in law's illiberal overstatement or elaboration.

"The rule of law" is a modern catchphrase, but law can be overstated as though everyone holds the same view, as though there is a common attitude, when in

DOI: 10.4324/9781003527886-4

fact this is not the case.[4] And law can be manipulated to bring about ends that are far from just. The rule of law creates an ostensive fairness while it enables practical injustice. When the emphasis is on the law, an unconstructive adjuvant blind eye radically partitions law from circumstantial reasonableness. Promoting bureaucratic procedural justice, law sanctions an adversarial atomistic idea of human relations, and enables the wealthy and shrewd to manoeuvre to their own advantage.[5]

I am concerned when people value conformity and law abidingness more, and first-order moral reasoning less. I balk when Rawls claims that principles of right and justice define virtue, and extensionally that virtue is a desire to act in accord with these principles.[6] On the Rawlsian account, rules are the primary element in moral life, and people are virtuous when they are inclined to rule-following. Recalling Aristotle who reasoned: "it is a characteristic of man that he alone has any sense of good and evil, of just and unjust, and the like, and the association of living beings who have this sense makes a family and a state,"[7] I place a greater weight on ideas of human conscience, and I argue that conscience should make a more substantial demand upon law. I accept, of course, that laws must safeguard the equal claim of all citizens to liberty. But it seems laws ought not deny realistic autonomy. By my lights, a reasonably good society does not overstate the law. A reasonably good society recognises the limit of law and allows space for moral discretion. Political rule is not limitless. Lawmakers must not treat the state as personal property and the citizens as things. Political rulers have a right to make laws, but not an unconditional right. Interrogating deep set liberal intuitions, Judith Shklar illuminates this claim in her essay, *The Liberalism of Fear.* Shklar explains liberalism's deep grounding in the over-riding aim to secure political conditions requisite to personal freedom.[8] Dispelling the false beliefs that liberalism is a dominant or widely accepted philosophy, or that liberalism is equivalent to modernity, Shklar sees the deep roots of liberalism in toleration. On Shklar's account, liberalism must be alert to the abuse of law to accomplish some political end.

The liberal state cannot base itself upon the notion of fundamental rights and human liberties, and yet ignore the way these rights are secured in practice. Liberalism depends upon a strong defense of equal rights and their legal protection. These ideas found clear expression in the Australian Senate,[9] in the 1985 *Report of the Australian Senate Standing Committee on Constitutional and Legal Affairs*,[10] and in the Australian House of Representatives when Dr. Cairns said:

> There must be room in a free and civilized community for an individual to decide for himself what's right and wrong.... If conscience is to amount to anything, the individual whether he happens to be wrong or right according to my standards or those of the Government ... should have his right to exercise his conscience protected. If conscience is to mean anything, it must be based upon the right of the individual to say what he believes is right and wrong....[11]

The Citizens and the State

In this section I give an overview of the liberal ideas which support my claim that law ought not force our most sincere and serious moral commitments, our conscience. I acknowledge the sovereign right of nations to model a state – its physical territory, institutions, constitution, and laws,[12] and I accept that law is the only human institution rightly claiming unlimited authority.[13] I am not in favour of weak government that cannot frame or carry out public policies and decisions made in conformity to the requirements of justice.[14] But I am concerned that the power of governments to make war, to kill, to indoctrinate, and otherwise to impair and variously wrong people is unconstrained and overwhelming.

The seventeenth-century philosopher, Thomas Hobbes, believed law served the state. In *De Cive*, Hobbes describes his thinking about the rights of states and the duties of citizens,[15] but it is in the *Leviathan* Hobbes offers the first organised modern theory of the state.[16] On the Hobbesian account, since the pre-political state of nature was dramatically and inevitably violent, people relinquish individual freedoms in exchange for collective security. The state, represented in the form of a sovereign or a sovereign government, has unimpeachable authority to make laws for the benefit of all.[17]

For Hobbes, the state of nature is a state of war and the life of man within it is dominated by the fear and danger of violent death: solitary, poor, nasty, brutish, and short. To escape these perils, people contract with a sovereign power.[18] On the Hobbesian account, this contract is an absolute transfer. People renounce and hand over their freedom and autonomy; they abandon and grant away individual liberty in exchange for security.[19]

Locke shapes a different course, and I follow it. Locke does not see the state of nature in the berserk, disturbed terms of Hobbes. For Locke, relations between human beings outside a legitimate political authority could be very far from awful. Locke supposed that though people quarrel over all manner of things, quarrels tend not to be hysterical and homicidal – in a word, Hobbesian. The resonance of this understanding is very great. For Locke, the greatest motive people have to form political society is not security, but advancement. This is not to disregard or to refute the claim of security, but rather to offer a more fine-tuned and proportionate consideration. Security is a reason for us to form political society, but for Locke it is not the overshadowing reason.

For Locke, the welfare of people and the progress of human society offered preponderate reason to set up political authority. Locke looked beyond the brute Hobbesian state of nature and declined to accept the Hobbesian conclusion that people might be unreservedly subject to sovereign power.[20] Where Hobbes emphasised the dependent and politically subordinate status of citizens, and the unchallengeable power of law, Locke acknowledged the inalienable rights inherent in citizens as people. On the Lockeian account, no legitimate government could exercise unfettered authority.[21] For Locke, the people entrust a strictly conditional political power to political representatives;[22] the people have a natural claim to the liberty of their conscience which government ought not infringe.[23]

In 1646 the Leveller, Richard Overton, foreshadowed Locke. At the height of the English Civil War, Overton contemplated the post-war political reform of England and offered up *An Arrow Against All Tyrants*, attesting to the natural equality of all people.[24] Claiming that all men are created equal and endowed by their creator with inalienable rights, the American *Declaration of Independence* (1776) and the French *Declaration of the Rights of Man and the Citizen* (1789)[25] offer important, harmonic weight to ideas which dissolved the divine legitimacy of kings and fostered the social contract as a vindication of political power. The idea of a social contract implies pre-political natural rights, which individuals seemingly consent to cede to the state. But of course, there is no real consent. Citizens have no opportunity to express consent or dissent. For this reason, natural rights are central to the consideration of political right.[26]

In the twentieth century, the philosopher John Rawls gave this discussion celebrated new momentum. Holding people equal as free citizens and moral persons,[27] Rawls made a case for justice, which he claimed to be effectuated when shared institutions and social arrangements were such that no citizen, without regard for social position or particular interest, might reasonably object.[28] Detailing the liberty of conscience among freedoms elemental to justice in society,[29] Rawls echoes Locke, who understood a free conscience to be the natural right of all people.[30]

In the liberal democracy today, we take it for granted that our intentions and conscientious deliberations are private and individual. We allow and tolerate difference of opinion and conscientious conviction. We recognise the imperative of moral obligation or conscientious commitment.[31] We accept that the state ought not infringe the individual conscience, even if the citizen serves as the general in supreme command. Foundational to liberalism, the claim of each person to the equal liberty of conscience is a golden thread. For the liberal, law does serve the state, but not in the dominating, unrestrained way of the Leviathan which Hobbes imagined.

The Idea of Law

Law is a social construction described by Joseph Raz as normative, institutionalised, and coercive. Normative since it serves, and is meant to serve, as a guide for human behaviour; institutionalised in that its application and modification are largely the work of institutions; and coercive since obedience is exacted by force.[32] In one way law supersedes custom, in another way law rests on custom, as a system of rules developed to effect a standardised means of social control.[33]

But law, though it understands custom and convention, can be inattentive to human moral concern and practical judgement. Pre-formed legal terms can ignore the facts of human existence. Plato made this point. In his *Statesman*, Plato says: law resembles some stiff-necked and ignorant person, who allows no one to do anything differently, or to ask any questions.[34] For Plato, law suffers a dearth of circumstantial reasonableness and moral sensitivity. He says since practically nothing in human affairs remains stable, it is unreasonable to expect law to act in the best interests of justice in all cases and for all time.[35]

Plato criticises a view of law which might be described as positivist. Following Ronald Dworkin, positivism insists law and ethics are wholly separate. In contrast, natural law theory holds that law and ethics share important common interests.[36] For the positivist, laws confer powers on people and impose duties or rules *because* they are posited and accepted.[37] Hart offers the example of chess. In chess, players move pieces according to rules, which are made and accepted as a standard for all who play the game. Just so in society, where laws represent a common standard and find expression in the normative terminology of "ought," "must," and "should," "right," and "wrong."[38]

But, as Nigel Biggar points out, the normative cachet of laws comes about, not since laws are posited, but because laws reflect the human condition. Laws are not born in a moral wasteland; they conform to human moral sensibility; "if that were not so, then Nuremberg was nothing but victors' vengeance dressed up in the fiction of 'justice.'"[39] Ronald Dworkin argues similarly that law must allow for human moral finesse and common-sense flexibility.[40] In this way, Dworkin stands with Biggar who describes moral realism, a view that human understanding of good and right does not depend upon legal prescription but is instead rooted "in the nature of things – in objective reality."[41] Lon Fuller follows the same tack when he describes a dichotomy between the moralities of "duty" and "aspiration." For Fuller, the morality of duty – the morality of posited law – speaks in the voice of the Old Testament and the Ten Commandments. For Fuller, posited law speaks in the terms of "thou shalt not" to defines negative duties, and to condemn people for their failings.[42]

In contrast, the morality of aspiration speaks to natural law ideas of individual merit and moral responsibility – in a word, virtue. In aspiration is the sort of indeterminate moral sensibility, elemental to ideas of conscience. The idea of aspiration gestures to the classical appreciation of human excellence, the certainty that the *telos* of human life was in excellence, the fullest realisation of individual powers.[43]

On Fuller's account, law which is insensitive to moral reasoning, fails to qualify as law. Fuller claimed, law cannot survive when it is severed from ordinary, common-sense ideas of justice and fairness.[44] Fuller, for whom natural law implicates the deep, formative, and unspoken moral values of a community,[45] recognised common sense, ordinary morality, external to law, makes law possible.[46] Acknowledging law's moral essence Fuller describes law's "core meaning."[47] His perspective is much larger than his positivist rival, H. L. A. Hart, who described a "core *settled* meaning,"[48] to imply standard connotations and approved interpretation. Fuller details the sort of meaning that comes from the deeper registers of conscience. He construes moral implication beyond prescription in words and beyond categorical rules and asks law to be *responsive* to lived experience. Arthur Leff captures the point when he says: "whenever we do set out to find 'the law' we are able to locate nothing more attractive, or more final than ourselves."[49] Law, in other words, derives its soul and significance from human life and from human moral concern. I support this view, the naturalist view. I see moral obligation beyond compliance with law. I am against positivist readings of law which enable executive power to behave illiberally and sidestep common-sense morality.

Executive Power in Australia

The character and compass of executive power are important because we want a well-adjusted system where illiberal abuses of executive power are minified. In Australia, the deep provenance of executive power is in the capricious, mysterious, inscrutable claim of Divine Right. Just as the origin of executive power is mysterious, so the limits are obscure. Terms such as "the Crown," or "Ministers (of the Crown)," involve the idea of executive power, but the margins and nature of the power are not clear.[50] In *Davis v. The Commonwealth* (1988) Mason CJ, Dean and Gaudron JJ observed that executive power is not defined in the Constitution.[51] And since executive power is not defined, limits on executive power are not demarcated. To all intents and purposes, the executive power amounts to the illiberal prerogative power of a crowned head, unless limited by statute or precedent.[52] In practice, the Australian Defence Force might be deployed on the personal say-so of the Prime Minister.[53]

Recent exercise of this power has been in warlike operations in Afghanistan since 2001, in the 2003 invasion of Iraq, in the 2015 decision to bomb Syria, in Australian maritime boarding operations in the Arabian Gulf since 1990, in counter piracy operations off Somalia since 2009, and in the 1999 temporary administration[54] of East Timor.[55]

Describing the way the Prime Minster, John Howard, committed the nation to war in 2003, Malcolm Fraser – himself a former Prime Minister – says:

> For whatever reason, it seems that the Prime Minister personally committed himself to President George W. Bush. Mr Howard was a strong leader and would have had no difficulty in persuading his government that participating in the war was necessary.[56]

The key word is "personal." On Mr. Fraser's account, promises made by Mr. Howard to commit Australia to war were personal promises, undertakings given without reference to Cabinet, or Parliament.

In Mr. Howard's words, sending Australian forces to Iraq was "the most controversial foreign policy decision taken by my government in the almost twelve years it held office."[57] Yet archival records show no Cabinet debate contemplated Australia's involvement in the war. Cabinet papers released in 2023 show Australia's immersion in the 2003 invasion of Iraq followed from the personal decision of Mr. Howard, without debate or review.

A Cabinet minute dated 18 March 2003 (two days before the Iraq invasion) describes an oral report from the Prime Minister. This oral report cited discussion between the Prime Minister and President Bush, and a request from the President, received on the morning of 18 March 2003, which asked "that Australia participate in military action by a coalition to disarm Iraq of its weapons of mass destruction, and advice that it was the intention of the President to issue a final ultimatum to Iraq shortly." The Cabinet Minute notes an Australian contingent has "pre-deployed" to the Middle East "fully prepared for involvement in any action against Iraq" and the need for *ex post facto* advice to parliament.[58] The Cabinet Minute testifies to the Prime Minister's personal decision to send Australia to war. The ostensible high-handed licence exercised by the Prime Minister and the seeming disinterest of Cabinet is astonishing. A one paragraph Cabinet minute dated 1 April 2003 (two weeks after the invasion of Iraq on 20 March) notes an "oral report by the Prime Minister on the progress of military operations in Iraq and the contribution made by the Australian Defence Force."[59] There is no record of debate, or question, or discussion. The record shows no interest in the long-term ramification of a war, decided upon by the Prime Minister. The record shows indifferent acceptance by Cabinet ministers of the Prime Minister's unilateral say-so.

Former Secretary of the Department of Defence, Paul Barratt, offers former Prime Minister, Tony Abbott, as a more recent example. In 2015 Prime Minister Abbott committed Australia to military action in Syria without Parliamentary debate and evidently without Cabinet discussion, on the basis of his unilateral decision.[60] On the face of it, the legislative apparatus sending Australia to war is section 8 (2) of the *Defence Act*: "the Chief of the Defence Force must comply with any directions of the [Prime] Minister." But behind the scenes the mechanism sending Australia to war is the Crown.[61]

At the deep level of why and wherefore, the Crown exercises a prerogative power which obtains from the doctrine of divine right. Technically separate from executive power, but executive in personality, the difference between executive and the prerogative power of the Crown is inaudible.[62] The Australian jurist, statesman, and polymath H.V. Evatt argued: "the [Crown] prerogative itself is … *par excellence* executive in character. For want of a better phrase, these prerogatives may, be called executive powers."[63] Evatt described the Crown – he may just as well have spoken of ministers – as "omnipotent."[64] Established in Renaissance political theology, the Crown prerogative speaks to irresistible, pervasive discretionary power;[65] a sort of Hobbesian authority without moral limit.[66] In *Mr. Bligh's Bad Language*, Greg Dening conveys an image of this overwhelming force. Dening describes how the Crown was an unquestioned supernatural legal-cultural artefact.[67] The Crown defined naval life. But beyond the quarterdeck, just as God was supposed to have spoken the world into existence, so the Crown spoke the world of man into life. The sovereign created the state. There was no theory of law, there was an unquestioned belief that law was in the word of the sovereign.[68] The ultimate, irrefutable power of the sovereign obtained from divine right which, in the bombast of James I, made the King: "God's Lieutenant on earth" with power to judge but judged only by God.[69]

Coined by Renaissance thinkers, the doctrine of divine right turned on the idea of "the King's two bodies." The Tudor legal theorist Edmund Plowden described the idea in 1571. In consideration of acts made by Edward VI whilst not yet of age, Plowden drew the distinction between the King's natural body, and the King's body politic. Whilst the natural body suffered from the infirmities and frailties common to people, the body politic was allegorical and perfect, constituted for the public welfare, and concerned with government.[70]

Like Plowden, Hobbes believed the sovereign embodies two persons, one natural and another political.[71] Shakespeare puts the point deftly, when he has Hamlet say to Rosencrantz (IV. ii): "The body is with the King, but the King is not with / the body. The King is a thing"[72] and in her accession speech Elizabeth I expressed the fiction of a perpetual, perfect, and divinely ordained Body politic inimitably:

> My Lords the law of Nature moveth mee to sorrowe for my Sister, the burthen that is fallen upon me maketh me amazed, and yet considering that I am Gods Creature, ordeyned to obey his appointment I will thereto Yelde, desiringe from the bottom of my harte that I may have assistance of his Grace to bee the Minister of his Heavenly Will in this office now committed to me, and as I am but one Bodye naturallye Considered though by his permission a Bodye Politique to Governe, so I shall desire you all my Lords / Chieffly you of the nobility euery one in his Degree and Power to be assistant to me, that I with my Rulinge and you with yo Service may make a good accompt to Almighty God and leave some comforte to our posteritye in Earth.[73]

Things changed after the "Glorious Revolution" of 1688 deposed James II and installed his daughter, Mary and her husband William of Orange. Requiring a promise to "Governe the People of this Kingdome of England and the Dominions thereto belonging according to the Statutes in Parlyament Agreed on and the Laws and Customs of the same," the *Coronation Oath Act* (1688) asserted the primacy of Parliament and inaugurated the constitutional monarchy. Together with the *Bill of Rights* (1689) – which declared the rights and liberties of the citizens – the *Coronation Oath Act* is elemental to the modern idea of responsible government.[74,75]

Following Sir Owen Dixon CJ, the idea of responsible government involves conflict between the supremacy of law, the supremacy of the Crown, and the supremacy of Parliament.[76] But the Crown, is uncontested as the organising principle and the defining symbol of political legitimacy.[77] Having the benefit of Crown prerogative, ministers are not limited by standards of integrity or sensibleness.[78] Ministers bear "no obligation to conform to the rules of natural justice,"[79] though they are limited by the law. Murphy J spoke to limitations imposed upon the executive by law in In *A v. Hayden* (1984), where he said:[80]

> The Executive power of the Commonwealth must be exercised in accordance with the *Constitution* and the laws of the Commonwealth. The Governor-General, the Federal Executive Council and every officer of the Commonwealth are bound to observe the laws of the land.... I restate these elementary principles because astonishingly one of the plaintiffs asserted through counsel that it followed from the nature of the executive government that it is not beyond the executive power, even in a situation other than war, to order one of its citizens to kill another person. Such a proposition is inconsistent with the rule of law. It is subversive of the *Constitution* and the laws. It is, in other countries, the justification for death squads.[81]

But law and the courts are not a fail-safe defence against political misdeed. In *Madzimbamuto v. Lardner-Burke* (1969), Reid LJ held:

> It is often said that it would be unconstitutional for the United Kingdom Parliament to do certain things, meaning that the moral, political and other reasons against doing them are so strong that most people would regard it as highly improper if Parliament did those things. But that does not mean it is beyond the power of Parliament to do such things. If Parliament chose to do any of them the courts would not hold the Act of Parliament invalid. [The courts are] only concerned with the legal powers of Parliament.[82]

In practice, Governments might pass laws which infringe basic democratic liberties and, unless law is unconstitutional, the courts are bound to enforce it. This is concerning since, as Judith Shklar says, we seek

> a properly equilibrated political system in which power [is] checked by power in such a way that neither the violent urges of kings, nor the arbitrariness of legislatures [might] impinge directly upon the individual in such a way as to frighten her and make her feel insecure in her daily life.[83]

Conclusion

Recognising few more consequential exercises of public power than committing a nation to war, this chapter has offered an overview of legal structures, assumptions, and conventions, which mean that ministers in the Westminster system might exercise executive power, illiberally and unconstrained by moral limit.

The Australian Constitution is largely mute concerning war. Section 51 of the Constitution empowers the federal parliament to pass laws with respect to "The naval and military defence of the Commonwealth and of the several States." Section 68 vests the Governor-General with the titular – but not actual – "command in chief" of the defence forces.[84] But the Constitution does not mention how the nation goes to war, or who declares war in Australia's name. By this silence, the Constitution reflects and ratifies assumptions of the Westminster tradition, according to which the Prime Minister has a prerogative. In other words, the Prime Minister may send the nation to war without reference to parliament, even without reference to the cabinet.

Ministers are not divine: they are politicians, and things within the minister's legal right are not necessarily within the minister's moral right. The political philosopher Harold Laski writes: "legally, an autocratic Czar may shoot down his subjects before the winter palace at Petrograd; but morally, it is condemnation that we utter."[85] We censure the high-handed, illiberal exercise of power. We are concerned that despite the human cost, the Australian Prime Minister might act like a tyrant king, without public, legislative, or judicial scrutiny or accountability, to send the country to war.[86] We should be uneasy. And we should be concerned that, trapped by law, which takes no account of moral limits, the general has no way out unless by resignation. The general is then implicated in crimes of obedience: acts "performed in response to orders from authority that [are] considered illegal or immoral by the larger community."[87]

Notes

1 Joseph Raz, *The Morality of Freedom* (Oxford: Clarendon Press, 2009), p. 21. Also pp. 17, 21, 23.
2 John Locke, "A Letter Concerning Toleration," in Ian Shapiro (ed.), *Two Treatises of Government and A Letter Concerning Toleration* (New Haven: Yale University Press, 2003), p. 246. Locke says: "… the liberty of conscience is every man's natural right."
John Rawls, *A Theory of Justice* (Cambridge, MA: The Belknap Press of Harvard University Press, 1999), p. 181. Rawls says justice depends upon the equal liberty of conscience.
John Rawls, "Kantian Constructivism in Moral Theory," in *Journal of Philosophy*, (1980) 77:9, pp. 515–572, 517, 526.
3 John Rawls, *A Theory of Justice* (Cambridge, MA: The Belknap Press of Harvard University Press, 1999), pp. xii, 6, 53, 173, 174, 177, 181, 197, 203, 243.
4 Paul Kahn, *Sacred Violence: Torture, Terror and Sovereignty* (Ann Arbor: University of Michigan Press, 2011), pp. 7, 9.
5 Morton J. Horwitz, "The Rule of Law: An Unqualified Human Good?" in *Yale Law Journal*, (1977) 86:3, pp. 561–566, 566.
6 John Rawls, *A Theory of Justice* (Cambridge, MA: The Belknap Press of Harvard University Press, 1999), p. 167.
7 Aristotle, "Politics," Bk. 1, Ch. 2, 1253a.15–18.
8 Judith Shklar, "The Liberalism of Fear," in Nancy L. Rosenblum (ed.), *Liberalism and the Moral Life* (Cambridge, MA: Harvard University Press, 1989), p. 21.
9 Commonwealth of Australia *Parliamentary Debates*, Senate, 31 May 1983, p. 1027. In the liberal democracy, law "ought to reinforce the individual conscience." (Senator Michael Tate).
10 Senate Standing Committee on Constitutional and Legal Affairs, *Conscientious Objection to Conscripted Military Service*, (1985), p. 30.
11 Commonwealth of Australia, *Parliamentary Debates*, House of Representatives, 28 May 1968, p. 1618 (The Hon. Dr. Jim Cairns).
12 H.L.A. Hart, *The Concept of Law* (Oxford: Oxford University Press, 2012), p. 51.
Martin Loughlin, *The Idea of Public Law* (Oxford: Oxford University Press, 2004), p. 85.
13 Joseph Raz, *The Morality of Freedom* (Oxford: Clarendon Press, 2009), p. 76.
14 Judith Shklar, "The Liberalism of Fear," in Nancy L. Rosenblum (ed.), *Liberalism and the Moral Life* (Cambridge, MA: Harvard University Press, 1989), p. 30.
15 Quentin Skinner, "The State," in Terrence Ball, James Farr and Russell L. Hanson (eds.), *Political Innovation and Conceptual Change* (Cambridge: Cambridge University Press, 1989), p. 90.
16 Quentin Skinner, "The State," in Terrence Ball, James Farr and Russell L. Hanson (eds.), *Political Innovation and Conceptual Change* (Cambridge: Cambridge University Press, 1989), p. 126.
17 Thomas Hobbes (ed.), C.B. Macpherson, *Leviathan* (England: Penguin, 1985), Ch. 18 "Of the Rights of Soveraignes by Institution," pp. 228–229.
Thomas Hobbes (ed. and tr.), Richard Tuck and Michael Silverthorne, *On the Citizen* (Cambridge: Cambridge University Press, 2017), pp. 94, 95, 137.
18 John Dunn, *The History of Political Theory and Other Essays* (Cambridge: Cambridge University Press, 1996), p. 51.

19 Quentin Skinner, "The State," in Terrence Ball, James Farr and Russell L. Hanson (eds.), *Political Innovation and Conceptual Change* (Cambridge: Cambridge University Press, 1989), pp. 117, 118.
20 John Dunn, *The History of Political Theory and Other Essays* (Cambridge: Cambridge University Press, 1996), p. 53.
Alasdair MacIntyre, *A Short History of Ethics* (Indiana: University of Notre Dame Press, 2009), p. 157.
21 John Dunn, *The History of Political Theory and Other Essays* (Cambridge: Cambridge University Press, 1996), pp. 55, 56.
22 John Locke, "Second Treatise," in Ian Shapiro (ed.), *Two Treatises of Government and A Letter Concerning Toleration* (New Haven: Yale University Press, 2003), Ch. 9, "Of the Ends of Political Society and Government" §131, p. 156.
Emmanuel J. Sieyes, *What is the Third Estate?* (London: Pall Mall Press, 1963), pp. 122, 123.
Martin Loughlin, *The Idea of Public Law* (Oxford: Oxford University Press, 2004), p. 85.
23 Michael Walzer, "Citizenship," in Terrence Ball, James Farr and Russell L. Hanson (eds.), *Political Innovation and Conceptual Change* (Cambridge: Cambridge University Press, 1989), p. 215.
24 Richard Overton, *An Arrow against All Tyrants and Tyrany* (London: Martin Claw-Clergy, 1646), p. 2.
Alasdair MacIntyre, *A Short History of Ethics* (Indiana: University of Notre Dame Press, 2009), p. 153.
25 The *Declaration of Independence* is reprised in the American *Bill of Rights* and the French *Declaration of the Rights of Man and the Citizen*, each adopted in the summer of 1789. These texts trace their deep provenance in revolution and law from *Magna Carta* (1215), the *Petition of Right* (1628), the *Habeas Corpus Act* (1679) and the English *Bill of Rights* (1689).
26 Alasdair MacIntyre, *A Short History of Ethics* (Indiana: University of Notre Dame Press, 2009), p. 158.
Hannah Arendt, *The Origins of Totalitarianism* (Orlando, Austin, New York, San Diego, London: Harvest, 1994), p. 290.
27 John Rawls, "Kantian Constructivism in Moral Theory," in *Journal of Philosophy*, (1980) 77:9, pp. 515–572, 517.
28 John Rawls, "Kantian Constructivism in Moral Theory," in *Journal of Philosophy*, (1980) 77:9, pp. 515–572, 517.
29 John Rawls, *A Theory of Justice* (Cambridge, MA: The Belknap Press of Harvard University Press, 1999), p. 181.
John Rawls, "Kantian Constructivism in Moral Theory," in *Journal of Philosophy*, (1980) 77:9, pp. 515–572, 526.
30 John Locke, "A Letter Concerning Toleration," in Ian Shapiro (ed.), *Two Treatises of Government and A Letter Concerning Toleration* (New Haven: Yale University Press, 2003), p. 246.
31 John Rawls, "Kantian Constructivism in Moral Theory," in *Journal of Philosophy*, (1980), 77:9, pp. 515–572, 542.
32 Joseph Raz, *The Concept of a Legal System* (Oxford: Clarendon Press, 1980), p. 3.
33 Leslie Green, "Introduction," to H.L.A. Hart, *The Concept of Law* (Oxford: Oxford University Press, 2012), p. xv.
34 Plato, "Statesman," 294c, p. 338.
35 Plato, "Statesman," 294b, p. 338.
36 Ronald Dworkin, *Law's Empire* (Cambridge, MA: Belknap Press of the Harvard University Press, 1986), p. 98.
37 Hans Kelsen, *Pure Theory of Law* (Clark, NJ: Lawbook Exchange, 2009), p. 7.

38 H.L.A. Hart, *The Concept of Law* (Oxford: Oxford University Press, 2012), p. 57.
39 Nigel Biggar, *In Defence of War* (Oxford: Oxford University Press, 2014), p. 214.
Mary Follett, *Creative Experience* (New York: Peter Smith, 1951), p. 273. Follett says: laws "unfold within human experience, not by their own momentum apart from experience."
Martin Loughlin, *The Idea of Public Law* (Oxford: Oxford University Press, 2004), p. 51.
40 Ronald Dworkin, *Law's Empire* (Cambridge, MA: Belknap Press of the Harvard University Press, 1986), p. 104.
41 Nigel Biggar, *In Defence of War* (Oxford: Oxford University Press, 2014), p. 12. Also pp. 160, 225, 227.
42 Lon Fuller, *The Morality of Law* (New Haven and London: Yale University Press, 1969), p. 6.
43 Lon Fuller, *The Morality of Law* (New Haven and London: Yale University Press, 1969), pp. 5, 9.
44 Lon L. Fuller, "Positivism and Fidelity to Law: A Reply to Professor Hart," in *Harvard Law Review*, (1958) 71:4, pp. 630–672, 661.
45 James T. Johnson, *Just War and the Restraint of War* (New Jersey: Princeton University Press, 1984), p. 73.
46 Lon L. Fuller, "Positivism and Fidelity to Law: A Reply to Professor Hart," in *Harvard Law Review*, (1958) 71:4, pp. 630–672, 645, 656.
47 Lon L. Fuller, "Positivism and Fidelity to Law: A Reply to Professor Hart," in *Harvard Law Review*, (1958) 71:4, pp. 630–672, 663.
48 H.L.A. Hart, "Positivism and the Separation of Law and Morals," in *Harvard Law Review* (1958), 71:4, pp. 593–629, 607.
49 Arthur Leff, "Unspeakable Ethics, Unnatural Law," in *Duke Law Journal* (1979), 6, pp. 1229–1249, 1229, 1233 Leff cites the dissenting judgement of Holmes J in *Southern Pac. Co. v. Jensen* 244 US 205, 222 (1916).
50 Adam Tomkins, "The Struggle to Delimit Executive Power in Britain," in Paul Craig and Adam Tomkins (eds.), *The Executive and Public Law: Power and Accountability in Public Perspective* (Oxford: Oxford University Press, 2006), p. 16.
51 166 CLR 79, 92 per Mason CJ, Deane and Gaudron JJ.
52 *Ruddock v. Vadarlis* (1) [2001] 110 FCR 491, 495–496 (paragraph 9) per Black CJ.
George Winterton, "The Relationship Between Commonwealth Legislative and Executive Power," in *Adelaide Law Review*, (2004) 25, pp. 21–50, 21–22.
Adam Tomkins, "The Struggle to Delimit Executive Power in Britain," in Paul Craig and Adam Tomkins (eds.), *The Executive and Public Law: Power and Accountability in Public Perspective* (Oxford: Oxford University Press, 2006), p. 24.
Anne Twomey, *The Veiled Sceptre: Reserve Powers and Heads of State in Westminster Systems* (Cambridge: Cambridge University Press, 2018), p. 7.
Cameron Moore, *Crown and Sword: Executive Power and the Use of Force by the Australian Defence Force* (Australia: Australian National University Press, 2017), pp. 53, 55.
Noel Cox, "The Gradual Curtailment of the Royal Prerogative," in *The Denning Law Journal*, (2012) 25, pp. 1–19, 1.
Anthony H. Birch, *The British System of Government* (Oxford: Routledge, 1998), p. 40.
H.V. Evatt, *The Royal Prerogative* (Sydney: The Law Book Company Ltd, 1987), p. 12.
53 George Williams, "The Power to go to War: Australia in Iraq," in *Public Law Review*, (2004) 15:5, pp. 5–9, 5.
Phil Larkin and John Uhr, "Bipartisanship, Partisanship and Bicameralism in Australia's 'War on Terror:' Forcing limits on the extension of executive power," in John E. Owens and Riccardo Pelizzo (eds.), *The 'War on Terror' and the Growth of Executive Power* (London and New York: Routledge, 2010), p. 142.
Commonwealth of Australia, *Parliamentary Debates*, House of Representatives, 18 March 2003, pp. 12505–12506 (The Prime Minister) Mr. Howard announces to the

House that Australian troops have deployed to the Gulf in the campaign against Iraq. The deployment is a *fait accompli*, there is no debate.
James Brown, "Firing Line: Australia's Path to War," in *Quarterly Essay*, (2016) 62, p. 5.

54 Acting under Chapter VII of the UN Charter, the Security Council adopted resolution 1264 (1999) authorising a multinational force under a unified command structure to restore peace and security in East Timor.

55 Cameron Moore, *Crown and Sword: Executive Power and the Use of Force by the Australian Defence Force* (Australia: Australian National University Press, 2017), p. 1.

56 Malcolm Fraser, Preface to Alison Broinowski (ed.) *How Does Australia go to War: A Call for Accountability and Change* (Melbourne: Australians for War Power Reform, 2015), p. 4.

57 John Howard, *Iraq 2003: A Retrospective,* Speech, Lowy Institute, 9 April 2013.

58 National Archives of Australia Without Submission – Iraq: Authority for Australian Defence Force Military Action, Cabinet Decision JH03/0124/CAB, NAA: A14370, JH03/0124.
Margaret Swieringa, 'Howard ignored advice and went to war in Iraq', *The Sydney Morning Herald*, 12 April 2013. Margaret Swieringa, a former secretary to the federal parliamentary intelligence committee, argues that the government's justification for war was not supported by any Australian intelligence agency.

59 National Archives of Australia Without Submission – Iraq–Military Operations, Cabinet Decision JH03/0157/CAB, 1 April 2003, NAA: A14370, JH03/0157.

60 Paul Barratt, "The War Powers in Australia: Why Reform is Needed," in Alison Broinowski (ed.), *How Does Australia go to War: A Call for Accountability and Change* (Melbourne: Australians for War Power Reform, 2015), p. 36.
Jonathan Baily, "The Political Context: Why We Went to War and the Mismatch of Ends, Ways and Means," in Jonathan Bailey, Richard Iron, and Hew Strachan (eds.), *British Generals in Blair's Wars* (London: Ashgate, 2013), p. 6. Bailey describes the erosion of Westminster "cabinet government" as decision in is centralised in the office of the prime minister as a "quasi–White House."

61 Peter Gerangelos, "The Executive Power of the Commonwealth of Australia: Section 61 of the Commonwealth Constitution, 'Nationhood' and the Future of the Prerogative," in *Oxford University Commonwealth Law Journal*, (2012) 12:1, pp. 97–131, 101, 108, 113, 117.
Cameron Moore, *Crown and Sword: Executive Power and the Use of Force by the Australian Defence Force* (Australia: Australian National University Press, 2017), pp. 10, 89, 100, 251.
Anthony H. Birch, *The British System of Government* (Oxford: Routledge, 1998), p. 40.
Anne Twomey, *The Veiled Sceptre: Reserve Powers and Heads of State in Westminster Systems* (Cambridge: Cambridge University Press, 2018), p. 2.

62 H.V. Evatt, *The Royal Prerogative* (Sydney: The Law Book Company Ltd, 1987), p. 27 (Citing Pitt Corbett, *Government of Australia*, unpublished manuscript, Sydney University Law School, p. 148), p. 37.
Cameron Moore, *Crown and Sword: Executive Power and the Use of Force by the Australian Defence Force* (Australia: Australian National University Press, 2017), p. 48.

63 H.V. Evatt, *The Royal Prerogative* (Sydney: The Law Book Company Ltd, 1987), pp. 31, 116. But these executive powers remain, *in theory*, the personal prerogative of the Crown.
Spigelman CJ, "Public Law and the Executive," the 2010 Garran Oration, in *The Australian Journal of Public Administration*, (2010) 69:4, pp. 345–356, at p. 351.

64 H.V. Evatt, *The Royal Prerogative* (Sydney: The Law Book Company Ltd, 1987), p. 8, citing Dicey.

65 A.V. Dicey (ed.), J. W. F. Allison, *The Law of the Constitution* (Oxford: Oxford University Press, 2013), p. 39.

H.V. Evatt, *The King and His Dominion Governors: A Study of the Reserve Powers of the Crown in Great Britain and the Dominions* (London: Oxford University Press, 1936), p. 1.
Cameron Moore, *Crown and Sword: Executive Power and the Use of Force by the Australian Defence Force* (Australia: Australian National University Press, 2017), p. 3.

66 Martin Loughlin, *The Idea of Public Law* (Oxford: Oxford University Press, 2004), p. 22.

67 Greg Dening, *Mr. Bligh's Bad Language: Passion, Power and Theatre on the Bounty* (Cambridge: Press Syndicate of the University of Cambridge, 1992), p. 19.

68 Paul Kahn, *Sacred Violence: Torture, Terror and Sovereignty* (Ann Arbor: University of Michigan Press, 2011), p. 27. Tense changed.

69 James Craigie (ed.) *Minor Prose Works of King James VI and I: Daemonologie, the Trve Lawe of Free Monarchies, A Counterblaste to Tobacco, A Declaration of Sports* (Edinburgh: Scottish Text Society, 1982), p. 69.

70 Ernst H. Kantorowicz, *The King's Two Bodies: A Study in Mediaeval Political Theology* (Princeton, NJ: Princeton University Press, 1997), p. 7, citing Edmund Plowden, *Commentaries or Reports* (London, 1816), p. 2122.

71 Thomas Hobbes (ed.), C.B. Macpherson, *Leviathan* (England: Penguin, 1985), Ch. 23 "Of the Publique Ministers of Sovereign Power," p. 289.

72 William Shakespeare, "Hamlet," in George Clark and William Aldis Wright (eds.), *The Works of William Shakespeare* (London: MacMillian and Co., 1866) (iv: ii), p. 834.

73 Allison Heisch, "Queen Elizabeth 1: Parliamentary Rhetoric and the Exercise of Power," in *Signs*, (1975) 1:1, pp. 31–55, 33. Citing Stow Manuscript 361 folio 1, British Museum.

74 Isaacs J acknowledged that the idea of responsible government has its provenance in the 1688 Bill of Rights, in *The State of New South Wales v. The Commonwealth* (The Wheat Case) (1915) 20 CLR 54. Isaacs J said (at 89) that the Executive power is subject "only to the conventions of responsible government."
H.V. Evatt, *The King and His Dominion Governors: A Study of the Reserve Powers of the Crown in Great Britain and the Dominions* (London: Oxford University Press, 1936), pp. 12, 20.
Arthur B. Keith, *Responsible Government in the Dominions* (Three Volumes, volume one) (Oxford: Clarendon Press, 1912), p. 147.
Ryder v Foley (1906) 4 CLR 422, 432 *per* Griffith CJ.
Horne v. Barber (1920) 27 CLR 494, 500 *per* Isaacs J.
Snedden v. State of New South Wales (2012) NSWCA 351.
The State of South Australia v. The State of Victoria (1911) 12 CLR 667, 719 *per* Isaacs J: citing Lord Mansfield in *Campbell v. Hall* (1774) 98 ER 1045.

75 In brief, "responsible government" means ministers act in the name of the Crown and do the acts of governing under the gaze of Parliament. But in practice, parliamentary scrutiny is notional since ministers *tend* in general to act and inform Parliament afterwards.

76 Sir Robin Cooke, "The Suggested Revolution Against the Crown," in *Essays on the Constitution* (Wellington, New Zealand: Brookers, 1995), p. 29.

77 Noel Cox, "The Gradual Curtailment of the Royal Prerogative," in *The Denning Law Journal*, (2012) 25, pp. 1–19, 1, 7, 10–11.
Uriel Abulof, "Public Political Thought: Bridging the Sociological-Philosophical Divide in the Study of Legitimacy," in *British Journal of Sociology*, (2016) 67:2, pp. 371–391, 371.
Rodney Barker, *Political Legitimacy and the State* (Oxford: Clarendon Press, 1990), p. 144.

78 Ultimately the High Court is the arbiter of reasonableness. Thus section 75 (v) of the *Constitution* specifies that in all matters, in which a writ of Mandamus or prohibition or

an injunction is sought against an officer of the Commonwealth; the High Court shall have original jurisdiction.

79 *Coutts v. The Commonwealth* (1985) 157 CLR 91, 94 *per* Mason ACJ.

80 (1984) 156 CLR 532.

81 (1984) 156 CLR 532, 562 per Murphy J.

82 Martin Loughlin, *The Idea of Public Law* (Oxford: Oxford University Press, 2004), p. 25. *Madzimbamuto v. Lardner-Burke* [1969] 1 AC 645, 723 per Reid LJ.

83 Judith Shklar, "Political Theory and the Rule of Law," in Allan C. Hutchinson and Patrick Monahan (eds.), *The Rule of Law: Ideal or Ideology* (Toronto, Calgary, Vancouver: Carswell, 1987), p. 4.

84 Rob McLaughlin, "The Impact of the 'Civilianisation' of Military Administrative Law on the 'Command Power,'" in Alison Duxbury and Matthew Groves (eds.), *Military Justice in the Modern Age* (Cambridge: Cambridge University Press, 2016), p. 141. *Marks v. The Commonwealth* (1964) 111 CLR 549, 565 *per* Windeyer J. The Governor General's prerogative powers are not the effectual powers of command. *The Australian Constitution* ss. 62, 63, 64. *Acts Interpretation Act* 1901 (Cth), s. 16A(b). *Millar v. Bornholt* 177 FCR 67, 76–77 *per* Logan J. *Coutts v. The Commonwealth* (1985) 157 CLR 91, 109 *per* Deane J: The Governor General's powers are exercisable *only* on the advice of the executive. The Governor General is thus a representation of the way the actual generals – who serve as Chief of the Defence Force – are utterly subaltern to politics. Sir Ninian Stephen, "The Role of the Governor General as Commander in Chief of the Australian Defence Forces," in *The Defence Force Journal: Journal of the Australian Profession of Arms*, (1983) 43, pp. 3–9, 9.

85 Harold J. Laski, *Authority in the Modern State* (New Haven: Yale University Press, 1919), p. 42.

86 Michael Head and Kristian Boehringer, *The Legal Power to Launch War: Who Decides?* (Oxford: Routledge, 2019), p. 1.

87 H.C. Kelman and V.L. Hamilton, *Crimes of Obedience* (New Haven and London: Yale University Press, 1989), p. 46.

References

Australian Cases

A v. Hayden (1984) 156 CLR 532.

Coutts v. The Commonwealth (1985) 157 CLR 91.

Davis v. Commonwealth (1988) 166 CLR 79.

Horne v. Barber (1920) 27 CLR 494.

Marks v. The Commonwealth (1964) 111 CLR 549.

Millar v. Bornholt 177 FCR 67.

Ruddock v. Vadarlis (1) [2001] 110 FCR 491.

Ryder v. Foley (1906) 4 CLR 422.

Snedden v. State of New South Wales (2012) NSWCA 351.

The State of New South Wales v. The Commonwealth (The Wheat Case) (1915) 20 CLR 54.

The State of South Australia v. The State of Victoria (1911) 12 CLR 667.

United Kingdom Cases

Madzimbamuto v. Lardner-Burke [1969] 1 AC 645.

Journal Articles

Abulof, Uriel. "Public Political Thought: Bridging the Sociological-Philosophical Divide in the Study of Legitimacy," in *British Journal of Sociology*, (2016) 67:2, pp. 371–391.

Brown, James, "Firing Line: Australia's Path to War," in *Quarterly Essay*, (2016) 62, p. 5.

Cox, Noel. "The Gradual Curtailment of the Royal Prerogative," in *The Denning Law Journal*, (2012) 25, pp. 1–19.

Fuller, Lon. "Positivism and Fidelity to Law: A Reply to Professor Hart," in *Harvard Law Review*, (1958) 71:4, pp. 630–672.

Gerangelos, Peter. "The Executive Power of the Commonwealth of Australia: Section 61 of the Commonwealth Constitution, 'Nationhood' and the Future of the Prerogative," in *Oxford University Commonwealth Law Journal*, (2012) 12:1, pp. 97–131.

Hart, H.L.A. "Positivism and the Separation of Law and Morals," in *Harvard Law Review*, (1958) 71:4, pp. 593–629.

Heisch, Allison. "Queen Elizabeth 1: Parliamentary Rhetoric and the Exercise of Power," in *Signs*, (1975) 1:1, pp. 31–55.

Horwitz, Morton J. "The Rule of Law: An Unqualified Human Good?" in *Yale Law Journal*, (1977) 86:3, pp. 561–566.

Leff, Arthur A. "Unspeakable Ethics, Unnatural Law," in *Duke Law Journal*, (1979) 6, pp. 1229–1249.

Rawls, John. "Kantian Constructivism in Moral Theory," in *Journal of Philosophy*, (1980) 77:9, pp. 515–572.

Spigelman CJ "Public Law and the Executive," the 2010 Garran Oration, in *The Australian Journal of Public Administration*, (2010) 69:4, pp. 345–356.

Stephen, Sir Ninian. "The Role of the Governor General as Commander in Chief of the Australian Defence Forces," in *The Defence Force Journal: Journal of the Australian Profession of Arms*, (1983) 43, pp. 3–9, 9.

Williams, George. "The Power to go to War: Australia in Iraq," in *Public Law Review*, (2004) 15:5, pp. 5–9.

Winterton, George. "The Relationship Between Commonwealth Legislative and Executive Power," in *Adelaide Law Review*, (2004), 25, pp. 21–50.

Books

Arendt, Hannah. *The Origins of Totalitarianism* (Orlando, Austin, New York, San Diego, London: Harvest, 1994).

Aristotle, "Politics," (ed.) Jonathan Barnes, in *The Complete Works of Aristotle* (Princeton, NJ: Princeton University Press, 1995).

Bailey, Jonathan, Iron, Richard, and Strachan, Hew (eds.) *British Generals in Blair's Wars* (London: Ashgate, 2013).

Ball, Terrence, Farr, James and Hanson, Russell L. (eds.) *Political Innovation and Conceptual Change* (Cambridge: Cambridge University Press, 1989).

Barker, Rodney. *Political Legitimacy and the State* (Oxford: Clarendon Press, 1990).

Biggar, Nigel. *In Defence of War* (Oxford: Oxford University Press, 2014).

Birch, Anthony H. *The British System of Government* (Oxford: Routledge, 1998).

Broinowski, Alison (ed.) *How Does Australia go to War: A Call for Accountability and Change* (Melbourne: Australians for War Power Reform, 2015).

Cooke, Sir Robin. "The Suggested Revolution Against the Crown," in *Essays on the Constitution* (Wellington, New Zealand: Brookers, 1995).

Craig, Paul and Tomkins, Adam (eds.) *The Executive and Public Law: Power and Accountability in Public Perspective* (Oxford: Oxford University Press, 2006).

Craigie, James (ed.) *Minor Prose Works of King James VI and I: Daemonologie, the Trve Lawe of Free Monarchies, A Counterblaste to Tobacco, A Declaration of Sports* (Edinburgh: Scottish Text Society, 1982).

Dening, Greg. *Mr. Bligh's Bad Language: Passion, Power and Theatre on the Bounty* (Cambridge: Press Syndicate of the University of Cambridge, 1992).

Dicey, A.V. (ed.) J.W.F. Allison, *The Law of the Constitution* (Oxford: Oxford University Press, 2013).

Dunn, John. *The History of Political Theory and Other Essays* (Cambridge: Cambridge University Press, 1996).

Duxbury, Alison and Groves, Matthew (ed.) *Military Justice in the Modern Age* (Cambridge: Cambridge University Press, 2016).

Dworkin, Ronald. *Law's Empire* (Cambridge, MA: Belknap Press of the Harvard University Press, 1986).

Evatt, H.V. *The King and His Dominion Governors: A Study of the Reserve Powers of the Crown in Great Britain and the Dominions* (London: Oxford University Press, 1936).

Evatt, H.V. *The Royal Prerogative* (Sydney: The Law Book Company Ltd, 1987).

Follett, Mary. *Creative Experience* (New York: Peter Smith, 1951).

Fuller, Lon. *The Morality of Law* (New Haven and London: Yale University Press, 1969).

Hart, H.L.A. *The Concept of Law* (Oxford: Oxford University Press, 2012).

Head, Michael and Boehringer, Kristian. *The Legal Power to Launch War: Who Decides?* (Oxford: Routledge, 2019).

Hobbes, Thomas. (ed.) C.B. Macpherson, *Leviathan* (England: Penguin, 1985).

Hobbes, Thomas. (ed. and tr.) Richard Tuck and Michael Silverthorne, *On the Citizen* (Cambridge: Cambridge University Press, 2017).

Hutchinson, Allan C. and Monahan, Patrick (eds.) *The Rule of Law: Ideal or Ideology* (Toronto, Calgary, Vancouver: Carswell, 1987).

Johnson, James T. *Just War and the Restraint of War* (New Jersey: Princeton University Press, 1984).

Kahn, Paul. *Sacred Violence: Torture, Terror and Sovereignty* (Ann Arbor: University of Michigan Press, 2011).

Kantorowicz, Ernst H. *The King's Two Bodies: A Study in Mediaeval Political Theology* (Princeton, NJ: Princeton University Press, 1997).

Keith, Arthur B. *Responsible Government in the Dominions* (Three Volumes, volume one) (Oxford: Clarendon Press, 1912).

Kelman, H.C. and Hamilton, V.L. *Crimes of Obedience* (New Haven and London: Yale University Press, 1989).

Kelsen, Hans. *Pure Theory of Law* (Clark, NJ: Lawbook Exchange, 2009).

Laski, Harold J. *Authority in the Modern State* (New Haven: Yale University Press, 1919).

Locke, John. (ed.) Ian Shapiro, *Two Treatises of Government and A Letter Concerning Toleration* (New Haven: Yale University Press, 2003).

Loughlin, Martin. *The Idea of Public Law* (Oxford: Oxford University Press, 2004).

MacIntyre, Alasdair. *A Short History of Ethics* (Indiana: University of Notre Dame Press, 2009).

Moore, Cameron, *Crown and Sword: Executive Power and the Use of Force by the Australian Defence Force* (Australia: Australian National University Press, 2017).

Overton, Richard. *An Arrow against All Tyrants and Tyrany* (London: Martin Claw-Clergy, 1646).

Owens, John E. and Pelizzo, Riccardo (eds.) *The 'War on Terror' and the Growth of Executive Power* (London and New York: Routledge, 2010).
Plato, "Statesman," in John M. Cooper (ed.), *Plato: Complete Works* (Indianapolis and Cambridge: Hackett, 1997).
Rawls, John. *A Theory of Justice* (Cambridge, MA: The Belknap Press of Harvard University Press, 1999).
Raz, Joseph. *The Concept of a Legal System* (Oxford: Clarendon Press, 1980).
Raz, Joseph. *The Morality of Freedom* (Oxford: Clarendon Press, 2009).
Rosenblum, Nancy L. (ed.) *Liberalism and the Moral Life* (Cambridge, MA: Harvard University Press, 1989).
Shakespeare, William. "Hamlet," in George Clark and William Aldis Wright (eds.), *The Works of William Shakespeare* (London: MacMillian and Co., 1866).
Sieyes, Emmanuel J. (tr. and ed.) M. Blondel and S.E. Finer, *What is the Third Estate?* (London: Pall Mall Press, 1963).
Twomey, Anne. *The Veiled Sceptre: Reserve Powers and Heads of State in Westminster Systems* (Cambridge: Cambridge University Press, 2018).

Commonwealth of Australia Parliamentary Debates

Commonwealth of Australia, *Parliamentary Debates*, House of Representatives, 28 May 1968, p. 1618 (The Hon. Dr. Jim Cairns).
Commonwealth of Australia *Parliamentary Debates*, Senate, 31 May 1983, p. 1027 (Senator Michael Tate).
Commonwealth of Australia, *Parliamentary Debates*, House of Representatives, 18 March 2003, pp. 12505–12506 The Hon. The Prime Minister Mr. Howard).

Commonwealth of Australia Committee Hansard

Senate Standing Committee on Constitutional and Legal Affairs, *Conscientious Objection to Conscripted Military Service* (1985).

Australian Government Documents

National Archives of Australia Without Submission – Iraq: Authority for Australian Defence Force Military Action, Cabinet Decision JH03/0124/CAB, NAA: A14370, JH03/0124.
National Archives of Australia Without Submission – Iraq–Military Operations, Cabinet Decision JH03/0157/CAB, 1 April 2003, NAA: A14370, JH03/0157.

Newspapers

Swieringa, Margaret, 'Howard ignored advice and went to war in Iraq', *The Sydney Morning Herald*, 12 April 2013. https://www.smh.com.au/opinion/howard-ignored-advice-and-went-to-war-in-iraq-20130411-2ho5d.html

Public Statements

Howard, John. *Iraq 2003: A Retrospective,* Speech, Lowy Institute, 9 April 2013. https://www.lowyinstitute.org/publications/iraq-2003-retrospective

5 Conscience – Some Things will be Morally Impossible

All things being equal, people should obey the law. But laws, even when right in all other respects, should not infringe the liberty of conscience[1] In a liberal society, law should accommodate citizens as autonomous and morally conscientious persons.[2] Thus, in *R v. John* (1974), Roskill LJ confirmed the duty of the courts to defend the freedom of conscience.[3] In this chapter, I offer a detailed outline of "conscience," to throw light on my contention that law should enable the general to refuse unconscionable political direction.

Some Things Are Unconscionable

We understand that something might be morally impossible. We understand that when we say something is unconscionable, we mean it is subjectively impermissible.[4] Simply put, something is unconscionable *for us* when we deeply believe it to be unconscionable, when we reach the farthest reach of our moral horizon. Sophocles gestures to this moral frontier when he has Antigone ignore the order of Creon, ruler of Thebes, to leave the body of Polyneices unburied and dishonoured:

Ismene: Would you bury him, when it is forbidden in the city?
Antigone: He is my brother – and yours too. I will not prove false to him / It is not for [Creon] to keep me from my own / Let me endure this terror. No suffering of mine will be enough to make me die ignobly.[5]

As conscience rises above mere preference, so unconscionable is a more demanding term than aversion. We recognise, as Cicero says: "there are activities, some so degrading and others so criminal, that no man of wisdom would perform them, even to save his country."[6] I ask for reform of the law so as the general in supreme command might resist political direction of this type. But I do not expect the general to be whiter than snow. I recognise, not everything which is conventionally wrong or unjust or illegal will be unconscionable. Since we live in the world as we know it, we must expect deliberate trespass, deliberate harms – cases of dirty hands – cases where following their all-things-considered moral duty people feel they *must* over-ride orthodox moral margins.

DOI: 10.4324/9781003527886-5

Moral margins cannot be defined in explicit and categorical terms. But in the term unconscionable there is a limit, the farthest reach of a moral concept. The term "unconscionable" describes something so unjust, excessive, or unreasonable, it exceeds our moral range of view. The term connotes an especially weighty, binding moral force: the most deciding, most urgent, most morally conclusive limits people put upon themselves. And as well, "unconscionable" involves the shared moral knowledge of people who establish their moral identity in community.

These limits are known. Their infringement is recognised. But these limits are not categorical, clear cut, and specifiable in explicit statutes and proscriptions. This sort of ambiguity is not unusual. We know from Wittgenstein that there is no such thing as a logically perfect language.[7] We know from Wittgenstein; we can use concepts with precision and yet not know their unambiguous and definitive character.[8] The content of unconscionable acts cannot be specified. But unconscionable acts will be recognised for what they are. There will be, either in the contemplation of certain acts, or in meeting the possibility of certain acts, what Bernard Williams describes as a "moral incapacity."

Describing moral incapacity, Williams describes "the incapacity to do a certain thing knowingly."[9] For Williams this is "the kind of incapacity that is in question when we say of someone, usually in commendation of him, that he could not act or was not capable of acting in certain ways."[10] Moral incapacity is grounded in character or moral disposition.[11] Bernard Williams speaks of integrity, the deep registers of our moral identity.[12] These deep, ingenerate moral sensitivities are not rehearsed. They are not specific, and not necessarily in advance of a situation or set of circumstances. Williams says: "'I can't" can present at once as a decision, and as a discovery. Decision obtains at the conclusion of a deliberation. Discovery comes at the rush, out of nowhere, to ambush us when we are confronted by the possibility of an act.[13] In short and in practice, moral incapacity presents as an expression of moral temperament and deliberation *in the circumstances*. For some people, no matter the acuteness of a crisis or the demands of an emergency, some things will be inconceivable. No matter the exigency of the moment or the practical workability of an act, for some people, some things will be unconscionable – they will be morally impossible.[14]

Conscience and Virtue

In the term "conscience" and in kindred terms "conscientious," "unconscionable," "public conscience," "good conscience," and the like, I reference an intuitive, common-sense, overtly credible idea which engages notions like integrity and virtue.

I reference and associate these ideas in a common-sense way. By my lights, people act well when they respond to the moral demands of circumstances and choose to do certain things, in order to *be* conscientious or, in another word, "virtuous."[15] For the virtuous person, Philippa Foot says "certain considerations, not necessarily abidance with law or with conventions arising from law, count as reasons for action."[16]

Seeded in ancient philosophy, virtue achieved modern philosophical life when, in 1958, G.E.M. Anscombe described how "anyone who has read Aristotle's *Ethics* and has also read modern philosophy must have been struck by the great contrasts between them." Anscombe explained how "the term 'moral,' which we have in direct inheritance from Aristotle, just doesn't seem to fit, in its modern sense into an account of Aristotelian ethics."[17] This is because, Anscombe explains, between Aristotle and us came Christianity, with its *law* conception of ethics.[18] Anscombe expressed the modern frustration with deontological ideas of sin and with juridical ideas of guilt. Taking from Anscombe, it is reasonably self-evident and common sensibly clear that the person we would describe as "good" is the sort of person we might also describe as just, fair, conscientious, principled, or honourable and the like.[19] I am persuaded by Anscombe, and her argument for individual merit and moral responsibility resonates throughout this book. Anscombe acknowledges virtue, which obtains from the deliberate endeavour to do right and well. She recognises the conclusive importance of intention, the deep reasons, the purpose we have for acting.[20]

But our moral reasons, our intentions, our conscience, our sense of duty, or virtue are contoured by circumstances, they are not solipsistic. These feelings and ideas are ours, but they are not ours alone, detached or unrelated to the world.[21] Reasons for which we act go beyond individual moral identity to implicate the relationship people share with others.[22] As Charles Taylor says, one self is only a self among other selves; "a self cannot be described without reference to those who surround it."[23] This thinking is in the word conscience. Derived from the Latin *con* – meaning together and *scientia* – meaning privity of knowledge, or knowledge within ourselves, conscience implicates a mutual awareness or shared knowledge, a socially constructed moral acumen.[24] People act well or virtuously or conscientiously when they fulfil role moralities as best they can. Shakespeare makes the point in *Hamlet* when he has Polonius say to Laertes: "[A]bove all: to thine ownself be true / And it must follow, as the night the day / Thou canst not then be false to any man" (I: iii).[25] The point is, we do not want our acts to be agreeable just for us. Ideas of conscience and virtue account for overlying and extending contexts, for the intersecting and overlapping claims of the various publics within which people act.[26] The human disposition to be virtuous is a propensity to want certain things, to react in certain ways, to use moral notions such as obligation, and to promote certain outcomes.[27] We recognise that certain ideas offer a justification for our action, and we want to engage as well as we can with the world.[28] In short, we want to be "conscientious" in a general, all-things-considered sense. Conscience implies a shared moral knowledge and recognises that people establish their moral identity in community. Recognising a person might not be properly understood in isolation, but only in the circumstances which give shape and colour to moral obligations,[29] Walzer says it is from the political community that people receive a second life, a moral life, which connects the individual to the larger order.[30] Joseph Raz describes how moral reasons apply to people *in* the roles they occupy.[31]

Conscience and Common-Sense Intention

Rawls details the liberty of conscience among freedoms elemental to justice in society. But Rawls does not offer a detailed outline of "conscience." On my account, conscience is not distinguished by objectively right or wrong responses to moral questions. As I mean it, conscience is distinguished by intention; a cultivated practical wisdom, a considered evaluation, a set of moral skills that stems from a deliberate attentiveness to the deep registers of our moral mind and to the whole of the circumstances. This does not mean our conscience offers an objective index to moral right and wrong. Practical reality means it is a caricature to paint conscience as an infallible guide to objectively right action. If the correct picture of morality is a pluralistic one – and I think it is – then conscience cannot be a dependable guide to morally right action. A pluralistic morality precludes the possibility of unqualified right answers. But conscience is more than a relativistic source of self-satisfaction.[32]

As I use the term, conscience implicates an intention to do well, even when a response is quick, instinctual, and unstudied. We act "in good conscience" when we seek to do well, to do right and rightly. Following Philippa Foot, I agree "there is no criterion of practical rationality that is *not* derived from goodness of the will,"[33] which means acting with the purpose or objective of doing the right thing.[34,35]

Of course, even the sincerest, most deeply held unfeigned moral commitments might be misguided. But it is impossible to imagine any act could be taken to be good in the absence of a good will,[36] which is not taken to be good on account of the effect, but on account of the intention.[37] To underline the point, we can say that to act badly, deliberately in contravention of our conscience, is a very radical form of badness. It is impossible to suppose that a person might act well in doing what he or she saw as evil.[38] This argument speaks to an everyday awareness of good will and obligation which is within the common-sense untaught grasp of ordinary people. To reference ordinary unexceptional turns of phrase, our run-of-the-mill sense of conscience and goodwill underpins a language which allows us to say, "I owe it to him" or "I should play my part."[39] The point is, ideas of good conscience and right intention are not fantastical, outlandish, or bizarre. As a rule, people appreciate a right intention and a good conscience. As a rule, people do not wrangle with conceptual fine points; they do not delve among the legal implications or the devious sub-meaning of words. There is a stock competence for discerning moral obligation; an almost intuitive sense of "the right thing to do." This is why when we think something is morally right or desirable, we do not stop to work out complicated reasons.[40] People have, as Rawls writes, an ordinary common-sense grasp of the good, the adjacent ideas of justice and fairness, and a desire to act rightly in an all-things-considered sense.[41]

In short: the ideas of good conscience and right intention speak to ordinary moral intuitions, the conventional, fine-spun human acumen, which enables people to understand circumstances, to distinguish right from wrong, and to make commitments. People from every walk of life all know well enough how to settle daily questions about the character and intellect of the individuals with whom they deal. Ordinary people discern motives and see jokes. They have learned how to apply in concrete situations such mental-conduct epithets as "careful," "stupid," "logical," "unobservant," "ingenious," "vain," "methodical," "credulous," "witty," "self-controlled," and a thousand others.[42]

Though it is ordinarily right to follow familiar, native moral intuitions,[43] sometimes we will find our moral intuitions vexed and disordered. When this happens, we think deeply to form a deliberate intention to do right and rightly.[44] The implication is: when *prima facie* reasons for compliance seem at odds with the deep registers of conscience, the general must determine what it will be to act rightly. By my lights, law should allow such autonomous morally responsible action. Autonomy, says Joseph Raz, is deeply rooted in liberal culture.[45] For Raz, autonomy implies a certain minimum rationality, the capacity to set and achieve goals, and a reasonable range of objectively valuable options.[46]

The ideal of personal autonomy is the idea of people controlling their own fortune, through successive decisions.[47] But autonomy does not imply utter control, since the autonomous person is only a part author of life events. Autonomy does not involve unobstructed success in a life plan, but the absence of improper coercion.[48] The conditions requisite for autonomy are complex. But in general, autonomy involves commonplace mental ability, and freedom to choose deliberately from an adequate range of options.[49]

Autonomous moral action is self-directed, independent, purposeful and not the result of social pressure or the knee-jerk reaction to social circumstances. Autonomy involves free and purposeful decision. Acting autonomously, people decide, they give deliberate expression to intention and moral disposition. When acting autonomously, people may decide or intend to act well or poorly: virtuously or scurrilously. But the point is, people decide, they form their intentions for themselves.[50] This account of autonomy is consistent with the version of moral responsibility offered up by Jessica Wolfendale, who says for an agent to be morally responsible the agent has the basic capacity to reflect on available options, to act upon choices and to control behaviours. Ideas of responsibility and autonomy do not entail that agents always exercise these capacities as perhaps they should.[51]

Conscience and Public Credibility

As I speak of it, conscience involves a common-sense-civic or public credibility. But public credibility does not set a claim of conscience beyond question.

There are many examples throughout history and today where communities have shared objectionable beliefs and exercised abhorrent practices under the cover of "good conscience." Communities have practiced sexism, racism, segregation, slavery, torture, and genocide, without believing these practices to be unconscionable. The Holocaust is the paradigm case; countless people involved in planning and perpetrating genocide did not feel the pangs of conscience (quite the opposite, in some cases). William Shirer makes the point:

> Eichmann, according to one of his henchmen, said just before the German collapse, that 'he would leap laughing into the grave because the feeling he had five million people on his conscience would for him be a sort of extraordinary satisfaction.'[52]

But, on my account, rather than undermine the concept of "conscience," Eichmann's ghoulish joyfulness demonstrates that there are limits to reasonableness.

Of course, when Eichmann played his part in the Holocaust, his repugnant views were common in government, in the military, and in society. Eichmann was representative and unextreme. But it would not be reasonable now, for a person to hold and to act on these awful views. Illustrating the point that a claim of "conscience" must be publicly credible, Christopher Cowley offers the example of the racist doctor. Cowley notes the utter censure of racism in modernity. Racism cannot reasonably stand as a reason or justification for any public policy or statement. Even in non-public discourse, racist remarks are questionable if they are not repugnant. Obviously, racism persists as an unpleasant feature of society, but racists can no longer express their racism in mainstream public if they have serious ambitions for public office or approval. Typically, racist views, or other unattractive opinions, are disguised under the cover of a publicly sustainable false or tangential argument. For example, homophobes might express dislike of homosexuality under the disguise of claims that gay marriage will imperil the welfare of children. Just so, a racist doctor would not attempt to offer a patient's skin colour as a sufficient reason for not treating them. Another, publicly defendable, reason will be offered. In contrast, a doctor can refer to the wrongness of abortion as an intelligible reason for refusing a patient, without thereby losing moral and intellectual credibility. There is real and publicly assertable debate about abortion. A doctor might reasonably claim to bear a conscientious objection to the practice. In contrast, a claim of conscientious objection to people of a certain ethnicity or background is not viable in public.[53]

The intuitive substance of conscience is detectable in the conventions, declarations, and statements which followed from our reaction against Nazism. Today the international conventions speak to unnamed "common principles,"[54] for "fundamental human rights,"[55] elemental human "freedoms,"[56] for "the inherent dignity and the equal and inalienable rights of all people," for "freedom, justice and peace in the world" and against "barbarous acts which have outraged the conscience of mankind."[57] These cosmopolitan catchphrases find legal approval in the judgement at Nuremberg, and resonate in the doctrine of universal jurisdiction which asserts the power of national courts to try the citizens of any country for certain egregious offences, regardless of where these offences were committed.[58] Gerry Simpson says: "certain acts are offences against the whole of humanity or, indeed, the very idea of humanity. They shock the conscience of mankind,"[59] they offend against common-sense and routine ideas of human decency and rightness.

The Cost of Conscience

At section 4, the *Defence Act* says conscientious belief "involves a fundamental conviction of what is morally right and morally wrong, whether or not based on religious considerations; [which] is so compelling in character [a person] is duty bound to espouse it." The Act speaks to a matter of fact, practical understanding of deep moral sense and conviction. Conscience correlates with the conviction a certain course of conduct is right.[60]

But beyond conviction or intention, conscience involves the preparedness to bear a cost. Kimberlee Brownlee says, a "person who has a conscientious moral conviction has a sincere and serious moral commitment that she is willing both to articulate to others and to bear the costs for holding."[61] Brownlee offers an example from Robert Bolt's play, *A Man for All Seasons*. The exchange is between Sir Thomas More and the Duke of Norfolk. More has just resigned as Lord Chancellor since he cannot support the *Act of Supremacy* that will make the King head of the Church of England:

Norfolk: Does this make sense? You'll forfeit all you've got – which includes the respect of your country – for a theory?

More: [replies hotly] The Apostolic Succession of the Pope is … [he stops: interested] … Why, it's a theory, yes; you can't see it, can't touch it, it's a theory. But what matters to me is not whether it's true or not, but that I believe it to be true, or rather not that I *believe* it, but that *I* believe it….[62]

Standing to bear the costs of moral beliefs – which include costs to his family – More demonstrates an idea of conscience which is more demanding than a claim of mere moral awareness or disposition, and he demonstrates moral good must be more than a consolation prize, the easement for worldly reward.[63]

Law Should Accommodate Conscience

In his book *Moral Principles and Political Obligations*, A. J. Simmons asks us to discard the maxim that, all things being equal, we should obey the political authorities.[64] Simmons goes further than I do. On the account I offer, all things being equal, people should obey the law; but law should accommodate the citizens as autonomous persons and the authors of their own moral lives. This is especially important in the case of the citizen serving as the general in supreme command. Joseph Raz underlines the point when he says the killing and subjugation of people must never be taken lightly, even in those regrettable cases where killing and subjugation are necessary and justified. No matter the reason or justification, the act of killing, or the unambiguous responsibility for killing, or even the tangential or collateral implication in killing have profound repercussion and significance for the people who are involved. Hence the right to object to such acts on conscientious grounds, takes precedence over the legal obligation to take part in them.[65]

More generally, law should accommodate conscience for the wellbeing of liberal democracy.[66] Repressive law is desolating. Liberalism withers when law abidingness comes to be "pragmatic acquiescence;"[67] the morally listless response to political coercion.[68] Repressive law drives conformance, not law abidingness.[69] Mary Follett describes mere consent, which is not actually confirmative or unforced,[70] but a pragmatic long-suffering response to power.

Laws enable, regulate, or restrict the activities and progress of people. Laws are a public institution. Following from law, social conventions, habits, proprieties, and processes give lived expression to abstract ideas of justice. Laws exert a needed and determining effect upon society, and the conduct of people in society. In a well-functioning liberal democracy law treats people with concern and respect, as moral persons, and fosters generally considerate social forms. Ronald Dworkin reminds us that government has an obligation to treat the citizens with a proper moral concern, as responsible, independent, conscientious, well-intentioned people who can form and act on intelligent conceptions of how their lives should be lived. And government must not merely treat people with concern and respect, but with equal concern and respect. In a reasonably good, liberal democratic society, the citizens benefit from equal justice. Opportunity must be offered fairly, and all citizens must bear a fair share. No citizen should bear a greater burden or a more onerous obligation than others.[71]

Law has a critical importance, but law should not force us to do what is unconscionable. In his play *A Man for All Seasons,* Robert Bolt demonstrates the imperative of conscience when he has Sir Thomas say: "I neither could nor would rule my King. But there's a little … little area … where I must rule myself."[72] This idea is restated when Bolt has Sir Thomas reprove the Duke of Norfolk. Norfolk wants More to swear a legal oath in contradiction of a spiritual commitment. More says: "when we stand before God, and you are sent to Paradise for doing according to your conscience, and I am damned for not doing according to mine, will you come with me, for fellowship?"[73] On trial for his life, Thomas More said: "in things touching conscience, euery true and good subject is bounde to haue respect to his saide conscience and to his soule than to any other thing in all the world beside."[74] Set against the edifice of medieval piety and monarchy; the dissolution of abbeys and the immolation of heretics, More offers the phrase "true and good subjects," as a gesture to the law's crucial and central place,[75] but most clearly and most memorably he lets us see that morality depends upon an independent good will.[76]

Conclusion

Very far from vague ideas of preference or inclination, I have described conscience in stringent terms, referencing our most sincere and serious moral commitment. On my account, a claim of conscience is a claim about what *must* be done, and a claim about what *must not* be done. Conscientious reasons are conclusive, they are trump cards.[77] A conscientious conviction is a defining feature of our moral lives, as deep-seated and unshakable as knowing our name.

But the idea of conscience, though it speaks to moral disposition is not disjoined from histories, from communities and cultures, or from nations and global society. My thinking about conscience educes Scanlon's imperative to recognise the moral knowledge and the moral identity which come when people live in community. Scanlon says: "an act is wrong if its performance under the circumstances would be disallowed by any set of principles for the general regulation of behaviour that no-one could reasonably reject."[78] Where Scanlon says "wrong," I say "unconscionable." We might use words apart from unconscionable. We might, for example, say "unjustified," "unjustifiable," "wrongful," or "unwarranted." But the gist of those terms rises above the merely "wrongful" to the higher standard of moral impossibility. When I argue that generals should have space in law to refuse executive direction which is "unjustified," or "wrongful," I mean generals should have space in law to refuse direction which is "unconscionable" – that is, so seriously objectionable that it is morally repugnant.

The idea that something might be morally repugnant or morally impossible gestures to a conscientious commitment which is so strong and so deeply impressed that it is beyond debate or contest. In Rawlsian terms I contend law should accommodate the liberty of conscience. Specifically, I argue for a limited or controlled exception so generals might act upon their deepest commitments. I do not ask for a global or unrestricted allowance for conscientious objection. Thus, when I argue for an exception so generals might refuse executive direction they consider unconscionable, I am not asking to open the door to unconstrained or indulgent free will. Rather, I look to reform so generals might act with reasonable independence; with a mind to principles which find their best expression in the Martens Clause.

Notes

1 Joseph Raz, *The Authority of Law: Essays on Law and Morality* (Oxford: Clarendon Press, 1979), p. 286.
2 Joseph Raz, *The Morality of Freedom* (Oxford: Clarendon Press, 2009), pp. 17, 21, 23.
3 *R v. John* (1974) 2 All ER 561, 564 *per Roskill LJ.*
Jeremy Horder, *Excusing Crime* (Oxford: Oxford University Press, 2004), p. 200.
4 Seth Lazar, "In Dubious Battle: Uncertainty and the Ethics of Killing," in *Philosophical Studies*, (2018) 175, pp. 859–883, 861.
5 Sophocles, *Antigone*, Lines: 51–52, 54, 110–113.
6 Cicero, *On Obligations* (Oxford University Press: Oxford, 2008), I, 159, p. 53.
7 Ludwig Wittgenstein (tr.) C.K. Ogden with an introduction by Bertrand Russell, *Tractatus Logico-Philosophicus* (New York: Dover, 1999), paragraph 3.323, p. 41.
8 Ludwig Wittgenstein (tr.), G.E.M. Anscombe, P.M.S. Hacker and Joachim Schulte, *Philosophical Investigations* (United Kingdom: Wiley Blackwell, 2009), § 66, p. 36.
9 Bernard Williams, "Moral Incapacity," in *Proceedings of the Aristotelian Society* (New Series), (1993) 93, pp. 59–70, 62.
10 Bernard Williams, "Moral Incapacity," in *Proceedings of the Aristotelian Society* (New Series), (1993) 93, pp. 59–70, 59.
11 Bernard Williams, "Moral Incapacity," in *Proceedings of the Aristotelian Society* (New Series), (1993) 93, pp. 59–70, 60, 66
12 Bernard Williams, "A Critique of Utilitarianism," in J.J.C. Smart and Bernard Williams (eds.), *Utilitarianism: For and Against* (Cambridge: Cambridge University Press, 2008), pp. 82, 104.
13 Bernard Williams, "Moral Incapacity," in *Proceedings of the Aristotelian Society* (New Series), (1993) 93, pp. 59–70, 66.
14 Bernard Williams, "Practical Necessity," in *Moral Luck* (Cambridge: Cambridge University Press, 1999) p. 127.
15 Philippa Foot, *Natural Goodness* (Oxford: Clarendon Press, 2010), p. 24.
16 Philippa Foot, *Natural Goodness* (Oxford: Clarendon Press, 2010), p. 12.
17 G.E.M. Anscombe, "Modern Moral Philosophy," in *Philosophy* (1958), 33:124, pp. 1–19, 1.
18 G.E.M. Anscombe, "Modern Moral Philosophy," in *Philosophy* (1958), 33:124, pp. 1–19, 5.

G.E.M. Anscombe, *Intention* (Cambridge, MA and London: Harvard University Press, 2000) p. 78.

19 G.E.M. Anscombe, "Modern Moral Philosophy," in *Philosophy*, (1958) 33:124, pp. 1–19, 16.

20 G.E.M. Anscombe, *Intention* (Cambridge, MA and London: Harvard University Press, 2000), p. 9.
G.E.M. Anscombe, "Modern Moral Philosophy," in *Philosophy,* (1958) 33:124, pp. 1–19, 12.
Jeff McMahan, *Killing in War* (Oxford: Clarendon Press, 2009), p. 110.

21 Charles Taylor, *Sources of the Self* (Cambridge: Cambridge University Press, 1992). pp. 4–5, 26, 28.

22 Christine M. Korsgaard, *The Sources of Normativity* (Cambridge: Cambridge University Press, 2014), pp. 131–166.
Mulford Q. Sibley, "Conscience, Law, and the Obligation to Obey," in *The Monist*, (October 1970) 54:4, pp. 556–586, 558.

23 Charles Taylor, *Sources of the Self* (Cambridge: Cambridge University Press, 1992), p. 35.

24 Kimberley Brownlee, *Conscience and Conviction: The Case for Civil Disobedience* (Oxford: Oxford University Press, 2015), p. 52. Mulford Q. Sibley, "Conscience, Law, and the Obligation to Obey," in *The Monist*, (October 1970) 54:4, pp. 556–586, 556, 558.

25 William Shakespeare, "Hamlet," in George Clark and William A. Wright (eds.), *The Works of William Shakespeare* (London: MacMillian and Co., 1866), p. 816.

26 Bernard Williams, *Ethics and the Limits of Philosophy* (Cambridge, MA: Harvard University Press, 1985), p. 37.

27 Bernard Williams, *Ethics and the Limits of Philosophy* (Cambridge, MA: Harvard University Press, 1985), p. 50.

28 Immanuel Kant, (tr.) E. B. Ashton, *On the Old Saw: That May be Right in Theory, but it Won't Work in Practice* (Philadelphia: University of Pennsylvania Press, 1974), p. 43.

29 F.H. Bradley, "My Station and its Duties," in *Ethical Studies* (Oxford: Clarendon Press, 2006), pp. 173–174, 183.
T.H. Green, "Principles of Political Obligation" in Paul Harris and John Morrow (eds.), *Lectures* (Cambridge: Cambridge University Press, 1986), pp. 13, 16, 17, 18.

30 Michael Walzer, *Obligations: Essays on Disobedience, War and Citizenship* (Cambridge, MA: Harvard University Press, 1970), pp. 5, 91, 112, 121, 129, 131.

31 Joseph Raz, "Incorporation by Law," in *Legal Theory*, (2004) 10, pp. 1–17.

32 Kimberley Brownlee, *Conscience and Conviction: The Case for Civil Disobedience* (Oxford: Oxford University Press, 2015), pp. 54, 66.

33 Philippa Foot, *Natural Goodness* (Oxford: Clarendon Press, 2010), p. 11.

34 Philippa Foot, *Natural Goodness* (Oxford: Clarendon Press, 2010), p. 12.

35 This would seem to be the thinking behind *The Defence Act* s. 51S which has the effect of relieving a Defence Force member who acts "in good faith" from criminal or civil liability for failure to act in accord with a Division 3, 4, or 5 obligation. Such obligations obtain under the terms of Part IIIAAA of the Act, when the Defence Force is "called out" under in order to protect Commonwealth interests, or to protect the interests of the states of the self-governing territories.

36 Immanuel Kant (ed. and tr.), Mary Gregor and Jens Timmerman, *Groundwork of the Metaphysics of Morals* (Cambridge: Cambridge University Press, 2012), §4.393, p. 9.

37 Immanuel Kant (ed. and tr.), Mary Gregor and Jens Timmerman, *Groundwork of the Metaphysics of Morals* (Cambridge: Cambridge University Press, 2012), §4.394, p. 10.
Philippa Foot, *Natural Goodness* (Oxford: Clarendon Press, 2010), p. 14.
Charles de Secondat, Baron de Montesquieu (ed.), Anne M. Cohler, Basia C. Miller, and Harold Stone, *The Spirit of the Laws* (Cambridge: Cambridge University Press, 2016), Part 1, Ch. 6, "How virtue is replaced in monarchical government," p. 26.

38 Philippa Foot, *Natural Goodness* (Oxford: Clarendon Press, 2010), p. 74.

39 Philippa Foot, *Natural Goodness* (Oxford: Clarendon Press, 2010), p. 44.
40 R.M. Hare, "War and Peace," in *Essays on Political Morality* (Oxford: Clarendon Press, 1998), pp. 65, 97.
41 John Rawls, *Political Liberalism* (New York: Columbia University Press, 2005), p. 86.
42 Gilbert Ryle, *The Concept of Mind* (United States: University of Chicago Press, 2002), p. 7.
43 R.M. Hare, "Utility and Rights," in *Essays on Political Morality* (Oxford: Clarendon Press, 1998), p. 98.
44 R.M. Hare, "Justice and Equality," in *Essays on Political Morality* (Oxford: Clarendon Press, 1998), pp. 183, 188.
45 Joseph Raz, "Autonomy, Toleration and the Harm Principle," in Ruth Gavison (ed.), *Issues in Contemporary Legal Philosophy* (Oxford: Clarendon Press, 1987), p. 313.
46 Joseph Raz, *The Morality of Freedom* (Oxford: Clarendon Press, 2009), pp. 372, 373.
47 Joseph Raz, "Autonomy, Toleration and the Harm Principle," in Ruth Gavison (ed.), *Issues in Contemporary Legal Philosophy* (Oxford: Clarendon Press, 1987), p. 314. Joseph Raz, *The Morality of Freedom* (Oxford: Clarendon Press, 2009), p. 369.
48 Joseph Raz, *The Morality of Freedom* (Oxford: Clarendon Press, 2009), p. 371.
49 Joseph Raz, "Autonomy, Toleration and the Harm Principle," in Ruth Gavison (ed.), *Issues in Contemporary Legal Philosophy* (Oxford: Clarendon Press, 1987), p. 314.
50 Bernard Williams, *Ethics and the Limits of Philosophy* (Cambridge, MA: Harvard University Press, 1985), p. 7.
51 Jessica Wolfendale, "Performance-Enhancing Technologies, and Moral Responsibility in the Military," in *The American Journal of Bioethics*, (2008) 8:2, pp. 28–38, 29.
52 William Shirer, *The Rise and Fall of the Third Reich* (New York: Simon & Schuster, 2011), p. 978.
53 Christopher Cowley, "A Defence of Conscientious Objection in Medicine: A Reply to Schuklenk and Savulescu," in *Bioethics*, (2016) 30:5, pp. 358–364, 360.
54 Franklin D. Roosevelt, *Selected Speeches of President Franklin D. Roosevelt* (Florida: Red and Black, 2010), p. 158.
Robert E. Sherwood, *Roosevelt and Hopkins: An Intimate History* (New York: Harper and Brothers, 1948), p. 507.
55 *Charter of the United Nations*.
56 Robert E. Sherwood, *Roosevelt and Hopkins: An Intimate History* (New York: Harper and Brothers, 1948), p. 507.
57 Preamble of the *Universal Declaration*.
58 Blackstone, *Commentaries on the Laws of England* (Chicago: Blackstone Institute, 1915), p. 106.
Attorney General of the Government of Israel v. Eichmann, 36 IRL 5, 26. *R v. Bow St Metropolitan Stipendiary Magistrate and Ors. ex parte Pinochet Ugarte* – a set of three constitutional law judgements by the House of Lords. The judgements concerned former Chilean dictator Augusto Pinochet, who claimed state immunity prevented his extradition from the United Kingdom to Spain to face charges that his regime tortured Spanish citizens to death. The first judgement – [2000] 1 AC 61 – found Pinochet was liable to be extradited from the United Kingdom to Spain for crimes which were so heinous that they exceeded the bounds of any diplomatic immunity. The third and final judgement – [2000] 1 AC 147 – confirmed that Pinochet was not entitled to claim state immunity. But the Home Secretary (Jack Straw) deemed Pinochet unfit for trial and allowed his return to Chile.
59 Gerry Simpson, *Law War and Crime* (Cambridge: Polity, 2007), p. 46.
60 Mulford Q. Sibley, "Conscience, Law, and the Obligation to Obey," in *The Monist*, (October 1970) 54:4, pp. 556–586, 556.
61 Kimberley Brownlee, *Conscience and Conviction: The Case for Civil Disobedience* (Oxford: Oxford University Press, 2015), pp. 1, 126, 160.
62 Kimberley Brownlee, *Conscience and Conviction: The Case for Civil Disobedience* (Oxford: Oxford University Press, 2015), p. 15.

63 Bernard Williams, *Ethics and the Limits of Philosophy* (Cambridge, MA: Harvard University Press, 1985), pp. 174, 195.
64 A. John Simmons, *Moral Principles and Political Obligations* (Princeton, NJ: Princeton University Press, 1979), p. 200.
65 Joseph Raz, "Bound by Their Conscience," in *Haaretz*, 31 December (2003) cited in Kimberley Brownlee, *Conscience and Conviction: The Case for Civil Disobedience* (Oxford: Oxford University Press, 2015), p. 145.
66 Kimberley Brownlee, *Conscience and Conviction: The Case for Civil Disobedience* (Oxford: Oxford University Press, 2015), p. 168.
Jeremy Horder, *Excusing Crime* (Oxford: Oxford University Press, 2004), p. 199.
67 David Held, "Power and Legitimacy in Contemporary Britain," in Gregor McLennan, David Held and Stuart Hall (eds.), *State and Society in Contemporary Britain: A Critical Introduction* (Cambridge: Polity Press, 1984), p. 301.
68 John S. Mill, "On Liberty," in Mark Philp and Frederick Rosen (eds.) *On Liberty, Utilitarianism and Other Essays* (Oxford: Oxford University Press, 2015), p. 8.
69 Antonio Gramsci (ed. and tr.) Q. Hoare and G.N. Smith, *Selections from the Prison Notebooks* (London: Lawrence and Wishart, 1971), pp. 12, 55.
Stuart Hall "The rise of the representative/interventionist state 1880s–1920s," in Gregor McLennan, David Held and Stuart Hall (eds.), *State and Society in Contemporary Britain: A Critical Introduction* (Cambridge: Polity Press, 1984), p. 11.
70 Mary Follett, *Creative Experience* (New York: Peter Smith, 1951), p. 222.
71 Ronald Dworkin, *Taking Rights Seriously* (Cambridge, MA: Harvard University Press, 1978), pp. 272–273.
72 Robert Bolt, *A Man for All Seasons* (New York: Vintage Books, 1990), Act One, p. 59. (Ellipses in the original.)
73 Robert Bolt, *A Man for All Seasons* (New York: Vintage Books, 1990), Act Two, p. 132.
74 Peter Ackroyd, *The Life of Thomas More* (New York: Nan A. Talese/Doubleday, 1998), p. 400.
75 Robert Bolt, *A Man for All Seasons* (New York: Vintage Books, 1990) Act One, p. 66.
76 Bernard Williams, *Ethics and the Limits of Philosophy* (Cambridge, MA: Harvard University Press, 1985), p. 7.
Immanuel Kant (ed. and tr.), Mary Gregor and Jens Timmerman, *Groundwork of the Metaphysics of Morals* (Cambridge: Cambridge University Press, 2012), §4.440, p 51. For Kant, "autonomy of the will is the supreme principle of morality."
77 Yossi Nehushtan and John Danaher "The Foundations of Conscientious Objection: Against Freedom and Autonomy," *Jurisprudence*, (2018) 9:3, pp. 541–565, 542.
78 T.M. Scanlon, *What We Owe to Each Other* (Cambridge, MA: Harvard University Press, 2000), p. 153.

References

United Kingdom Cases

R v. Bow St Metropolitan Stipendiary Magistrate and Ors. ex parte Pinochet Ugarte [2000] 1 AC 61 (Pinochet No. 1).

R v. Bow St Metropolitan Stipendiary Magistrate and Ors. ex parte Pinochet Ugarte [2000] 1 AC 147 (Pinochet No. 3).

R v. John (1974) 2 All ER 561.

Israeli Cases

Attorney General of the Government of Israel v. Eichmann, 36 IRL 5 (District of Jerusalem, 1961).

Journal Articles

Anscombe, G.E.M. "Modern Moral Philosophy," in *Philosophy*, (1958) 33:124, pp. 1–19.

Cowley, Christopher. "A Defence of Conscientious Objection in Medicine: A Reply to Schuklenk and Savulescu," in *Bioethics*, (2016) 30:5, pp. 358–364.

Lazar, Seth. "In Dubious Battle: Uncertainty and the Ethics of Killing," in *Philosophical Studies*, (2018) 175, pp. 859–883.

Nehushtan, Yossi and Danaher, John. "The Foundations of Conscientious Objection: Against Freedom and Autonomy," *Jurisprudence*, (2018) 9:3, pp. 541–565.

Raz, Joseph. "Incorporation by Law," in *Legal Theory*, (2004) 10, pp. 1–17.

Sibley, Mulford Q. "Conscience, Law, and the Obligation to Obey," in *The Monist*, (1970) 54:4, pp. 556–586.

Williams, Bernard. "Moral Incapacity," in *Proceedings of the Aristotelian Society* (New Series), (1993) 93, pp. 59–70.

Wolfendale, Jessica. "Performance-Enhancing Technologies, and Moral Responsibility in the Military," in *The American Journal of Bioethics*, (2008) 8:2, pp. 28–38.

Books

Ackroyd, Peter. *The Life of Thomas More* (New York: Nan A. Talese/Doubleday, 1998).

Anscombe, G.E.M. *Intention* (Cambridge, MA and London: Harvard University Press, 2000).

Blackstone, Henry W. *Commentaries on the Laws of England* (Chicago: Blackstone Institute, 1915).

Bolt, Robert. *A Man for All Seasons* (New York: Vintage Books, 1990).

Bradley, F.H. *Ethical Studies* (Oxford: Clarendon Press, 2006).

Brownlee, Kimberley. *Conscience and Conviction: The Case for Civil Disobedience* (Oxford: Oxford University Press, 2015).

Cicero. *On Obligations*, (tr.) P.G. Walsh (Oxford: Oxford University Press, 2008).

Dworkin, Ronald. *Taking Rights Seriously* (Cambridge, MA: Harvard University Press, 1978).

Follett, Mary. *Creative Experience* (New York: Peter Smith, 1951).

Foot, Philippa. *Natural Goodness* (Oxford: Clarendon Press, 2010).

Gavison, Ruth. (ed.) *Issues in Contemporary Legal Philosophy* (Oxford: Clarendon Press, 1987).

Gramsci, Antonio. (ed. and tr.) Q. Hoare and G.N. Smith, *Selections from the Prison Notebooks* (London: Lawrence and Wishart, 1971).

Hare, R.M. *Essays on Political Morality* (Oxford: Clarendon Press, 1998).

Harris, Paul and Morrow, John (eds.) *Lectures* (Cambridge: Cambridge University Press, 1986).

Horder, Jeremy. *Excusing Crime* (Oxford: Oxford University Press, 2004).

Kant, Immanuel. (tr.) E.B. Ashton, *On the Old Saw: That May be Right in Theory, but it Won't Work in Practice* (Philadelphia: University of Pennsylvania Press, 1974).

Kant, Immanuel. (ed. and tr.) Mary Gregor and Jens Timmerman, *Groundwork of the Metaphysics of Morals* (Cambridge: Cambridge University Press, 2012).

Korsgaard, Christine M. *The Sources of Normativity* (Cambridge: Cambridge University Press, 2014).

McLennan, Gregor, Held, David and Hall, Stuart (eds.) *State and Society in Contemporary Britain: A Critical Introduction* (Cambridge: Polity Press, 1984).

McMahan, Jeff. *Killing in War* (Oxford: Clarendon Press, 2009).

Mill, John S. (ed.) Mark Philp and Frederick Rosen, *On Liberty, Utilitarianism and Other Essays* (Oxford: Oxford University Press, 2015).
Montesquieu, Charles and Secondat Baron. (eds.) Anne M. Cohler, Basia Carolyn Miller, and Harold Stone, *The Spirit of the Laws* (Cambridge: Cambridge University Press, 2016).
Rawls, John. *Political Liberalism* (New York: Columbia University Press, 2005).
Raz, Joseph. *The Authority of Law: Essays on Law and Morality* (Oxford: Clarendon Press, 1979).
Raz, Joseph. *The Morality of Freedom* (Oxford: Clarendon Press, 2009).
Roosevelt, Franklin D. *Selected Speeches of President Franklin D. Roosevelt* (Florida: Red and Black, 2010).
Ryle, Gilbert. *The Concept of Mind* (United States: University of Chicago Press, 2002).
Scanlon, T.M. *What we Owe to Each Other* (Cambridge, MA: Harvard University Press, 2000).
Shakespeare, William. "Hamlet," in George Clark and William A. Wright (eds.), *The Works of William Shakespeare* (London: MacMillian and Co., 1866).
Sherwood, Robert E. *Roosevelt and Hopkins: An Intimate History* (New York: Harper and Brothers, 1948).
Shirer, William. *The Rise and Fall of the Third Reich* (New York: Simon & Schuster, 2011).
Simmons, A. John. *Moral Principles and Political Obligations* (Princeton, NJ: Princeton University Press, 1979).
Simpson, Gerry. *Law War and Crime* (Cambridge: Polity, 2007).
Smart, J.J.C. and Williams, Bernard. *Utilitarianism: For and Against* (Cambridge: Cambridge University Press, 2008).
Sophocles, *Antigone* (eds.) David Grene and Richmond Lattimore, *The Complete Greek Tragedies*, Volume. II (Chicago and London: University of Chicago Press, 1992).
Taylor, Charles. *Sources of the Self* (Cambridge: Cambridge University Press, 1992).
Walzer, Michael. *Obligations: Essays on Disobedience, War and Citizenship* (Cambridge, MA: Harvard University Press, 1970).
Williams, Bernard. *Moral Luck* (Cambridge: Cambridge University Press, 1999).
Williams, Bernard. *Ethics and the Limits of Philosophy* (Cambridge, MA: Harvard University Press, 1985).
Wittgenstein, Ludwig. (tr.) C.K. Ogden with an introduction by Bertrand Russell, *Tractatus Logico-Philosophicus* (New York: Dover, 1999).
Wittgenstein, Ludwig. (tr.). G.E.M. Anscombe, P.M.S. Hacker and Joachim Schulte, *Philosophical Investigations* (United Kingdom: Wiley Blackwell, 2009).

6 For All of Us, As One of Us – The General is Equal as a Citizen

In 1962, delivering the Lees-Knowles lectures at Cambridge University, the Western Australian-born British General Sir John Winthrop Hackett coined the phrase "unlimited liability."[1] As an expressive term, unlimited liability has come to be a commonplace, describing the soldier's commitment to "almost unlimited service"[2] and to "risk death for his country."[3] Taking things to a brute conclusion, the philosopher Colm McKeogh argues that the unlimited liability turns people into "non-persons, instruments [or] things."[4] McKeogh presumes a difference in the status of human rights: he does not think it possible that society might treat citizens who volunteer to serve wrongly. For McKeogh, soldiers are property which the executive can treat as it pleases. On my account, McKeogh's claim is horrible and mistaken.

In this chapter I dispute with the "unlimited liability" (so-called). I argue that in a liberal democracy, just as some things cannot be taken away so some things cannot be given up. There are limits to consent. When a citizen offers military service, the citizen cedes many rights of individual autonomy to the state – but not every right. Citizens cannot sign away their conscience and the fact of their being responsible for acts within their power.

I reason that a reasonable, liberal society will respect the limits of voluntarism and the value of autonomy. I admit democracy has significant moral value worth protecting, and I accept the state must impose on the citizen in order to safeguard critical common interests. But even though the sovereign power is very great, there are limits on its exercise.[5] To treat the general differently, to deny the elemental rights of citizens is illiberal and unmerited.

Equal Justice

After Rawls, the distinction between institutional and interactional moral analysis has come to differentiate justice from ethics.[6] Justice, being concerned with institutional analysis, denominates a moral assessment associated with law, social conventions, and institutions which are basic to democracy. In this section I overview ideas which mean democratic society will, so far as possible, honour the rights of citizens who are equal as moral beings worthy of concern and respect.

DOI: 10.4324/9781003527886-6

Following Locke,[7] Rawls recognised the free conscience as a primary good and constitutional essential.[8] For Rawls, the equal liberty of conscience stands among the most basic points of social justice.[9] On the Rawlsian argument if any principle can be agreed to, it must be that of equal liberty, since this is the idea which enables individuals to interpret and to meet moral obligations, and it is this idea which enables the democracy to accommodate the various interests and obligations of citizens.[10]

Without conscience, moral responsibility amounts to nothing more than compliance with the law. To act morally is to act autonomously. Moral decision, obtains from wilful, deliberate, intention, or motive. It cannot be a moral act when I merely comply, or when I am forced, or required. A reasonable, liberal, and democratic society takes the moral convictions of citizens seriously and enables individuals to examine and to act upon deeply held beliefs.[11] In practice, such a society will pay attention to institutional structures, and to the offices that comprise those institutions, in order to minimise the chance that citizens bear unreasonable moral burdens. An unreasonable moral burden is understood to bring about occasions in which non-compliance with the law is the only morally acceptable course of action.[12]

When legislation curtails liberty of conscience, legislation abrades a prerequisite democratic foundation. States bear an obligation to structure legislative frameworks and public policy with a mind to justice. This obligation is dishonoured in Australian legislation which compels the general to abide by any direction from politics without a moral second thought. The trespass is made plain by J.S. Mill who describes the injustice of using people as "mere human instruments for firing cannon or thrusting bayonets in the service and for the selfish purposes of a master."[13]

I contend the commitment made by the citizen who serves as general is wide, but it is not infinite and not expected to be infinite. The general has promised to serve the democracy. The burden of supreme command is great, but the general stands among us. The general is not somehow different from the rest of us; not greater than the rest of us, and not lesser than the rest of us. The general shares, in Locke's words, the "perfect freedom" and "the equality of men by nature."[14] Like all soldiers, the general serves all of us as one of us. To treat the general differently, to deny elemental rights of citizenship fails to bear out basic liberal democratic principles. In the liberal democracy, each person is understood to possess an inviolability which might not be sacrificed even to the welfare of the greater society. In other words, the loss of basic freedoms by some is not made right since others enjoy a greater good. Justice does not agree that sacrifices imposed on the few are outweighed by the advantages shared by many.[15] A properly functioning liberal society offers each citizen equal justice under the law. This is the point of John Donne's truism: "no man is an island,"[16] and the crux of the famous oration where Pericles says democracy favours the many, instead of the few.

In the democracy, laws – whether on the statute book or part of an unwritten code – afford the equal justice which is basic to society.[17] Unkindly, Plato said, democracy distributes equality to equals and non-equals.[18] More charitably,

Michael Walzer says democracy replaces the idea of "some" with the idea of "all."[19] The point is the democratic idea of a "citizen" has taken over from the idea of the aristocrat. Rights, to which the aristocracy once laid exclusive claim, have come to be the rights of all. Following from claims of equal citizenship, democracy gives real-world life to the idea of equal justice. In chapter 40, *Magna Carta* puts the idea in few famous words: "to no one will we sell, to no one deny, or delay, right or justice." Described by Lord Denning as "the greatest constitutional document of all times – the foundation of the freedom of the individual against the arbitrary authority of the despot,"[20] and by William Pitt the Elder as "the Bible of the English Constitution,"[21] *Magna Carta* inaugurated the Enlightenment declarations which define modern political society. Once understood in metaphysical terms to be ordained by God, outside the political order, and incapable of formulation or annulment by law, equality came to be practical and realisable when people asserted it. Hannah Arendt explains that in the liberal democracy, equality is the result of human organisation guided by the principle of justice. We are not born equal; we become equal as members of a group on the strength of our decision to guarantee ourselves mutually equal rights.[22]

Without the protections and constraints of law, equality between people is the sort of unimpeded dissolution Edmund Burke described as disorderly and destructive.[23] As we like it, political society depends on protections offered by, and conditions worked out by people and imposed by law.[24] Even so, political institutions must respect citizens as autonomous individuals. The democracy suffers when the free conscience of the citizens is coerced.[25] But conscience *is* coerced by Australian legislation, which says the general must comply with any political direction. The legislation presumes the general is not an equal citizen. On the terms of legislation, the general is a subjacent mechanism of mere instrumental political value. In *The Crown of Wild Olive*, John Ruskin reviles this sort of using.[26] Ruskin asks us to remember that war concerns people. Society cannot rightly "set unhappy peasant pieces upon the chequer of forest and field," thence to sit "on the sides of the amphitheatre … [and] urge peasant millions into gladiatorial war."[27]

Volunteering and Consent

John Locke, in many ways the father of modern democracy,[28] says political society depends upon the consent of citizens who devolve some independence to the government to assure their enjoyment of liberty and property.[29] However, Locke was mindful that this devolution was conditional and did not entail the impoverishment of individuals or the surrender of inalienable freedoms.[30] In the summary offered by Kant: "every man has inalienable rights which he cannot give up, even if he would."[31] In a reasonable, liberal society, as some things cannot be taken away, so some things cannot be given up. It is not sufficient to assert that since volunteers consent to the rigours of military service, there can be nothing unjust about demands which are imposed.

Volunteering to serve, soldiers assume a moral obligation. Moral obligation obtains from the chosen act of volunteering – from the deliberate shouldering of duties, some explicit and some implied. Moral obligation obtaining from voluntarism differs from positional legal duties involved in military service. In his book, *Moral Principles and Political Obligations*, A.J. Simmons reasons that if we consider the case of a conscript, then surely the conscript has no moral obligation to those who have forced him. He is no doubt obliged to obey – since there are the tender mercies of military discipline. But any suggestion that there are moral obligations seems absurd. Even volunteers to military service do not bear the sort of moral obligation people often assume to be borne. For Simmons: it is not legally defined positional "military duties" which bind, but rather the autonomous voluntary obligation to discharge those positional military duties.[32] The distinction is between positional, legally defined duties, and moral obligations. Positional or legal obligations are quite different from moral obligations. To speak of "legal obligations" is to reference the requiring rules imposed by the legal system. But the mere existence of such rules is not sufficient to establish a moral requirement. Certainly, there might be a moral obligation to obey the law, but this moral obligation is quite a different thing from a legal onus.[33]

Choosing to serve, citizens elect to meet specified, positional duties: they assume for themselves a moral obligation to obey explicit laws. Citizens also assume implied obligations, which are obtained from custom and convention. But volunteers do not surrender citizenship and the liberty of conscience which is elemental to justice in a democracy.

> If a soldier [even a general] admitted that the acceptance of money or even the taking of an oath obligated him to kill and be killed, he would be turning himself into a mere instrument of the state or of the mercenary captain who hires him.[34]

Volunteering military service, people retain the rights of citizens, *inter alia* the right to preserve their own interests. Even volunteering, as we remember from Hobbes, there are some rights which cannot be abandoned or signed away under any circumstances.[35]

Harvard philosopher Michael Sandel illustrates this point. Sandel describes how most countries allow the donation of organs for transplantation in life-saving procedures; though the sale of organs is not allowed.[36] Similarly, self-ownership does not extend so far that the state allows individuals to sell themselves into slavery. Laws which recognise the possibility of rape in marriage offer a further illustration. In committing to marriage, a person makes a special, panoptic, and exclusive promise. Yet, even freely entering into marriage, a person is seen to be incapable of giving away the advantages of personhood and the right to consent or to renounce consent. So it is when people volunteer military service.

When people volunteer military service, they expect to meet military duties. Some of these duties are ordinary and dull. Others are morally trying. Since people who volunteer for military service know something of that which will be expected of them, we can reasonably say that some – even many – things will be consented to. Yet not everything can be consented to; and some things might be objected to.[37]

Jeff McMahan says the person who volunteers for military service is much like the person who walks voluntarily through a dangerous neighbourhood. Such a person accepts the risk of being mugged, but such a person does not consent to being mugged.[38] Walking in the dangerous neighbourhood a person does not give permission that others may mug him. In fact, even when a person properly aware of risk chooses to walk in a dangerous neighbourhood, it is reasonable for such a person to hold an animated objection to mugging. Similarly, the volunteer soldier might accept some risks in the service of some causes, whilst maintaining a lively objection to other risks and other causes.

The philosopher Christopher Cowley offers up the case of the obstetrician who objects to abortion.[39] On its face, the illustration seems to be a *non sequitur*. Since obstetrics is that branch of medicine concerned with pregnancy and the genitourinary tract, it seems unrealistic to suppose an obstetrician might object conscientiously to a procedure which is integral to the specialism. Even if we allow that prospective obstetricians embark upon medical training with only a partial grasp of the professional demands involved, we might reasonably assume that deliberate progression from medical student to medical specialist implies consent to all the profession may ask. The prospective obstetrician could drop out before becoming a doctor, or switch specialisation before becoming an obstetrician. Since opportunities to avoid obstetrics and the dilemma inherent in the procedure of abortion are declined, we might say the obstetrician has accepted the rules of the game. We might say it is too late to object once the procedure is encountered in real life. We might say, given the state pays most of the cost of medical training, and given the state supports the practice of medicine in public hospitals, the state is entitled to insist obstetricians provide services for which they have been trained. But such a response would miss the point.

We don't object conscientiously simply since we feel pangs of moral discomfit, because something is not quite our cup of tea. We object conscientiously since we feel deep moral obligation. For the obstetrician, moral reaction against abortion obtains from a commitment to the invisible foetus, without separate voice and dependent upon us. As Cowley explains, the obstetrician bears a conscientious objection to abortion which is not a quirk, not contingent, not some quaint debating society artifice, and not the derivative of theological dogma. The example shows conscientious objection as a long way from bizarre or idiosyncratic, but connected profoundly to the profession of medicine and to the doctor as healer. For the obstetrician as Cowley describes her, pregnancy is not an illness or an injury which might be resolved through a procedure.[40]

Asking us to recognise the moral commitment of the obstetrician to the dependent foetus, Cowley does not dismiss the moral claims of prospective mothers or the moral obligation obstetricians bear to mothers in need of specialist care. Rather, he asks us to grapple with polysemous moral obligation, and he asks us to recognise the power of moral commitment. Cowley shows that, though people consent to render duties, they do not sign away their conscience. Consent to meet duties does not relieve people from ordinary moral limits or excuse moral wrongdoing. Relatedly, in a reasonable, liberal, and democratic society, law ought not force us to flout the deep registers of our conscience.

Obligations and Law

Obligations to comply with just laws enacted under a just constitution are uncontroversial. The real question concerns the extent to which citizens are bound when laws go too far. When the basic structure of society is reasonably just, the injustice of a law does not offer a *prima facie* reason for conscientious refusal. Rather, laws should be binding, provided they do not surpass the reasonably evident limits of injustice. Equally, legal validity does not offer sufficient reason for obedience to a law.[41] Since we see that unjust laws, unjust policies, and unjust institutions are not on a par,[42] our idea of justice is characterised by circumstantial reasonableness, in other words, by a common-sense understanding of right.[43] In every community, the obligation to obey the laws must be tempered by a larger, standing determination to serve justice not power.[44]

Making these remarks, I disagree with the argument offered up by A.J. Simmons in *Moral Principles and Public Obligations*. Simmons claims that if "the unjust institution does not happen to be doing violence to *me*, I can freely consent to its authority."[45] When he makes this claim, Simmons forgets the veil of ignorance, conceived by Rawls to ensure no one is advantaged or disadvantaged by natural chance or the contingency of social circumstances. For Rawls, the principles of justice are the principles of fairness, given the circumstances. For Rawls, principles of justice are agreed in a spirit of even-handedness, with a standing, over-all, inclusive sense of rightfulness.[46] I agree with Rawls when he observes that an individual who finds that he enjoys seeing others in positions of distress or disadvantage should understand that this enjoyment is ill-found. It is discreditable to take pleasure in the misery, deprivation, or poverty of others, since this is a pleasure which contravenes the basic principles of justice as fairness.[47]

Taking from Rawls, I believe it would be implausible to consent to an unjust institution on the basis that only other people suffered. To my mind, it is unreasonable to claim that Nazi officers were morally obligated to their unjust state – since the state did not treat them inhospitably. To my mind, the unjust character of the Nazi state voids any moral obligation to obey; gross injustice inflicted upon so many innocents would have been sufficient to release any German from moral commitment to the Nazi state. The permeating flagrant and occult evil of autocratic and arbitrary forms of government means it is impossible for an obligation of obedience to arise from any consent or from any other acquiescence.[48] The obligation to obey or comply presupposes institutions are reasonably just in view of the circumstances. Thus, I seek the reform of legislation that stipulates generals *must* comply with *any* ministerial direction, since these are autocratic terms, which deny the general the liberty of conscience which is elemental to the basic structure of society.[49]

To put this in other words, the democracy's public legitimacy should not increase the state's coercive influence. The state might insist on some things, but there are limits. Just as the state cannot force a person to contravene the deep registers of conscience, so an individual cannot transfer rights of autonomy to the state, cease thereby to be an autonomous agent, and thus become exempt from moral constraints.[50]

Power of the State

The modern volunteer military is at a critical remove from politics,[51] and from the society it serves. Few people have experience of military service, few people are concerned by the conditions of military service, and few people are keen or even prepared to serve. Rousseau gives voice to the concern that the fabric of society and the state is weakened as soon as public service ceases to be the concern of citizens, who pay tax but little else.[52]

Such a country is like the Omelas conceived by Ursula le Guin. The people in Omelas are genuinely happy. They enjoy festivals, a wonderful farmers' market, and magnificent architecture.[53] But, in a basement, there is a room. There is no window. In one corner there are mops with stiff, clotted, foul-smelling heads. The floor is dirt, a little damp to the touch. There is a child, prisoner in the room. It looks about six but is actually ten. It is feeble-minded. Perhaps it was born defective, or perhaps made an imbecile through fear, malnutrition, and neglect.[54]

Occasionally the door opens, and people look in. One of them may kick the child to make it stand. The others never come close. The child is fed corn meal and grease and given water. It sits, naked in its own excrement, encrusted and ulcerated, and does not speak. The child used to cry out, "please let me out, I will be good"[55] but now it makes only a kind of moaning.

The people of Omelas know about the child, and they know it must be there since their happiness, the beauty of their city, the tenderness of their friendships, the health of their children, the wisdom of their scholars, the skill of their makers, even the abundance of their harvest and the kindly weather of their skies, depend wholly on this child's abominable misery.

Offering the story of Omelas I offer a rhetorical challenge to utilitarian law which treats the general improperly as morally imperceptive and insensible, incapable of forming deep moral convictions, and capable of nothing except unquestioning obedience. Offering the metaphor, I recognise liberal democratic governments can engage in rights abuses and liberal societies, acculturated to the usual way of doing things, can be guilty of needs-neglect.[56]

Obviously, the state must impose some things in the common interest. But state authority can only go so far. As French CJ said in *Pape v. Commissioner of Taxation* (2009), the executive power cannot reasonably be confined to a constitutional museum; it must serve the purposes of national government.[57] But the political obligation to maintain order does not mean the state has licence to do whatever it wants, such as Hobbes argued in *De Cive* when he claimed the executive can do no wrong to the citizens.[58]

My argument takes after Locke, who acknowledges laws might go a long way when they are made for the public good.[59] But unlike Hobbes, Locke understands there are limits.[60] Locke accepts the right of the citizens to resist autocracy, to safeguard themselves and their own interests.[61] He says, "the liberty of man in society, is to be under no other legislative power, but that established by consent."[62] In *Anarchy, State and Utopia*, Robert Nozick makes a similar case when he reasons that though individuals might *choose* to undergo some pain or sacrifice for a greater benefit, society does not have a claim on some for the sake of the majority.[63]

Nozick argues that the most extensive state that can be justified is the state which will impose minimally upon people whilst ensuring justice.[64] Offering a more minimal conception of the state than Rawls might accept, Nozick agrees with Rawls insofar as he says the state should acknowledge uninfringeable human rights. I agree. The state should regard the citizens as inviolate individuals who may not be used as mere tools, or means.[65]

Yet, in Australian legislation, the claims of the executive are over-riding. Stipulating that the Chief of the Defence Force *must* comply with *any* directions of the Minister, the *Defence Act* presumes the general to be a morally trivial hireling. Thomas Hurka excuses this overstep of executive power by claiming that enlistment implies a universal consent, a global surrender of rights, and an unconditional promise to serve in any and all wars the government may direct.[66] But in fact, consent is not given once, for all time, and for all things.[67] When soldiers enlist as soldiers, and when the general accepts appointment as Chief of the Defence Force, the consent is a consent to serve the state. But the consent is not an unqualified consent to the state using them in *any* war, for *any* reason.

Service not Servitude

Citizens freely offer service as soldiers. They enlist to serve the common good. But they do not enlist in servitude; to be military chattels, bondservants, or villeins. Remembering that what can be said of soldiers applies even more strongly to generals: soldiers are not slaves. Soldiers are citizens entitled to the rights and liberties secured to citizens by law. This view was endorsed by the Australian High Court in *Re Tracey: ex parte Ryan* (1989)[68] where Mason CJ, Wilson and Dawson JJ cited Lord Mansfield CJ in *Burdett v. Abbot* (1812) with approval: "A soldier is gifted with all the rights of other citizens." Assuming the obligation of a soldier does not dissolve the rights and duties of an ordinary civilian citizen.[69] Likewise, in his 1867 *Commentaries Upon Martial Law,* Finlason argued: "Soldiers are not the less citizens and entitled to the rights of citizens … and of those rights they cannot be deprived, except upon the ground of paramount necessity, with reference to the safety of the community."[70] *Halsbury's Laws of England* maintains likewise: "Officers and men of the royal forces, by becoming subject to naval, military or air force law, do not divest themselves of the civil rights and duties of citizens in general."[71]

In his 1832 *Charge to the Bristol Grand Jury on a Special Commission*, Lord Tindal CJ made things plain: "the law acknowledges no distinction … between the soldier and the private individual."[72] Though soldiers are soldiers, they are also citizens. Just as soldiers bear the obligations of citizenship, so they are entitled to the privileges of citizenship in liberal society. This argument was made resonant by Lord Atkin in *Liversidge v. Anderson* (1942).[73] His Honour found laws must speak the same language in war as in peace; the language of individual liberty and worth, not the language of political repression.[74] Likewise, Locke says the practical stringencies of military discipline cannot infringe upon the requisites of justice.[75] Powers must not be used to harm people. Citizens and soldiers are alike entitled to equal justice.[76]

Conclusion

We are not genetically liberal. We are not naturally immune to horrible ideologies and injustice.[77] We are protected from wrongs by ideas and by the political institutions which are inspired by our ideas. We cannot afford to be cavalier about these ideas. We must take liberalism seriously. Liberalism will fail if we merely look on. We must seek to express liberal thinking in real-world action.

We are protected from wrongs by ideas and by the political institutions which are inspired by our ideas. Governments must operate to safeguard the state and they must use powers to do this. But governments can use coercive power unduly and they will beget tremendous evil unless they are prevented. There are limits. When law enjoins generals from their conscience and denies them status as moral beings worthy of concern and respect, the democracy imposes too much. Such law must be reformed.

Notes

1 Lt. Gen Sir John Winthrop Hackett, *The Profession of Arms: The 1962 Lees Knowles Lectures Given at Trinity College Cambridge* (London: Times Publishing, 1962), p. 63.
2 Nicholas Keijzer, *Military Obedience* (Alpena an den Rijn, Netherlands: Sijthoff & Noordhoff, 1978), p. 32.
3 Mark Osiel, *Obeying Orders: Atrocity, Military Discipline and the Law of War* (New Brunswick and London: Transaction, 2002), p. 65.
4 Colm McKeogh, *Innocent Civilians: The Morality of Killing in War* (Great Britain: Palgrave, 2002), p. 12.
5 Thomas Hobbes (ed.), C.B. Macpherson, *Leviathan* (England: Penguin, 1985), Ch. 21, p. 269.
6 Thomas Pogge, *Politics as Usual: What Lies Behind the Pro-Poor Rhetoric* (Cambridge: Polity, 2010), p. 16.
7 John Locke, "A Letter Concerning Toleration," in Ian Shapiro (ed.), *Two Treatises of Government and A Letter Concerning Toleration* (New Haven: Yale University Press, 2003), p. 246. "The liberty of conscience is every man's natural right."
8 John Rawls, *Justice as Fairness: A Restatement* (Cambridge, MA: The Belknap Press of Harvard University Press, 2001), pp. 28, 58.
9 John Rawls, *A Theory of Justice* (Cambridge, MA: The Belknap Press of Harvard University Press, 1999), pp. 181, 182.
10 John Rawls, *A Theory of Justice* (Cambridge, MA: The Belknap Press of Harvard University Press, 1999), p. 181.
11 John Rawls, *A Theory of Justice* (Cambridge, MA: The Belknap Press of Harvard University Press, 1999), p. 181.
12 Kimberley Brownlee, *Conscience and Conviction: The Case for Civil Disobedience* (Oxford: Oxford University Press, 2015), p. 102.
13 John S. Mill, "The Contest in America," in *Fraser's Magazine for Town and Country*, (1862) 65:386, pp. 258–268, 268.
14 John Locke, "Second Treatise," in Ian Shapiro (ed.), *Two Treatises of Government and A Letter Concerning Toleration* (New Haven: Yale University Press, 2003), Ch. 2, "Of the State of Nature," §4–§5, p. 101.
15 John Rawls, *A Theory of Justice* (Cambridge, MA: The Belknap Press of Harvard University Press, 1999), p. 3.
16 John Donne, "Nunc Lento Sonitu Dicunt, Morieris," Meditation xvii in, *Devotions Upon Emergent Occasions and Death's Duel* (New York: Vintage Books, 1999), p. 103.
17 Thucydides, "History of the Peloponnesian War," in Robert B. Strassler (ed.), *The Landmark Thucydides* (New York: Free Press, 2008), 2.37.1, p. 112.

18 Plato, *Republic*, 558c.
19 Michael Walzer, *Thick and Thin: Moral Argument at Home and Abroad* (Indiana: University of Notre Dame Press, 2012), pp. 53, 54.
20 Danny Danziger and John Gillingham, *1215: The Year of Magna Carta* (New York, London, Toronto, Sydney: Touchstone, 2005), p. 268.
21 Danny Danziger and John Gillingham, *1215: The Year of Magna Carta* (New York, London, Toronto, Sydney: Touchstone, 2005), p. 268.
22 Hannah Arendt, *The Origins of Totalitarianism* (Orlando, Austin, New York, San Diego, London: Harvest, 1994), p. 301.
23 J.C.D. Clark, "Introduction" to Edmund Burke (ed.), J.C.D. Clark, *Reflections on the Revolution in France* (Stanford, CA: Stanford University Press, 2001), p. 33.
24 Edmund Burke (ed.), J.C.D. Clark, *Reflections on the Revolution in France* (Stanford, CA: Stanford University Press, 2001), p. 152.
25 Michael Walzer, *Obligations: Essays on Disobedience, War and Citizenship* (Cambridge, MA: Harvard University Press, 1970), p. 141.
26 John Ruskin, *The Crown of Wild Olive: Four Lectures on Industry and War* (London: George Allen and Unwin Ltd, 1915), p. 127.
27 John Ruskin, *The Crown of Wild Olive: Four Lectures on Industry and War* (London: George Allen and Unwin Ltd, 1915), p. 127.
28 Ian Shapiro, "John Locke's Democratic Theory," in John Locke (ed.), *Two Treatises of Government and A Letter Concerning Toleration* (New Haven: Yale University Press, 2003), pp. 309–340.
29 John Locke, "Second Treatise," in Ian Shapiro (ed.), *Two Treatises of Government and A Letter Concerning Toleration* (New Haven: Yale University Press, 2003), Ch. 8, "Of the Beginning of Political Societies," §95, pp. 141–142.
John Locke, "A Letter Concerning Toleration," in Ian Shapiro (ed.), *Two Treatises of Government and A Letter Concerning Toleration* (New Haven: Yale University Press, 2003), p. 243.
30 John Locke, "Second Treatise," in Ian Shapiro (ed.), *Two Treatises of Government and A Letter Concerning Toleration* (New Haven: Yale University Press, 2003), Ch. IV, "Of Slavery," §23, p. 110.
John Locke, "Second Treatise," in Ian Shapiro (ed.), *Two Treatises of Government and A Letter Concerning Toleration* (New Haven: Yale University Press, 2003), Ch. 4, "Of Slavery," §22, pp. 109–110. Also: Ch. 7, "Of the Beginning of Political Societies," §94, p. 141.
31 Immanuel Kant (tr.), E.B. Ashton, *On the Old Saw: That May be Right in Theory, but it Won't Work in Practice* (Philadelphia: University of Pennsylvania Press, 1974), p. 72.
32 A. John Simmons, *Moral Principles and Political Obligations* (Princeton, NJ: Princeton University Press, 1979), p. 22.
33 A. John Simmons, *Moral Principles and Political Obligations* (Princeton, NJ: Princeton University Press, 1979), p. 23.
Michael Walzer, *Obligations: Essays on Disobedience, War and Citizenship* (Cambridge, MA: Harvard University Press, 1970), p. 89:
34 Michael Walzer, *Obligations: Essays on Disobedience, War and Citizenship* (Cambridge, MA: Harvard University Press, 1970), p. 85.
35 Thomas Hobbes, (ed.) C.B. Macpherson, *Leviathan* (England: Penguin, 1985), Ch. 14, p. 192.
36 Michael Sandel, *Justice: What's the Right Thing to Do?* (New York: Farrar, Straus and Giroux, 2010), p. 70.
37 Kimberley Brownlee, *Conscience and Conviction: The Case for Civil Disobedience* (Oxford: Oxford University Press, 2015), pp. 111–112.
38 Jeff McMahan, *Killing in War* (Oxford: Clarendon Press, 2009), p. 52.
39 Christopher Cowley, "A Defence of Conscientious Objection in Medicine: A Reply to Schuklenk and Savulescu," in *Bioethics*, (2016) 30:5, pp. 358–364.

40 Christopher Cowley, "A Defence of Conscientious Objection in Medicine: A Reply to Schuklenk and Savulescu," in *Bioethics*, (2016) 30:5, pp. 358–364, 362.
41 John Rawls, *A Theory of Justice* (Cambridge, MA: The Belknap Press of Harvard University Press, 1999), 308.
42 John Rawls, *A Theory of Justice* (Cambridge, MA: The Belknap Press of Harvard University Press, 1999), p. 309.
43 John Rawls, *A Theory of Justice* (Cambridge, MA: The Belknap Press of Harvard University Press, 1999), p. 41.
44 Immanuel Kant (tr.), E.B. Ashton, *On the Old Saw: That May be Right in Theory, but it Won't Work in Practice* (Philadelphia: University of Pennsylvania Press, 1974), p. 73.
45 A. John Simmons, *Moral Principles and Political Obligations* (Princeton, NJ: Princeton University Press, 1979), p. 78.
46 John Rawls, *A Theory of Justice* (Cambridge, MA: The Belknap Press of Harvard University Press, 1999), p. 11.
47 John Rawls, *A Theory of Justice* (Cambridge, MA: The Belknap Press of Harvard University Press, 1999), pp. 27–28.
48 John Rawls, *A Theory of Justice* (Cambridge, MA: The Belknap Press of Harvard University Press, 1999), p. 96.
49 John Rawls, *A Theory of Justice* (Cambridge, MA: The Belknap Press of Harvard University Press, 1999), p. 53. At p. 177 Rawls says: "individuals have this basic liberty [of conscience] when they are free to pursue their moral, philosophical, or religious interests without legal restrictions."
50 Jeff McMahan, "Collectivist Defenses of the Moral Equality of Combatants," in *Journal of Military Ethics*, (2007) 6:1, pp. 50–59, 54.
51 Eliot A. Cohen, *Supreme Command, Soldiers Statesmen and Leadership in Wartime* (New York: Anchor Books, 2003), p. 11.
52 Jean-Jacques Rousseau (ed.), Susan Dunn, *The Social Contract and The First and Second Discourses* (New Haven and London: Yale University Press, 2002), Book III, Ch. 15, p. 220.
53 Ursula Le Guin, "The Ones who Walk Away from Omelas," in Ann Charters (ed.), *The Story and its Writer: An Introduction to Short Fiction* (Boston: Bedford St. Martin's, 2003), p. 903.
54 Ursula Le Guin, The Ones who Walk Away from Omelas," in Ann Charters (ed.), *The Story and its Writer: An Introduction to Short Fiction* (Boston: Bedford St. Martin's, 2003), p. 904.
55 Ursula Le Guin, "The Ones who Walk Away from Omelas," in Ann Charters (ed.), *The Story and its Writer: An Introduction to Short Fiction* (Boston: Bedford St. Martin's, 2003), p. 905.
56 Kimberley Brownlee, *Conscience and Conviction: The Case for Civil Disobedience* (Oxford: Oxford University Press, 2015), p. 195.
57 (2009) 238 CLR 1, 160 per French CJ.
58 Thomas Hobbes (ed. and tr.), Richard Tuck and Michael Silverthorne, *On the Citizen* (Cambridge: Cambridge University Press, 2017), Ch. VII "On Three Kinds of Commonwealth: Democracy, Aristocracy and Monarchy," §14, p. 97.
59 John Locke, "Second Treatise," in Ian Shapiro (ed.), *Two Treatises of Government and A Letter Concerning Toleration* (New Haven: Yale University Press, 2003), Ch. 4, "Of Slavery," §22, pp. 109–110. Also: Ch. 7, "Of the Beginning of Political Societies," §94, p. 141. Ch. 2, "Of the State of Nature," §3, p. 101. Ch. 13, "Of the Subordination of the Powers of the Commonwealth," §149, p. 166. Ch. 14, "Of Prerogative," §161, p. 172: So far as the executive power acts for the common good, it is never to be questioned.
60 John Locke, "Second Treatise," in Ian Shapiro (ed.), *Two Treatises of Government and A Letter Concerning Toleration* (New Haven: Yale University Press, 2003), Ch. 2, "Of the State of Nature," §13, pp. 105–106.

61 John Locke, "Second Treatise," in Ian Shapiro (ed.), *Two Treatises of Government and A Letter Concerning Toleration* (New Haven: Yale University Press, 2003), Ch. 19, "Of the Dissolution of Government," §232, p. 202.
62 John Locke, "Second Treatise," in Ian Shapiro (ed.), *Two Treatises of Government and A Letter Concerning Toleration* (New Haven: Yale University Press, 2003), Ch. 4, "Of Slavery," §22, pp. 109–110. Also: Ch. 7, "Of the Beginning of Political Societies," §94, p. 141.
63 Robert Nozick, *Anarchy, State and Utopia* (New York: Basic Books, 2013), p. 33.
64 Robert Nozick, *Anarchy, State and Utopia* (New York: Basic Books, 2013), p. 149.
65 Robert Nozick, *Anarchy, State and Utopia* (New York: Basic Books, 2013), pp. 333–334.
66 Thomas Hurka, "Liability and Just Cause," in *Ethics and International Affairs*, (2010) 21:2, pp. 199–218, 210, 211.
67 Michael Walzer, *Obligations: Essays on Disobedience, War and Citizenship* (Cambridge, MA: Harvard University Press, 1970), p. xiii–xiv.
68 (1989) 166 CLR 518 at 546.
69 (1812) 4 Taunt 401 at 449–450; 128 ER 384 at 403.
70 William F. Finlason, *Commentaries Upon Martial Law* (London: Stevens and Sons, 1867), p. 48. Also pp. 99–100, 104.
71 "Royal Forces" in Viscount Hailsham (ed.), *Halsbury's Laws of England* (London: Butterworth, 1938), vol. 28, paragraph 1396, p. 677.
72 Sir Nicholas Conygham Tindal "Charge Delivered to the Grand Jury of the County of the City of Bristol by the Rt. Hon. Sir Nicholas Conygham Tindal Knight, Lord Chief Justice of Her Majesty's Court of Common Pleas at Westminster on Monday the 2nd January 1832 Under the Special Commission Issued into that County," in W.H. Somerton (ed.), *A Narrative of the Bristol Riots,* (Bristol: The Mercury Office, no date).
A.V. Dicey (ed.), E.C.S. Wade, *Introduction to the Study of the Law of the Constitution* (MacMillan: London, 1961), pp. 300–301.
73 (1942) AC 206.
74 (1942) AC 206, 244 *per* Atkin LJ.
75 John Locke, "Second Treatise," in Ian Shapiro (ed.), *Two Treatises of Government and A Letter Concerning Toleration* (New Haven: Yale University Press, 2003), Ch. 11, "On the Extent of the Legislative Power," §135, p. 159; §139, p. 162; Ch. 19, "Of the Dissolution of Government," §221, p. 197.
76 John Locke, "Second Treatise," in Ian Shapiro (ed.), *Two Treatises of Government and A Letter Concerning Toleration* (New Haven: Yale University Press, 2003), Ch. 4, "Of Slavery," §22, pp. 109–110. Also: Ch. 7, "Of the Beginning of Political Societies," §94, p. 141. Ch. 18, "Of Tyranny," §210, p. 192. Ch. 11, On the Extent of the Legislative Power," §142, p. 163; Ch. 14, "Of Prerogative," §164, p. 173.
77 Jeff McMahan, *Killing in War* (Oxford: Clarendon Press, 2009), p. 3.

References

Australian Cases

Davis v. Commonwealth (1988) 166 CLR 79.
Pape v. Commissioner of Taxation (2009) 238 CLR 1.

United Kingdom Cases

Burdett v. Abbot (1812) 128 ER 384.
Liversidge v. Anderson (1942) AC 206.

Journal Articles

Cowley, Christopher. "A Defence of Conscientious Objection in Medicine: A Reply to Schuklenk and Savulescu," in *Bioethics*, (2016) 30: 5, pp. 358–364.

Hurka, Thomas. "Liability and Just Cause," in *Ethics and International Affairs*, (2010) 21:2, pp. 199–218.

McMahan, Jeff. "Collectivist Defenses of the Moral Equality of Combatants," in *Journal of Military Ethics*, (2007) 6:1, pp. 50–59.

Books

Arendt, Hannah. *The Origins of Totalitarianism* (Orlando, Austin, New York, San Diego, London: Harvest, 1994).

Brownlee, Kimberley. *Conscience and Conviction: The Case for Civil Disobedience* (Oxford: Oxford University Press, 2015).

Burke, Edmund (ed.) J.C.D. Clark. *Reflections on the Revolution in France* (Stanford, CA: Stanford University Press, 2001).

Charters, Ann (ed.) *The Story and its Writer: An Introduction to Short Fiction* (Boston: Bedford St. Martin's, 2003).

Cohen, Eliot. *Supreme Command, Soldiers Statesmen and Leadership in Wartime* (New York: Anchor Books, 2003).

Danziger, Danny and Gillingham, John. *1215: The Year of Magna Carta* (New York, London, Toronto, Sydney: Touchstone, 2005).

Donne, John. *Devotions Upon Emergent Occasions and Death's Duel* (New York: Vintage Books, 1999).

Finlason, William F. *Commentaries Upon Martial Law: with special reference to its regulation and restraint: with an introduction containing comments upon the Charge of the Lord Chief Justice by the author of the 'Treatise upon martial law."* (London: Stevens and Sons, 1867). (Making of Modern Law: Reproduction from Harvard Law School Library).

Hackett, Lt. Gen Sir John Winthrop. *The Profession of Arms: The 1962 Lees Knowles Lectures Given at Trinity College Cambridge* (London: Times Publishing, 1962).

Hailsham, Viscount (ed.) *Halsbury's Laws of England* (London: Butterworth, 1938).

Hobbes, Thomas. (ed.) C.B. Macpherson, *Leviathan* (England: Penguin, 1985).

Hobbes, Thomas. (ed. and tr.) Richard Tuck and Michael Silverthorne, *On the Citizen* (Cambridge: Cambridge University Press, 2017).

Kant, Immanuel (tr.) E.B. Ashton, *On the Old Saw: That May be Right in Theory, but it Won't Work in Practice* (Philadelphia: University of Pennsylvania Press, 1974).

Keijzer, Nicholas. *Military Obedience* (Alpena an den Rijn, Netherlands: Sijthoff & Noordhoff, 1978).

Locke, John. (ed.) Ian Shapiro, *Two Treatises of Government and A Letter Concerning Toleration* (New Haven: Yale University Press, 2003).

McKeogh, Colm. *Innocent Civilians: The Morality of Killing in War* (Great Britain: Palgrave, 2002).

McMahan, Jeff. *Killing in War* (Oxford: Clarendon Press, 2009).

Mill, John S. "The Contest in America," in *Fraser's Magazine for Town and Country*, (1862) 65:386, pp. 258–268.

Nozick, Robert. *Anarchy, State and Utopia* (New York: Basic Books, 2013).

Osiel, Mark. *Obeying Orders: Atrocity, Military Discipline and the Law of War* (New Brunswick and London: Transaction, 2002).

Plato, "Republic," in John M. Cooper (ed.) *Plato: Complete Works* (Indianapolis and Cambridge: Hackett, 1997).

Pogge, Thomas. *Politics as Usual: What Lies Behind the Pro-Poor Rhetoric* (Cambridge: Polity, 2010).

Rawls, John. *A Theory of Justice* (Cambridge, MA: The Belknap Press of Harvard University Press, 1999).

Rawls, John. *Justice as Fairness: A Restatement* (Cambridge, MA: The Belknap Press of Harvard University Press, 2001).

Rousseau, Jean-Jacques (ed.) Susan Dunn, *The Social Contract and The First and Second Discourses* (New Haven and London: Yale University Press, 2002).

Ruskin, John. *The Crown of Wild Olive: Four Lectures on Industry and War* (London: George Allen and Unwin Ltd, 1915).

Sandel, Michael. *Justice: What's the Right Thing to Do?* (New York: Farrar, Straus and Giroux, 2010).

Simmons, A. John. *Moral Principles and Political Obligations* (Princeton, NJ: Princeton University Press, 1979).

Somerton, W.H. (ed.) *A Narrative of the Bristol Riots on the 29th, 30th and 31st of October, 1831, Consequent on the Arrival of the Recorder, Sir C. Wetherell to open the Commission of Assize with full particulars of the burning of Bridewell, the Gaol, the Toll House, Gloucester County Prison, the Bishop's Palace, the Mansion House, Custom House, Excise Office, and Nearly Fifty Houses in Queens-Square, King Street, Little King Street, Prince's Street etc., etc."* (Bristol: The Mercury Office, no date).

Thucydides, "History of the Peloponnesian War," in Robert B. Strassler (ed.), *The Landmark Thucydides* (New York: Free Press, 2008).

Walzer, Michael. *Obligations: Essays on Disobedience, War and Citizenship* (Cambridge, MA: Harvard University Press, 1970).

Walzer, Michael. *Thick and Thin: Moral Argument at Home and Abroad* (Indiana: University of Notre Dame Press, 2012).

Australian Government Documents

Anonymous. *Leadership in the Australian Defence Force*: (Australian Defence Doctrine Publication 00.6), (Commonwealth of Australia, 2007).

7 More Than a Postman – The General's Singular Burden

There is only one general. In supreme command the general acts explicitly and distinctively alone; individual responsibility is not dissolved or made obscure by the collective. The general is not anonymous. The entire spread-out chain of command is unified in the general. It is the general who offers the only connection between the military and politics. The general bears the obligations of office alone.

The general is not like the soldier who might refuse to fight, knowing others are willing. The general is not like a doctor who might act on a conscientious objection since another doctor offers the procedure. The general is not like a clerk who can act on a nasty prejudice, since more open-minded clerks are happy to deal with all people. The general is distinctively and importantly different. But the special responsibility of the general – the supreme military commander – has been unexamined.

In this chapter I speak to the special role responsibilities of the general. I accept the general will be asked to do morally problematic things. But I argue the general should not be forced. Law should offer the general a right to refuse unconscionable direction so resignation or non-conformity with law are not the only morally acceptable courses of action.

The General

Augustine says the soldier is merely a sword, the blameless tool of politics.[1] Similarly, Michael Walzer says soldiers are subject to coercive institutional forces, acculturated to law abidingness, acculturated to feel obedience is a patriotic duty. Thus, we might say that when soldiers fight an unjust war, there is no moral cloud over them so long as they abide by the *jus in bello* rules.[2]

The general is different. Serving in supreme command, the general presents as a single figure. The general is not merely one soldier among many soldiers, or even one officer among many officers. The general is distinctive. The general has a special office, a special expertise, and special responsibilities. Famously, Dennis F. Thompson spoke of the problem of many hands. He said:

> Because many different officials contribute in many different ways to decisions and policies of government, it is difficult even in principle to identify

DOI: 10.4324/9781003527886-7

> who is morally responsible for political outcomes. Even if we can decide that a policy is morally wrong, we may not be able to locate anyone who made it.[3]

The general is different. Positioned at the intersection of law, politics, and public interest, and central to the exercise of national power, the general bears a singular burden. Only the general might turn political direction in to military command and set the armed forces in motion to war. But scholarship has paid insufficient attention to the general, and to the relationship between the general and the state.

Referring to Rommel, Walzer describes generals as servants.[4] He puts generals and soldiers on the same footing, asking us to consider them alike as patriots, dependable citizens answering the call of the nation. Walzer says, since we recognise the moral burdens of citizenship, "we don't blame a soldier, even a general, who fights for his own government."[5] But in fact we do hold generals especially accountable. The trials at Nuremberg bear witness.

High Expectations

We expect the general to bear a profound public responsibility. We expect the general to resist political direction which infringes – following the Martens forms – "the laws of humanity and the dictates of public conscience."

Of course, history offers countless cases where invidious beliefs have enjoyed public credibility. Nations have practised racism, slavery, torture, genocide, and unjust war without judging these things unconscionable. Indeed, the trials at Nuremberg highlight the problem of asserting that there is a shared understanding of what counts as unconscionable. Many Nazis did not see the genocide or the unjust war they waged as reprehensible. Indeed, since it was a popular movement, the horrors of Nazism suggest we have strong reason to doubt any intuitive moral sense or any so-called "public conscience."[6]

But I do not associate "the laws of humanity" or "the public conscience" with the hateful populist rallying cries of awful, extreme, and dangerous movements. On my account, "conscience" and "public conscience" involve an ideal. An ideal is a paradigm of excellence around which we can orient our attention and seek to effect non-trivial changes in perspective and practice. The practical implication is in the connotation of "unconscionable." Unconscionable acts do not derive their character from specification in law, but from plain, inherent monstrosity. Thus, David Estlund is understood when he says that though we might not judge soldiers harshly when they obey the order to fight an unjust war, we cannot assume that soldiers are never acting wrongly when they obey orders to fight. In Nazi Germany, for example, it is reasonable to assume that some soldiers had their doubts about the justification for a war of aggression.[7]

Estlund sees the ordinary soldier bears an obligation beyond the conventions of obedience. *A fortiori*, what may be said of soldiers might be said of the general. Like the political representative described by Edmund Burke, the general bears an over-riding onus to exercise moral judgement.[8] For the general, conscientious decision must account for the unspecified common-sense ideals, for which millions died in the Second World War. Individual obligation is not dissolved by the imperatives of politics or law and the conventions which obtain.[9] As Robert Nozick says: "some bucks stop with each of us."[10] For the general, the buck is the unique, exceptional moral responsibility for the military command which will mobilise the armed forces to war. This singular moral responsibility is at odds with the legal responsibility set down in section 8 (2) of the Australian *Defence Act* which says: "the Chief of the Defence Force must comply with any directions of the Minister." The legislation offers a constitutional power to the convention that "when the military man receives a legal order from an authorised superior, he does not argue, he does not hesitate, he does not substitute his own view; he obeys instantly."[11] More than a shibboleth, the convention of unquestioning obedience is borne out in the case law. In *Commonwealth v. Quince* (1944)[12] Williams J described obedience as the "first, second and third duty of a soldier, at all times."[13] In *McBride* (2023) obedience was found to denominate military duty.[14]

But though obedience is indispensable,[15] the onus of military service is not the same for all people, without regard for positional duties, or circumstances. When formal expectations diverge in non-trivial ways from morality, the general has a moral obligation to follow the path of moral responsibility.[16] On my account, a liberal democratic society will enable this sort of conscientious moral action.

Military Discipline

In the military, freedoms are restricted in foreseeable common-sense ways. But too often, militaries overstate unreflective obedience, and turn soldiers into marionettes, heedlessly obedient to destructive authority.[17]

In the *Introduction to the Study of the Law of the Constitution*, A.V. Dicey recognises the practical problem which follows from the military fetish for discipline-and-obedience. Dicey says: a soldier is liable to be shot by a court-martial if he disobeys an order, or hanged by a judge and jury if he obeys it.[18] Dicey (though he speaks of soldiers and the *in bello* duty of obedience to superior orders) recognises the dreadful life-and-death tension between conscience and positional obligation, which Robert Bolt fictionalised in his play *A Man for all Seasons*. Famously, Bolt has Sir Thomas More say: "when statesmen forsake their own private conscience for the sake of their public duties … they lead their country by a short route to chaos."[19] More recognised that beyond abidance with law, larger duties involve an allusive and elevated sense of moral properness, honour, or chivalry.[20] Bolt would have Thomas More agree with the Chief of the German General Staff, Colonel General Ludwig Beck. Expressing his resistance to Hitler and trying to avert war, General Beck saw limits to political obligation where conscience, knowledge, and responsibility forbade carrying out an order.[21]

At Nuremberg, Sir Hartley Shawcross, the British chief prosecutor, said likewise: "there comes a point where a man must refuse to answer to his leader if he is also to answer to his conscience."[22] Similarly, the United States chief prosecutor, Justice Jackson, acknowledged "common sense" demanded prosecution of those who possess great power and employ it for "evils which leave no home in the world untouched."[23] Underlining evil as a moral concept, not a legal one, Jackson saw: "the foundation of the law must be morality and the fundamental question of the trial was that of individual moral responsibility."[24] Jackson dismissed the notion that only states could be held responsible before international law. "Men who exercise great power cannot be allowed to shift their responsibility on to the fictional being, the State."[25] Famously, the United States prosecutor Telford Taylor said "a man who commits crimes cannot plead as a defence that he committed them in uniform."[26]

Taylor foretold argument from the German generals who claimed to be "pure technicians." Dismissing this fantasy, Taylor argued that such a claim amounts to

> saying that military men are a race apart from and different from the ordinary run of the mill human beings – men above and beyond the moral and legal requirements that apply to others, incapable of exercising moral judgement on their own behalf.[27]

But generals are not a race apart. Generals cannot plead as a defence that they were in uniform, acting for the state. In the 1940 case of *Shaw Savill & Albion Co Ltd v. Commonwealth*,[28] Starke J said:

> a public officer cannot defend himself by alleging generally that he has acted from necessity in the public interest and for the defence of the realm, whether he has or has not the express or implied command of the Crown.[29]

Generals know what they *ought* to do, just as well as we do: and we know that evil follows the *reductio* of unquestioning obedience. Stanley Milgram makes the evil of obedience plain when he explains that between 1933 and 1945, millions were systematically slaughtered on command. Gas chambers were built, death camps were guarded, daily quotas of corpses were produced with industrial efficiency. These inhumane policies may have originated in the mind of a single person, but they could only have been carried out on a massive scale if a very large number of people obeyed orders.[30]

Today, the mind-numbing horror of the Final Solution is muffled by the passage of years, made a *mise-en-scene* to a high-handed conceit that we are insulated from evil, that things are so very *legal* now. People say, "things were different then." People assume the Nazi monstrousness would not be possible today. But arguments like this depend upon the vain hallucination that in the twenty-first century we have a sort of special ethical prowess. The disquieting reality is that modern soldiers are not congenitally unsimilar from the Nazis. Just like the Nazis were conditioned, modern soldiers are conditioned by the military institution to shape up and observe the golden rules. Obedience is embedded as a shaping feature of the institutional culture in which routine, compliance, and unctuous snivelling set the dominant tone. Typically, we do not find heroic figures resisting unconscionable misdeeds. Neither do we tend to find people exploit institutional power. The most usual military figure is the forceless jobsworth who strives to avoid initiative and confect the impression of competence.[31]

The modern re-enactment of immoral conformability is in the 2014 report of the United States Senate Select Committee on Intelligence, which notes systemic conventions of obedience to command enabled torture.[32] Gerry Simpson, professor of law at the University of Melbourne, draws things together. Simpson sees the foundation of morally culpable behaviour in larger, shaping collective or social contexts. Simpson sees that the obtruding, constraining, requiring force of law and the conventions which obtain can make obedience to orders and compliance with the law look like moral responsibility.[33] But moral responsibility is different from obedience, and different from compliance with the law. I accept moral responsibility is autonomous.[34] I agree when Robert Nozick says the best institutions allow people freedom to act in good conscience, to do the right thing in the circumstances.[35]

I dispute that law might rightly force the general's conscience and compel obedience. I contend there is no case where the weight of conscience disappears. I contend that if a positional duty is binding, it is because there are moral grounds to meet that positional duty.[36] Overshadowing the positional obligation of compliance, lies the onus of personal responsibility and the need for moral judgement.

But unquestioning obedience is precisely the end and the effect of legislation that seems to rubber stamp the regressive memes of military life. Among the lessons of Nuremberg, we do not have to look hard to see law should make it feasible for generals to resist political injustice.

A Moral Obligation to Resist Injustice

In the aftermath of the Second World War, the Nuremberg trials transformed international law and endowed a juridical touchstone.[37] Despite different legal traditions and dissimilar political approaches, four nations were united in the need to prosecute "crimes of obedience," those atrocities which occur when orders exceed the bounds of morality or law, and morally repressed generals can discern no option but to do as they are told.[38]

The Nuremberg Tribunal recognised "moral value in fixing responsibility in a field of anonymous irresponsibility"[39] and dissolved any distinction between perpetration and accomplice liability.[40] The German officers were found guilty as perpetrators – not as mere accomplices. They were unable to claim, as Adolf Eichmann tried to claim, that they were paying the price for the glass someone else broke.[41] The convicted officers were found *personally* responsible for the signature or issuance of orders that violated the laws and customs of war.[42] These officers observed explicit laws but mishandled moral obligations. Recognising civilisation as "the real complaining party,"[43] Justice Jackson acknowledged that barbarism, dreadful beyond the capacity of legal definition, offended the common moral sense of all people.[44] To be clear: generals were hanged at Nuremberg *not for crimes* set out on any statute book, but for iniquity – for *moral wrong*. Generals hanged at Nuremberg had complied with constitutional laws. Generals were hanged since they failed to resist political misdirection, and their acts in giving expression to political villainy were unconscionable. In his opening address, United States Chief Prosecutor, Robert Jackson, a Justice of the United States Supreme Court, said:

> The wrongs which we seek to condemn and punish, have been so calculated, so malignant and so devastating, that civilisation cannot tolerate their being ignored, because it cannot survive their being repeated.[45]

At the heart of the Nuremberg proceedings was genocide, the "crime with no name."[46] Used in the indictment of the International Military Tribunal, "genocide" was not a legal expression. The Polish lawyer Raphael Lemkin coined the word in 1944.[47] The term obtains from the Greek "*genos*," meaning "race," or "tribe," and "*cide*," which means, "kill," in Latin.[48] Genocide did not serve as an organising legal concept. Genocide served to capture the moral profanation of the Holocaust; an atrocity which escaped definition in law.[49] At Nuremberg, the enormity of evil-doing not demarcated by law was contained in the prosecution of crimes against humanity.[50] As Hersch Lauterpacht explains, crimes against humanity are crimes regardless of whether they were committed in accordance with and in obedience to national law. Crimes against humanity violate human rights to such a degree that the law of the State which ordered the wrongdoing is irrelevant.[51]

By the indictment of crimes against humanity, the Tribunal acknowledged the common moral sense of mankind, and repudiated the established wisdom that compliance with law was sufficient. There was no other ground on which the Tribunal was so vulnerable to the charge of *ex post facto* lawmaking.[52] Göering sought to avert Nuremberg's legal invention and insisted: "[this] was our right! We were a sovereign state and that was strictly our business."[53] Answering, Justice Robert Jackson, said: "ordinarily we [would] not consider that the acts of a government toward its own citizens warrant our interference." Customarily there would be no basis for investigating "atrocities which were committed inside Germany, under German law, or even in violation of German law, by authorities of the German state."[54] But confronted with deviltry of an inhuman kind, and on a scale unimagined by the law, the Tribunal saw an unavoidable moral obligation. Writing in *The American Journal of International Law*, F.B. Schick noted that the prosecution of crimes against humanity is a substantial legal innovation since it disregards the rule of international law that no state shall intervene in the territorial sphere of another national legal order.[55] Recognising moral principles beyond the stipulation of law, the Tribunal accepted the overwhelming demands of unspecified high ideals. The Tribunal looked to moral ideas which are not organised and codified by law. For the Tribunal, the generals' bad move was in morally disinterested compliance with law and the failure to resist injustice. The expectation was the expectation of moral agency. R.M. Hare is direct: legal obligation does not entail moral obligation.[56] We feel no sympathy for the Nazi officer, because we understand that the legal duty to obey the command to kill innocent people is over-ridden by the moral obligation to disobey such a heinous order.[57]

Obedience to law and to command is the rock upon which states are built.[58] But, since Nuremberg, common sense moral doctrines have come to inform public international law and, at the same time, come to offer substantive sources of individual obligation.[59] We see the resonance of Nuremberg and the relevance of moral common sense in the International Court of Justice *Nuclear Weapons Advisory Opinion*.[60] Handed down in 1996, and the first *non-liquet*[61] pronounced by the Court,[62] the *Nuclear Weapons* case concerned the *legality* of the mass killing of innocents.[63] Confronted by the awfulness of total annihilation the triviality of lawyerly conjecture is breathtaking. The inevitably apocalyptic consequences of nuclear war make mannerly legal debate beside the point.[64] Thus, in the *Nuclear Weapons* case, Shahabuddeen J saw international delinquency beyond the axenic terms of law, in acts contrary to the ordinary sentiments of humanity which are even more exacting in peace than in war.[65]

Generals not Postmen

Independently responsible moral decision, important for soldiers, is especially significant for the general. Their fellow citizens trust the general in distinctive ways. Some of these citizens serve as soldiers; they are junior to the general and trust their lives will not be wasted in political folly. Some of these citizens are civilians; they trust the general to safeguard the blood and treasure of the nation and to avoid unconscionable wars. Generals are trusted in ways soldiers are not. We remember *King Henry V*, where the soldier Michael Williams says [IV: i]:

> If the cause be not good the [general] himself hath a heavy reckoning to make, when all those legs and arms and heads, chopped off in a battle, shall join together at the latter day and cry all: 'We died at such a place; some swearing, some crying for a surgeon, some upon their wives left poor behind them, some upon the debts they owe, some upon their children rawly left.... Now if these men do not die well, it will be a black matter for the [general] that led them to it.[66]

Shakespeare had Williams speak of the King, not the general. But the denotation of special responsibility seems the same. It is this special moral onus which makes service as the general so different from service as an ordinary soldier. Isolated from politics and immersed in the functioning of the military instrument, the soldier can do little about political injustice and executive over-reach.[67] We might believe that a soldier who had no hand in making war is inculpable for *ad bellum* villainy. But the general bears a different burden. The general links the executive and the military. Thus, since Nuremberg, the expectancy is that the general will resist the unsafe exercise of executive power; that they will not turn the military over to an unreasonable executive; that they will act morally. But the *Defence Act* makes the general a mere obedient toiler whose sole purpose is to turn the military over to the political will.

By my lights, since the general bears an obligation to resist unconscionable political direction, legislation should enable this sort of moral withstanding. In his book, *Dereliction of Duty*, H.R. McMaster[68] shows how generals must, in *exceptional* circumstances, resist the unconscionable exercise of executive power. McMaster considers the Joint Chiefs of Staff during Lyndon Johnson's presidency and describes "five silent men."[69] The Joint Chiefs, trapped in routines of bureaucratic deference by an alleged military code, were acquiescent and persuadable. These men were silent when they should have spoken, malleable when they ought to have been conscientious and uncompromising. Analysing the political calamity of Vietnam, the failings McMaster describes are uniquely human. Among many reinforcing shortcomings, the biggest was the failure by the Joint Chiefs to resist the morally unjustified exercise of executive power. Conforming reflexively to familiar and pervasive punctilios, the generals perpetuated the rococo habits of bureaucratic politesse and legalistic observance, which embellish military failure. The generals abdicated responsibility to exert constructive influence.[70]

The general bears special and demanding responsibilities. Above all, the general is expected to act morally, which means "autonomously" not merely in accord with the law or the prevailing conventions.[71] The general is expected to do more than issue military commands in the wake of political direction merely because law mandates obedience. Especially since Nuremberg, the general is counted on; expected to be more than a postman passing on orders without responsibility.[72] The general is expected to act morally and to set an example. The general is expected to lead. Robert McNamara, Secretary of Defense to Presidents Kennedy and Johnson during the Vietnam War, described the onerous burden of leadership. McNamara says: "leaders are supposed to lead, to resist pressures or forces … to understand more fully than others, the range of options and [the] implications of choosing such options."[73] On McNamara's view, generals are not expected to be the speechless instruments of political injustice or guile. But the general is not expected to be perfect, untainted, simon-pure.

Dirty Hands

When I argue for law reform so generals might exercise responsible agency, I do not expect generals to be beyond reproach. As Bernard Williams explains, sometimes answers in politics are very disagreeable and sometimes we do not want people to be simon-pure.[74] Citing from Sartre's play *Les Mains Sales*, Michael Walzer offers a richly textured analysis. Sartre has the Communist, Hoerderer, pose a rhetorical question: "'I have dirty hands right up to the elbows. I've plunged them in filth and blood. Do you think you can govern innocently?'"[75] In response Walzer offers: "My own answer is no; I don't think I could govern innocently."[76] Neither can generals be entirely innocent. General Sherman offers an example. Writing to James Calhoun (the Mayor of Atlanta) and to Councilmen Rawson and Wares (Representing the City Council of Atlanta) Sherman is explicit: Atlanta will be evacuated and destroyed. Acknowledging the distress his strategy would cause innocent civilians, Sherman nonetheless forced the evacuation of Atlanta before he burned the city. There was, reasoned Sherman, no other way. Atlanta could not be left untouched and able to sustain an armed resistance.[77]

Confronted by utilitarian failure, absolute principles must be over-ridden.[78] On occasion, it is a form of moral self-indulgence to refuse acts which would be conventionally impossible.[79] When the stakes are high and the cost of not acting is unendurable, it is often right to contravene conventional moral boundaries.[80] But it is not right to dirty one's hands without moral remorse or regret.[81] There should be a feeling of guilt, a felt moral residue, a sense approaching shame that things *needed* to be done.[82] Moralities should not be over-ridden without a care, reflexively, or merely in obedience to law or convention. I am cautious when Machiavelli argues that reprehensible actions may be justified by their effects, and that a good always justifies the action.[83] I am expressly wary when Machiavelli argues that national security justifies any level of injustice.[84] My approach is subtler. I follow the course shaped by Walzer and claim that moral standards are *pro-tanto*. Moral standards might be *over-ridden* but not erased when the consequences of not acting are immeasurably awful.[85] To be unequivocal, the sacrifice of principles might be justified only when there is no other course of action.

Even though people might contravene orthodox standards and deeply held moral commitments, people still act autonomously, and with a right intention. When they over-ride moral commitments, people make a *deliberate* choice. Morally responsible people *accept* the utilitarian calculation.[86] They *choose* to get their hands dirty.[87] To recall Kimberley Brownlee, a case of dirty hands is the case of a person who is willing to bear the costs of a serious moral commitment.[88] This cost is in remorse since, as Bernard Williams explains, the dirty feature persists as a remainder within the act.[89] Bernard Williams offers the example of Agamemnon, who sacrificed his daughter to appease the gods and thus save the expedition against Troy. Agamemnon acted to fulfil his responsibilities. Awake at night – not because of a doubt but because of a certainty – Agamemnon's agony is that of a general who acted *autonomously*, for the best as he saw it, knowing no better thing could have been done.[90]

The point is, I do not imagine moral action to be always legal, and unlike Kant, I do not suppose moral choice is the same for everyone. I go along with Philippa Foot and take moral action to follow from a rational sense of in-the-moment good will and right intention.[91]

In the *Groundwork*, Kant recognises moral action to be autonomous[92] and unencumbered by "alien causes."[93] But the Kantian picture insists on a rational *universal* basis for moral choice.[94] I dispute with Kant on this point. Insisting moral action must be universalisable, Kant makes the idea of moral responsibility absurd and imaginary. Kant offers an idea of moral choice lacking the self-interest, the understanding and the finesse of real people who deal with real situations. Kant's moral actors are improbably impartial, and without the independent personality which is elemental to moral choice.[95] But sometimes, it will not be rational to act according to an overall principle, to do the conventional thing – to obey the law, to give help when it is needed, to keep a promise or to speak the truth.[96] It is implausible that morality might be considered as universalisable without reference to circumstances and the people involved. Acts are right *for us* when they obtain from serious all things considered deliberation.[97] Recognising people as individuals with distinct characters, subject to uncertain and complex circumstances, we must accept autonomous moral action will sometimes be inconsistent with law and not necessarily universalisable.[98]

One Does not Pray to the Enemy's Gods

My critic will accept awful things must be done. But for my critic, it is the minister who does these things. The minister does not want to force the general, but circumstances make coercion imperative. For the minister, forcing the general (in which case it is the minister's hands which are dirty) is an entailment of responsible government. The general's job is to obey the law. But my critic invokes Huntington's normal theory, which accepts soldiers might be treated as means.

I claim that a reasonable, liberal democratic society will recognise generals as moral beings who bear burdensome moral duties. Such a society will allow generals moral space in law so that they might refuse unconscionable executive direction. In the words of Aharon Barak, formerly President of the Supreme Court of Israel, sometimes a democracy must fight with one hand tied behind its back. The democracy must safeguard the freedom of the individual conscience and accept the voice of dissent. At the end of the day, these basic freedoms fit the democracy to overcome its enemies.[99]

As Paul Kahn explains, the hardboiled, unidealistic business of winning wars will place ideals under stress. But fundamental ideals ought not be forsaken. One does not pray to the enemy's gods for success in war. One lives and dies with one's own faith, and our faith is in democratic ideals not the oppressive, suppressive dogmas of despotism.[100]

Conclusion

War is a deliberate, devastating, shocking circumstance; for which politics is the *fons et origio* but for which the general bears a special responsibility. In this chapter, I have argued that the general bears a responsibility to act morally, which means autonomously.[101] Yet law impedes generals who seek to be attentive to moral obligation. Section 8 (2) of the Australian *Defence Act* stipulates: "the Chief of the Defence Force *must* comply with *any* directions of the Minister." Law presumes the priority of law and puts generals "on a level with wood and earth and stones."[102] Drafted in 1903, the *Defence Act* expects no more of the general than compliance. The legislation treats generals as postmen; expecting them to pass executive direction on without a moral second thought. By my lights, this approach is naïve and unsound.

Commanding a war is not morally trivial; not the sort of thing for which moral responsibility might be extirpated by law, and not the sort of thing which might rightly be coerced by law. A reasonably good society will view war seriously and honour the general's special moral responsibility. Such a society will offer the general a right to refuse unconscionable direction so that resignation or non-conformity with law are not the only morally acceptable courses of action.

Notes

1 Augustine (tr.), Henry Bettenson, *Concerning the City of God Against the Pagans* (England: Penguin, 1984), Book 1, Ch. 21, p. 32.
2 Michael Walzer, *Just and Unjust Wars: A Moral Argument* (New York: Basic Books, 2000), pp. 38–40.
David Estlund, "On Following Orders in an Unjust War," in *The Journal of Political Philosophy*, (2007) 15:2, pp. 213–234, 226.
3 Dennis F. Thompson, *Political Ethics and Public Office* (Cambridge, MA: Harvard University Press, 1987), p. 40.
4 Michael Walzer, *Just and Unjust Wars: A Moral Argument* (New York: Basic Books, 2000), p. 39.
5 Michael Walzer, *Just and Unjust Wars: A Moral Argument* (New York: Basic Books, 2000), p. 39.
6 Mark Osiel, *Obeying Orders: Atrocity, Military Discipline and the Law of War* (New Brunswick and London: Transaction, 2002), p. 3.
Celeste Bohlen, "Italy Convicts Ex-SS Officers in '44 Killings," in *The New York Times*, Wednesday, July 23, 1997, p. A4.
7 David Estlund, "On Following Orders in an Unjust War," in *The Journal of Political Philosophy*, (2007) 15:2, pp. 213–234, 226.
8 Edmund Burke: Speaking at the Conclusion of the Poll, at Bristol (3 November 1774) in *The Works of the Right Honourable Edmund Burke*, Vol. 1 (six Volumes) (London: Bell & Daldy, 1872), p. 447.
9 Jeff McMahan, "Collectivist Defenses of the Moral Equality of Combatants," in *Journal of Military Ethics*, (2007) 6:1, pp. 50–59, 51, 53.
10 Robert Nozick, *Anarchy, State and Utopia* (New York: Basic Books, 2013), p. 100.
11 Samuel P. Huntington, *The Soldier and the State: The Theory and Politics of Civil-Military Relations* (Cambridge, MA: Belknap Press of the Harvard University Press, 1981), p. 73.
General Sir John W. Hackett, "The Military in the Service of the State," in Malham M. Wakin (ed.), *War, Morality, and the Military Profession* (Boulder, CO: Westview Press, 1986), pp. 115–117.
12 (1944) 68 CLR 227.
13 (1944) 68 CLR 227, 254 per Williams J.
14 *R v. McBride* (2023) ACTSC 42.
R v. McBride (No. 2) (2023) ACTSC 330.
R v. McBride (2023) ACTSC 328.
15 Cameron Moore, *Crown and Sword: Executive Power and the Use of Force by the Australian Defence Force* (Australia: Australian National University Press, 2017), pp. 19, 115, 116.
16 Kimberley Brownlee, *Conscience and Conviction: The Case for Civil Disobedience* (Oxford: Oxford University Press, 2015), pp. 87, 95, 97.
17 Mary Wollstonecraft, *A Vindication of the Rights of Woman with Strictures on Political and Moral Subjects* (London: J. Johnson, 1792), pp. 26–27, 42–44, 264.
Jessica Wolfendale, *Torture and the Military Profession* (Hampshire: Palgrave MacMillan, 2007), p. 128.
Philip Zimbardo, *The Lucifer Effect: Understanding How Good People Turn Evil* (New York: Random House, 2007). In the influential 1971 Stanford Prison Experiment, Zimbardo explained how organisational systems can dominate and overcome individual agency to amplify the human proneness towards obedience.
18 A.V. Dicey (ed.), E.C.S. Wade, *Introduction to the Study of the Law of the Constitution* (London: MacMillan, 1961), p. 303.
19 Robert Bolt, *A Man for All Seasons* (New York: Vintage Books, 1990), Act One, p. 22.

20 Peter Ackroyd, *The Life of Thomas More* (New York: Nan A. Talese/Doubleday, 1998), p. 65.
21 William Shirer, *The Rise and Fall of the Third Reich* (New York: Simon & Schuster, 2011), p. 368.
22 Ann Tusa and John Tusa, *The Nuremberg Trial* (United States: Skyhorse, 2010), p. 178.
23 Ann Tusa and John Tusa, *The Nuremberg Trial* (United States: Skyhorse, 2010), p. 155.
24 Ann Tusa and John Tusa, *The Nuremberg Trial* (United States: Skyhorse, 2010), p. 155.
25 Ann Tusa and John Tusa, *The Nuremberg Trial* (United States: Skyhorse, 2010), p. 155.
Hersch Lauterpacht, *International Law and Human Rights* (United States: Archon Books, 1968), p. 6.
26 Telford Taylor, *The Anatomy of the Nuremberg Trials: A Personal Memoir* (New York: Skyhorse, 2013), p. 249.
Ann Tusa and John Tusa, *The Nuremberg Trial* (United States: Skyhorse, 2010), p. 436.
27 Telford Taylor, *he Anatomy of the Nuremberg Trials: A Personal Memoir* (New York: Skyhorse, 2013), pp. 252–253.
Ann Tusa and John Tusa, *The Nuremberg Trial* (United States: Skyhorse, 2010), p. 438.
28 (1940) 66 CLR 344. On 3 September 1940, M.V. *Coptic* was sailing from Brisbane to Newcastle NSW. The warship HMAS *Adelaide* was on the reciprocal course. There was a collision. Shaw Savill and Albion sued the Commonwealth for damages. The Court found, though the warship was on active operations (thus, darkened ship and at an high rate of speed), this did not relieve the officers from keeping a proper lookout, or from following the conventions of navigation at sea which were not made impossible by operations.
29 (1989) 66 CLR 344 per Starke J 355 citing; *Mackenzie-Kennedy v. Air Council* (1927) 2 K.B 517 at 532 and *Raleigh v Goschen* (1898) 1 Ch 73 at 77.
30 Stanley Milgram, *Obedience to Authority* (New York, HarperPerennial, 2009), p. 1.
31 Stanley Milgram, *Obedience to Authority* (New York, HarperPerennial, 2009). p. 187.
32 Senate Select Committee on Intelligence, *Committee Study of the Central Intelligence Agency's Detention and Interrogation Program*, chaired by Dianne Feinstein, United States Senate (2014), p. 56.
33 Gerry Simpson, *Law War and Crime*,(Cambridge: Polity, 2007), p. 2.
34 Bernard Williams, *Ethics and the Limits of Philosophy* (Cambridge, MA: Harvard University Press, 1985), p. 7.
35 Robert Nozick, *Anarchy, State and Utopia* (New York: Basic Books, 2013), pp. 327, 328.
36 A. John Simmons, *Moral Principles and Political Obligations* (Princeton, NJ: Princeton University Press, 1979), pp. 20, 21.
37 Gerry Simpson, *Law War and Crime* (Cambridge: Polity, 2007), pp. 57, 67, 72, 75, 133, 142.
Tara Helfman, "Francis Biddle and the Nuremberg Legacy: Waking the Human Conscience," in *The Journal Jurisprudence*, (2012) 15, pp. 353–372, 354.
Telford Taylor, *The Anatomy of the Nuremberg Trials: A Personal Memoir* (New York: Skyhorse, 2013), p. 226.
Ann Tusa and John Tusa, *The Nuremberg Trial* (United States: Skyhorse, 2010), p. 146.
38 H.C. Kelman and V.L. Hamilton, *Crimes of Obedience* (New Haven and London: Yale University Press, 1989), p. 46.

Brian Orend, *The Morality of War* (Canada: Broadview Press, 2006), p. 109.

39 Francis Biddle, "The R. A. F. Penrose Jr. Memorial Lecture," in Guenael Mettraux (ed.), *Perspectives on the Nuremberg Trial* (Oxford University Press: Oxford, 2008), p. 207.

40 James G. Stewart, "The End of 'Modes of Liability' for International Crimes," in *Leiden Journal of International Law*, (2012), 25:1, pp. 165–219, 170, f/n 17.
Philippe Sands, *East West Street* (Great Britain: Weidenfeld & Nicholson, 2016), p. 366.

41 James G. Stewart, "The End of 'Modes of Liability' for International Crimes," in *Leiden Journal of International Law*, (2012) 25:1, pp. 165–219, 171.

42 George Finch, "The Nuremberg Trial and International Law," in *American Journal of International Law*, (1947) 41:20, pp. 20–37, 21.
Hersch Lauterpacht, *International Law and Human Rights* (United States: Archon Books, 1968), p. 43.

43 Telford Taylor, *The Anatomy of the Nuremberg Trials: A Personal Memoir* (New York: Skyhorse, 2013), p. 171.
G.M. Gilbert, *Nuremberg Diary* (United States: Da Capo, 1995), p. 39.

44 George Finch, "The Nuremberg trial and International Law," in *American Journal of International Law*, (1947) 41:20, pp. 20–37, 20.
Ann Tusa and John Tusa, *The Nuremberg Trial* (United States: Skyhorse, 2010), p. 155.

45 Telford Taylor, *The Anatomy of the Nuremberg Trials: A Personal Memoir* (New York: Skyhorse, 2013), p. 167; Ann Tusa and John Tusa, *The Nuremberg Trial* (United States: Skyhorse, 2010), pp. 154–155.

46 William A. Schabas, *Genocide in International Law: The Crime of Crimes* (Cambridge: Cambridge University Press, 2000), p. 14.

47 William A. Schabas, *Genocide in International Law: The Crime of Crimes* (Cambridge: Cambridge University Press, 2000), pp. 14, 24.

48 Raphael Lemkin, *Axis Rule in Occupied Europe: Laws of Occupation, Analysis of Government, Proposals for Redress* (Washington, DC: Carnegie Endowment for World Peace, 1944), pp. xi, 79.
Raphael Lemkin, "Genocide as a Crime Under International Law," in *The American Journal of International Law*, (1947) 41:1, pp. 145–151, 147.
William A. Schabas, *Genocide in International Law: The Crime of Crimes* (Cambridge: Cambridge University Press, 2000), p. 25.

49 Donald Bloxham, "From the International Military Tribunal to the Subsequent Nuremberg Proceedings: The American Confrontation with Nazi Criminality Revisited," in *History: The Journal of the Historical Association*, (2013) 98:332, pp. 567–591, 584.

50 "Charter of the International Military Tribunal" in *American Bar Association Journal*, (1945), 31:9, pp. 454–457, 454, article 6(c).
George Finch, "The Nuremberg trial and International Law," in *American Journal of International Law*, (1947) 41:20, pp. 20–37, 22.
Philippe Sands, *East West Street* (Weidenfeld & Nicholson: Great Britain, 2016), *passim*.

51 Hersch Lauterpacht, *International Law and Human Rights* (United States: Archon Books, 1968), p. 36.

52 Ann Tusa and John Tusa, *The Nuremberg Trial* (United States: Skyhorse, 2010), p. 415.
Gerry Simpson, *Law War and Crime* (Cambridge: Polity, 2007), p. 19. Lord Hankey believed the trials in Nuremberg and Tokyo offended against the principle of retroactivity. The same objection lay against attempts to try the Kaiser in 1918. Also p. 115: "The accused at Nuremberg were tried and convicted on the basis of largely *ex post facto* laws either improvised for the trial itself (crimes against humanity) or imported from the United States (conspiracy)."

53 G.M. Gilbert, *Nuremberg Diary* (United States: Da Capo, 1995), p. 37. Also, p. 193. Gerry Simpson, *Law War and Crime* (Cambridge: Polity, 2007), pp. 94, 95, 97.
54 Luke Glanville, *Sovereignty and the Responsibility to Protect: A New History* (Chicago, London: University of Chicago Press, 2014), p. 147.
55 F.B. Schick, "The Nuremberg Trial and the International Law of the Future," in *American Journal of International Law*, (1947) 41:4, October, pp. 770–794, 785.
56 R.M. Hare, "Political Obligations," in *Essays on Political Morality* (Oxford: Clarendon Press, 1998), p. 9.
57 A. John Simmons, *Moral Principles and Political Obligations* (Princeton, NJ: Princeton University Press, 1979), p. 10.
58 Mark Osiel, *Obeying Orders: Atrocity, Military Discipline and the Law of War* (New Brunswick and London: Transaction, 2002), p. 98. Citing William James.
59 Gerry Simpson, *Law War and Crime* (Cambridge: Polity, 2007), pp. 34, 35, 37.
60 *Legality of the Threat or Use by a State of Nuclear Weapons in Armed Conflict*, International Court of Justice Advisory Opinion, International Court of Justice Reports 1996, General List No. 95, p. 226.
61 The term *non liquet* means "it is not clear" or "not proven."
62 Terry Gill, "The Nuclear Weapons Advisory Opinion of the International Court of Justice and the Fundamental Distinction Between the *Jus ad Bellum* and the *Jus in Bello*," in *Leiden Journal of International Law*, (1999) 12, pp. 613–624, 613.
Martti Koskenniemi, "Faith, Identity and the Killing of the Innocent: International Lawyers and Nuclear Weapons," in *Leiden Journal of International Law*, (1997) 10, pp. 137–162, 139, 140.
63 Martti Koskenniemi, "Faith, Identity and the Killing of the Innocent: International Lawyers and Nuclear Weapons," in *Leiden Journal of International Law*, (1997) 10, pp. 137–162, 137.
64 Martti Koskenniemi, "Faith, Identity and the Killing of the Innocent: International Lawyers and Nuclear Weapons," in *Leiden Journal of International Law*, (1997) 10, pp. 137–162, 146. See also f/n 17.
65 International Court of Justice Advisory Opinion, International Court of Justice Reports 1996, General List No. 95, p. 226, per Shahabuddeen J at p. 407. His Honour cited the opinion of Alvarez J in the *Corfu Channel* Case (I.C.J. Reports 1949, p. 45, separate opinion). Alvarez J stated the "characteristics of an international delinquency are that it is an act contrary to the sentiments of humanity."
Hersch Lauterpacht, *International Law and Human Rights* (United States: Archon Books, 1968), p. 38.
66 William Shakespeare, "King Henry V," in George Clark and William A. Wright (eds.), *The Works of William Shakespeare* (London: MacMillian and Co., 1866), Act IV, Scene 1, p. 456.
67 Dan Zupan, "A Presumption of the Moral Equality of Combatants," in David Rodin and Henry Shue (eds.), *Just and Unjust Warriors: The Moral and Legal Status of Soldiers* (Oxford: Oxford University Press, 2013), p. 218.
68 McMaster served as a Lieutenant General, an "ordinary general," a general officer, not as the Chief of the Defence Force which, in the United States would be described as the Chairman of the Joint Chiefs.
69 H.R. McMaster, *Dereliction of Duty: Lyndon Johnson, Robert McNamara, the Joint Chiefs of Staff and the Lies that Led to Vietnam* (New York: HarperPerennial, 1998), p. 330.
Thomas Ricks, *The Generals: American Military Command from World War II to Today* (New York: Penguin, 2012), pp. 254–255.
70 Harry G. Summers, Jr., *Historical Atlas of the Vietnam War* (Boston and New York: Houghton Mifflin, 19955), p. 86.
71 Bernard Williams, *Ethics and the Limits of Philosophy* (Cambridge, MA: Harvard University Press, 1985), p. 7.

72 Telford Taylor, *The Anatomy of the Nuremberg Trials: A Personal Memoir* (New York: Skyhorse, 2013), p. 493.
William Shirer, *The Rise and Fall of the Third Reich* (New York: Simon & Schuster, 2011), p. 867.
73 Robert S. McNamara, James G. Blight and Robert K. Brigham, *Argument Without End: In Search of Answers to the Vietnam Tragedy* (New York: Public Affairs, 1999), p. 7.
Robert S. McNamara, *In Retrospect: The Tragedy and Lessons of Vietnam* (New York: Vintage, 1995), p. 203.
74 Bernard Williams, "Politics and Moral Character," in *Moral Luck* (Cambridge: Cambridge University Press, 1999), p. 54.
Hannah Arendt, *The Human Condition* (Chicago & London: University of Chicago Press, 1998), p. 77.
75 Michael Walzer, "Political Action: The Problem of Dirty Hands," *Philosophy and Public Affairs* (1973) 2:2, pp. 160–180, 161.
76 Michael Walzer, "Political Action: The Problem of Dirty Hands," *Philosophy and Public Affairs* (1973) 2:2, pp. 160–180, 161.
77 William T. Sherman (ed.), Jean V. Berlin and Brooks D. Simpson, *Sherman's Civil War: Selected Correspondence of William T. Sherman, 1860–1865* (Chapel Hill, NC: University of North Carolina Press, 1999), pp. 707–709.
78 Michael Walzer, "Political Action: The Problem of Dirty Hands," *Philosophy and Public Affairs* (1973) 2:2, pp. 160–180, 161–162, 174.
Michael Walzer, "Emergency Ethics," in *Arguing About War* (New Haven: Yale University Press, 2004), p. 34.
79 Bernard Williams, "Utilitarianism and Moral Self-indulgence," in *Moral Luck* (Cambridge: Cambridge University Press, 1999), pp. 40, 44, 49.
Bernard Williams, "Politics and Moral Character," in *Moral Luck* (Cambridge: Cambridge University Press, 1999), p. 60.
80 Michael Walzer, "Political Action: The Problem of Dirty Hands," *Philosophy and Public Affairs* (1973) 2:2, pp. 160–180, 174.
81 Michael Walzer, "Political Action: The Problem of Dirty Hands," *Philosophy and Public Affairs* (1973), 2:2, pp. 160–180, 174.
82 Bernard Williams, "Ethical Consistency," in *Problems of the Self: Philosophical Papers 1956–1972* (Cambridge: Cambridge University Press, 1999), p. 172.
83 Nicolo Machiavelli (ed.), Bernard Crick, "Autocracy Essential to Reform," in *The Discourses* (England: Penguin, 1970), Bk. 1, Ch. 9, p. 132.
84 Nicolo Machiavelli (ed.), Bernard Crick, "That one's Country should be defended whether it entail ignominy or glory, and that it is good to defend it in any way whatsoever," in *The Discourses* (England: Penguin, 1970), Bk. 3, Ch. 41, p. 515.
85 Michael Walzer, *Just and Unjust Wars: A Moral Argument* (New York: Basic Books, 2000), p. 253.
86 Michael Walzer, "Political Action: The Problem of Dirty Hands," *Philosophy and Public Affairs* (1973) 2:2, pp. 160–180, 180.
87 Michael Walzer, "Political Action: The Problem of Dirty Hands," *Philosophy and Public Affairs* (1973) 2:2, pp. 160–180, 164, 175, 176.
88 Kimberley Brownlee, *Conscience and Conviction: The Case for Civil Disobedience* (Oxford: Oxford University Press, 2015), p. 1.
89 Bernard Williams, "Ethical Consistency," in *Problems of the Self: Philosophical Papers 1956–1972* (Cambridge: Cambridge University Press, 1999), p. 179.
Bernard Williams, "Politics and Moral Character," in *Moral Luck* (Cambridge: Cambridge University Press, 1999), p. 61.
90 Bernard Williams, "Ethical Consistency," in *Problems of the Self: Philosophical Papers 1956–1972* (Cambridge: Cambridge University Press, 1999), p. 173.
91 Philippa Foot, *Natural Goodness* (Oxford: Clarendon Press, 2010), p. 11.

92 Immanuel Kant (ed. and tr.), Mary Gregor and Jens Timmerman, *Groundwork of the Metaphysics of Morals* (Cambridge: Cambridge University Press, 2012), §4.431, p 43, §4.440, p 51.
93 Immanuel Kant (ed. and tr.), Mary Gregor and Jens Timmerman, *Groundwork of the Metaphysics of Morals* (Cambridge: Cambridge University Press, 2012), §4.446, p 56.
94 Immanuel Kant (ed. and tr.), Mary Gregor and Jens Timmerman, *Groundwork of the Metaphysics of Morals* (Cambridge: Cambridge University Press, 2012), §4.400 pp. 15–16, §4.401 pp. 16–17, §4.411 pp. 25–26, §4.413 p. 27, §4.434 p. 46, §4.448 p. 58.
95 Bernard Williams, "Persons, Character and Morality," in *Moral Luck* (Cambridge: Cambridge University Press, 1999), p. 5.
96 Philippa Foot, *Natural Goodness* (Oxford: Clarendon Press, 2010), p. 11.
97 Peter Winch, "The Universalizability of Moral Judgements," in *The Monist*, (1965) 49:2, pp. 196–214.
98 Bernard Williams, "Persons, Character and Morality," in *Moral Luck* (Cambridge: Cambridge University Press, 1999), p. 14.
99 Aharon Barak, "A Judge on Judging: The Role of a Supreme Court in a Democracy," in *Harvard Law Review*, (2002) 116:1, pp. 19–162, 148.
100 Paul Kahn, *Sacred Violence: Torture, Terror and Sovereignty* (Ann Arbor: University of Michigan Press, 2011), p. 18.
101 Bernard Williams, *Ethics and the Limits of Philosophy* (Cambridge, MA: Harvard University Press, 1985), p. 7.
Joseph Raz, *The Morality of Freedom* (Oxford: Clarendon Press, 2009), pp. 407–409.
Aristotle, "Nichomachean Ethics," Bk. III, 1110a 12–14.
102 Henry D. Thoreau, *Civil Disobedience* (San Bernardino, CA: Black and White, 2014), p. 5.

References

Australian Cases

The Commonwealth v. Quince (1944) 68 CLR 227.
R v. McBride (2023) ACTSC 42.
R v. McBride (No. 2) (2023) ACTSC 330.
R v. McBride (2023) ACTSC 328.
Shaw Savill & Albion Co Ltd v. Commonwealth (1940) 66 CLR 344.

United Kingdom Cases

Mackenzie-Kennedy v. Air Council (1927) 2 K.B 517.
Raleigh v. Goschen (1898) 1 Ch 73.

International Cases and Opinions

Legality of the Threat or Use by a State of Nuclear Weapons in Armed Conflict, International Court of Justice Advisory Opinion, International Court of Justice Reports 1996, General List No. 95.

Journal Articles

Barak, Aharon. "A Judge on Judging: The Role of a Supreme Court in a Democracy," in *Harvard Law Review*, (2002) 116:1, pp. 19–162.

Bloxham, Donald. "From the International Military Tribunal to the Subsequent Nuremberg Proceedings: The American Confrontation with Nazi Criminality Revisited," in *History: The Journal of the Historical Association*, (2013) 98:332, pp. 567–591.
"Charter of the International Military Tribunal" in *American Bar Association Journal*, (1945) 31:9, pp. 454–457.
Estlund, David. "On Following Orders in an Unjust War," in *The Journal of Political Philosophy*, (2007) 15:2, pp. 213–234.
Finch, George. "The Nuremberg Trial and International Law," in *American Journal of International Law*, (1947) 41:20, pp. 20–37.
Gill, Terry. "The Nuclear Weapons Advisory Opinion of the International Court of Justice and the Fundamental Distinction Between the *Jus ad Bellum* and the *Jus in Bello*," in *Leiden Journal of International Law*, (1999) 12, pp. 613–624.
Helfman, Tara. "Francis Biddle and the Nuremberg Legacy: Waking the Human Conscience," in *The Journal Jurisprudence*, (2012) 15, pp. 353–372.
Koskenniemi, Martti. "Faith, Identity and the Killing of the Innocent: International Lawyers and Nuclear Weapons," in *Leiden Journal of International Law*, (1997) 10, pp. 137–162.
Lemkin, Raphael. "Genocide as a Crime Under International Law," in *The American Journal of International Law*, (1947) 41:1, pp. 145–151.
McMahan, Jeff. "Collectivist Defenses of the Moral Equality of Combatants," in *Journal of Military Ethics*, (2007) 6:1, pp. 50–59.
Schick, F.B. "The Nuremberg Trial and the International Law of the Future," in *American Journal of International Law*, (October 1947) 41:4, pp. 770–794.
Stewart, James G. "The End of 'Modes of Liability' for International Crimes," in *Leiden Journal of International Law*, (2012) 25:1, pp. 165–219.
Walzer, Michael. "Political Action: The Problem of Dirty Hands," *Philosophy and Public Affairs*, (1973) 2:2, pp. 160–180.
Winch, Peter. "The Universalizability of Moral Judgements," in *The Monist* (1965), 49:2, pp. 196–214.

Books

Ackroyd, Peter. *The Life of Thomas More* (New York: Nan A. Talese/Doubleday, 1998).
Arendt, Hannah. *The Human Condition* (Chicago & London: University of Chicago Press, 1998).
Aristotle. "Nichomachean Ethics," in Jonathan Barnes (ed.), *The Complete Works of Aristotle* (Princeton, NJ: Princeton University Press, 1995).
Augustine, (tr.) Henry Bettenson *Concerning the City of God Against the Pagans* (England: Penguin, 1984).
Bolt, Robert. *A Man for All Seasons* (New York: Vintage Books, 1990).
Brownlee, Kimberley. *Conscience and Conviction: The Case for Civil Disobedience* (Oxford: Oxford University Press, 2015).
Burke, Edmund. *The Works of the Right Honourable Edmund Burke* Vol. 1 (six Volumes) (London: Bell & Daldy, 1872).
Dicey A.V. (ed.) E.C.S. Wade, *Introduction to the Study of the Law of the Constitution* (London: MacMillan, 1961).
Foot, Philippa. *Natural Goodness* (Oxford: Clarendon Press, 2010).
Gilbert, G.M. *Nuremberg Diary* (United States: Da Capo, 1995).
Glanville, Luke. *Sovereignty and the Responsibility to Protect: A New History* (Chicago, London: University of Chicago Press, 2014).

Hare, R.M. *Essays on Political Morality* (Oxford: Clarendon Press, 1998).
Huntington, Samuel P. *The Soldier and the State: The Theory and Politics of Civil-Military Relations* (Cambridge, MA: Belknap Press of the Harvard University Press, 1981).
Kahn, Paul. *Sacred Violence: Torture, Terror and Sovereignty* (Ann Arbor: University of Michigan Press, 2011).
Kant, Immanuel (ed. and tr.) Mary Gregor and Jens Timmerman, *Groundwork of the Metaphysics of Morals* (Cambridge: Cambridge University Press, 2012).
Kelman, H.C. and Hamilton, V.L. *Crimes of Obedience* (New Haven and London: Yale University Press, 1989).
Lauterpacht, Hersch. *International Law and Human Rights* (United States: Archon Books, 1968).
Lemkin, Raphael. *Axis Rule in Occupied Europe: Laws of Occupation, Analysis of Government, Proposals for Redress* (Washington, DC: Carnegie Endowment for World Peace, 1944).
Machiavelli, Nicolo (ed.) Bernard Crick, *The Discourses* (England: Penguin, 1970).
McMaster, H.R. *Dereliction of Duty: Lyndon Johnson, Robert McNamara, the Joint Chiefs of Staff and the Lies that Led to Vietnam* (New York: HarperPerennial, 1998).
McNamara, Robert S. *In Retrospect: The Tragedy and Lessons of Vietnam* (New York: Vintage, 1995).
McNamara, Robert S, Blight, James G and Brigham, Robert K. *Argument Without End: In Search of Answers to the Vietnam Tragedy* (New York: Public Affairs, 1999).
Mettraux, Guenael (ed.) *Perspectives on the Nuremberg Trial* (Oxford University Press: Oxford, 2008).
Milgram, Stanley. *Obedience to Authority* (New York, HarperPerennial, 2009).
Moore, Cameron, *Crown and Sword: Executive Power and the Use of Force by the Australian Defence Force* (Australia: Australian National University Press, 2017).
Nozick, Robert. *Anarchy, State and Utopia* (New York: Basic Books, 2013).
Orend, Brian. *The Morality of War* (Canada: Broadview Press, 2006).
Osiel, Mark. *Obeying Orders: Atrocity, Military Discipline and the Law of War* (New Brunswick and London: Transaction, 2002).
Raz, Joseph. *The Morality of Freedom* (Oxford: Clarendon Press, 2009).
Ricks, Thomas. *The Generals: American Military Command from World War II to Today* (New York: Penguin, 2012).
Rodin, David and Shue, Henry (eds.) *Just and Unjust Warriors: The Moral and Legal Status of Soldiers* (Oxford: Oxford University Press, 2013).
Sands, Philippe. *East West Street* (Great Britain: Weidenfeld & Nicholson, 2016).
Schabas, William A. *Genocide in International Law: The Crime of Crimes* (Cambridge: Cambridge University Press, 2000).
Shakespeare, William. "King Henry V," in William George Clark and William A. Wright (eds.), *The Works of William Shakespeare* (London: MacMillian and Co., 1866).
Sherman, William T. (ed.) Jean V. Berlin and Brooks D. Simpson, *Sherman's Civil War: Selected Correspondence of William T. Sherman, 1860–1865* (Chapel Hill, NC: University of North Carolina Press, 1999).
Shirer, William. *The Rise and Fall of the Third Reich* (New York: Simon & Schuster, 2011).
Simmons, A. John. *Moral Principles and Political Obligations* (Princeton, NJ: Princeton University Press, 1979).
Simpson, Gerry. *Law War and Crime* (Cambridge: Polity, 2007).
Summers, Harry G. Jr., *Historical Atlas of the Vietnam War* (Boston and New York: Houghton Mifflin, 1995).

Taylor, Telford. *The Anatomy of the Nuremberg Trials: A Personal Memoir* (New York: Skyhorse, 2013).
Thompson, Dennis F. *Political Ethics and Public Office* (Cambridge, MA: Harvard University Press, 1987).
Thoreau, Henry D. *Civil Disobedience* (San Bernardino, CA: Black and White, 2014).
Tusa, Ann and Tusa, John. *The Nuremberg Trial* (United States: Skyhorse, 2010).
Wakin, Malham M. (ed.) *War, Morality, and the Military Profession* (Boulder, CO: Westview Press, 1986).
Walzer, Michael. *Just and Unjust Wars: A Moral Argument* (New York: Basic Books, 2000).
Walzer, Michael. *Arguing About War* (New Haven: Yale University Press, 2004).
Williams, Bernard. *Ethics and the Limits of Philosophy* (Cambridge, MA: Harvard University Press, 1985).
Williams, Bernard. *Moral Luck* (Cambridge: Cambridge University Press, 1999).
Williams, Bernard. *Problems of the Self: Philosophical Papers 1956–1972* (Cambridge: Cambridge University Press, 1999).
Wollstonecraft, Mary. *A Vindication of the Rights of Woman with Strictures on Political and Moral Subjects* (London: J. Johnson, 1792).
Wolfendale, Jessica. *Torture and the Military Profession* (Hampshire: Palgrave MacMillan, 2007).
Zimbardo, Philip. *The Lucifer Effect: Understanding How Good People Turn Evil* (New York: Random House, 2007).

United States Government Documents

Committee Study of the Central Intelligence Agency's Detention and Interrogation Program, Senate Select Committee on Intelligence, chaired by Dianne Feinstein, United States Senate, (2014). https://fas.org/irp/congress/2014_rpt/ssci-rdi.pdf

Newspapers

Bohlen, Celeste. "Italy Convicts Ex-SS Officers in '44 Killings," in *The New York Times*, Wednesday, July 23, 1997, p. A4. https://timesmachine.nytimes.com/timesmachine/1997/07/23/269581.html?pageNumber=4

8 Let the General Say No – Moral Space in the Shadow of Law

I argue that law – and conventions collateral to law – should relax the categorical stipulation that the general *must* comply with *any* of the minister's directions. In this chapter I reiterate my argument and approach some likely objections.

I contend law should offer an exception, so the general in supreme command might refuse unconscionable political direction. This is not unusual. As Jeremy Horder explains, the first and normal way to accommodate individual moral sense and principle is through the creation of a specific exemption or exception when a law touches on matters likely to involve conscientious decision.[1] For example, law allows concessions in relation to self-defence, necessity, and conscientious objection.[2] These exclusions integrate moral reasons *within* law. They are dispensations, which recognise the limits of explicit legal defining and the need for circumstantial reasonableness. But law wholly regulates exceptions or dispensation for special cases.[3] The point is: for law to allow generals moral space to refuse unconscionable direction would not undermine law's authority. Rather, allowing generals to refuse would acknowledge that generals bear the burden of responsible choice *within* the confines of legal doctrine. On my account, law would allow generals to refuse *only* when direction is unconscionable, in contravention of the Martens forms, which speak of "the laws of humanity or the dictates of public conscience." The common-sense idea of unconscionable direction was made vivid in the Eichmann case, where the Israeli Attorney General said:

> The conscience of the world, speaking with the voice of the International Military Tribunal, [at Nuremberg] declared that orders contrary to the principle of conscience and morality, orders that violate the essential imperatives on which human society is based and negate the basic rules without which men cannot live together – such orders constitute no defence, legal or moral.[4]

Duty and Decision

The general bears a duty to obey laws which protect important moral values and make our lives possible. But the general also has a duty to decide, and a duty to refuse when direction is unconscionable. Massimo Renzo offers a metaphor, where a nurse stands for the general and a doctor represents the government. Doctors

DOI: 10.4324/9781003527886-8

place nurses under a *pro-tanto* duty to follow direction. But if the doctor asks the nurse to do something that is medically inattentive or unconscionable, the nurse bears a moral obligation to refuse so as to safeguard the interests of the patient.[5]

Hobbes would have the nurse obey. On the Hobbesian account, no law, no matter how iniquitous or unreasonable can be unjust. Law is a determining reason and an over-riding justification for action.[6] Joseph Raz would have the nurse obey – unless there was an exception. For Raz law is categorically authoritative.[7] For Raz there is no point in having laws and authorities unless the laws and the judgements of the authorities are binding.[8] But the authority of law does not close out exceptions. Recognising what Lon Fuller called "a morality external to law, which makes law possible,"[9] an exception, enables law to accommodate individual moral sense and circumstantial reasonableness.[10]

Accepting the value of independent thinking and professional detachment but recognising that the general must be subject to the civil power, we might reflect upon the standard Mason J applied in *Ansett Transport Industries (Operations) Pty. Ltd. v. Commonwealth.*[11] In this case, Mason J found the Regulations vest discretion in the Secretary of the Department, who is described as the "decision-maker." Thus, the Regulations contemplate decision by the Secretary. If the Secretary is bound by the Regulations to merely accept direction from the Minister, it cannot be said decision is the Secretary's decision. Rather, if the Secretary is compelled by the Regulations to act on the Minister's decision, the decision and consequent action are rightly attributed to the Minister.[12]

But independently conscientious decision does not mean decision-makers might be absolutely sovereign.[13] In *R v. Anderson ex parte Ipec Air Pty. Ltd*,[14] Kitto J found proper independent decision to be:

> According to the rules of reason and justice, not according to private opinion; according to law, and not humour, and within those limits within which an honest man, competent to discharge the duties of his office, ought to confine himself.[15]

Similarly, in *Minister for Immigration and Citizenship v. Li*[16] French CJ found: "reasonable minds may reach different conclusions about the correct or preferable decision,"[17] but reasonableness "cannot be construed as … arbitrary or capricious or to abandon common sense."[18] Reasonableness "reflects a limitation imputed to the legislature on the basis of which courts can say that parliament never intended to authorise that kind of decision."[19] Following French CJ, Hayne, Kiefel and Bell JJ found an unreasonable exercise of a discretion would be "arbitrary," unwarranted in the circumstances, and lacking an evident intelligible justification.[20]

These ideas hint to the way law might offer generals discretionary space. But to be clear: I am not contending for freedom from legal control. As Dixon J held in *Shrimpton v. The Commonwealth*[21]:

> Complete freedom from legal control is a quality which cannot … be given under our Constitution to a discretion [since such a discretion would be]

> capable of being exercised for purposes, or given an operation, which would or might go outside the power from which the law or regulation conferring the discretion derives its force.[22]

Voluntarism, Resignation, and Closed Doors

Of course, the general volunteered to enter the armed forces and, over the course of many years, voluntarily accepted successive promotions and cognate status. By continued service over years, we can assume the general understood and agreed to the obligation of discipline and obedience borne by serving members. But it is unsound to presume that the moral implication of voluntarism trumps all other moral duties. Kimberley Brownlee observes: "no decision to take up an office could be so well-informed, so prescient, that it could bind us to follow the dictates of the office no matter what."[23]

Of course, even accepting my remarks about voluntarism, people might say reform is unnecessary, since the general might resign. In fact, critics like James Dubik will say that the general has a moral obligation to resign, rather than do something unconscionable.[24] But symbolic loss and prodigiously burdensome practical consequences make resignation well-nigh impossible. This is a strong claim, but the record suggests it is not unreasonable since no Australian general has resigned on a matter of principle. And even if resignation entailed no practical consequence, such as the loss of a vast salary and a remarkable official residence, there are mental hurdles. Ordinary work, let alone military service at high rank, contributes to the psychology of personal identity, to reputation, and to social status. Resigning means severing a long-term commitment to military service. Once resigned, generals will have consigned a deep-rooted vocation (we presume) to the past.[25] It is unreasonable that law makes resignation the *only* option.

Of course, resignation may be avoidable since the general might refuse behind closed doors. But suggesting law reform is unnecessary since the general can resist political injustice behind closed doors places the general in the position of religious people, banned by law from the exercise of their faith and forced to practice rituals in secret and at odd hours.[26]

In practice it is sensible to presume many generals do refuse behind closed doors. Equally, we may reasonably suppose many generals do not refuse, even behind closed doors. But this is beside the point. Notwithstanding closed doors, refusal (conscientious objection) is *contra* the law. Since the law is constitutional and made justly, since obedience to law is important for well-functioning society, and since no person is above the law it seems unreasonable to claim law reform is unnecessary since the general might break the law behind closed doors. Besides, sooner or later the general will be offered Hobson's choice: comply, resign, or be relieved. Rightly, the minister will always have preponderant power, because in a well-balanced system the military must be subordinate to civil authority. But an exception would allow the general to refuse in plain sight; thus, to engage the democratic devoir to transparency.

Out From Behind Closed Doors

Section 11 of the *Reserve Bank Act* 1959 (Cth.) elucidates the democratic commitment to transparency. Dealing with differences of opinion between the Reserve Bank Board and the Government, the section prescribes that the Government shall always prevail. But the Section also prescribes that if the Government forces a conclusion on the Bank, the Government's reasons and the reasons of the Board of the Reserve Bank shall be set before both Houses of Parliament, and thus made public. Thus, the Reserve Bank Act is a damper on political impetuosity, and an instrument of democratic transparency. The Act appreciates that faced by public exposure of a subitaneous folly plan, the politician is likely to think twice, and perhaps recant. Asking law to accompany the general out from behind closed doors I think along similar lines.

It is important for the general to have legal room to refuse so the public might be alerted to the prospect of political folly, and the tragedy of avoidable unjust war. Transparency does not dissolve common sense, prudent tact, and discretion. Some things are appropriately private. Properly private exchange includes cabinet discussion and conversation the general will necessarily have with political figures.[27] Rather, transparency is an antidote to political deceit, to furtiveness, to sly concealment. It is important for the general to refuse in public so the public might have an opportunity to see and to defend against the political folly of an unjust war.

But transparency is not a first-order reason. Following Frances Kamm, I note the difference between doing something *because* it will have an effect and doing it *in order to* produce an effect.[28] I do not contend that the general refuse unconscionable direction in plain sight in order to make a public spectacle. I do not presume that creating a public spectacle is a first-order reason. I argue for law reform so as the general might refuse unconscionable direction from politics. I ask for law to allow the general to refuse in plain sight *because* executive direction is unconscionable. It would be wrong for the general to hold the elevation of public awareness as a first-order reason to refuse political injustice. But the general will anticipate the need of public spectacle.

In the democracy, our political experience is exercised by the vote.[29] But beyond participation at the ballot, democracy depends upon transparency. Public scrutiny, public hearings, public reasons, and a free press are cardinal to democracy.[30] The vote goes only part of the way, and it can be deluding, since by the time the citizens get to cast a vote, the damage is usually done. And in the case of going to war, the damage is usually irreversible.[31] Second, the vote is deluding since it hinges on the promise of politicians who decide for themselves how political power is used and how political power is portrayed. Politicians offer up scripted speeches to mass television audiences. Their staffs construct political image in formulated press releases, in orchestrated interviews, in affected social media chirrups, and on the party web page. There is nothing spontaneous or unstructured, nothing so honest as face-to-face contact, nothing human or unaffected, no undoubted accountability. The politicians oversee their own publicity. They are luxated from the people they claim to represent, and in charge of the conditions that keep them separate.

They organise and conduct political life on terms contrived to privilege secrets and self-interest. They shy away from proper disclosure and straightforward public notice. Or at least some politicians behave this way. In democracy, a small class of decisions depends upon secrecy. In some circumstances, secrecy is essential to critical ends. In some circumstances, it is right that politicians keep things quiet. But for the most part, openness is necessary.

To voice an opinion and exercise judgement; to participate properly in the democracy, in the decisions that set the terms of collective life, the people must *see* what is going on. To decide responsibly, the people must *see* so they might comprehend. By itself, the assumption that the citizens are politically engaged when they have a vote is too narrow. Democracy should be more attuned to the people's gaze, to the "type of sight that partakes of supervision, inspection, examination and scrutiny"[32] in order that the working of public institutions might be generally understood and generally agreed.[33]

When the people cannot see, they cannot know what officials have done, and they cannot be consequential participants in their democracy. To see is to believe, to understand, and to trust. This is Shakespeare's point when he has Othello say to Iago: "Be sure of it; give me the ocular proof … / Make me to see it…."[34] Actions which infringe upon the rights and freedoms of the citizens must withstand publicity.[35] It was thus, that in *The Iliad*, Achilles dismissed a delegation from Agamemnon: "Let him not beguile me / with words again"[36] "go back to the great men of the Achaians, / and take them this message"[37] Tell the Greeks in public, says Achilles, so as they might see their leader, Agamemnon, for what he is; so his chicanery might not be hidden. But though he refused, Achilles recognised Agamemnon as king: Achilles did not try to oust Agamemnon. Homer has Nestor, make this point when he says to Achilles: "… though you are the stronger man, and the mother who bore you was immortal, / yet this man [Agamemnon] is greater who is lord over more than you rule."[38]

Nestor makes plain that conscientious refusal and public disclosure do not rise to mutiny. The general remains subordinate to the executive and bears the risk of dismissal. But when political secrecy is not critical for reasons of carefulness and public responsibility, then secrecy is merely astucious, and the democracy is impoverished.[39]

The Military Machine

It is a paradox that the liberal democracy which values individual autonomy and opposes unduly coercive law is protected by a military which demands obedience without regard for individual conscience.[40] The deep provenance of military illiberalism is Machiavellian. For Machiavelli, *virtu* (not virtue, but political prowess or statecraft) demands ruthless pragmatism.[41] In Book XVII of *The Prince*, Machiavelli offers the example of Hannibal and Scipio. The army rebelled against Scipio, since he gave his soldiers more licence than is consistent with military discipline. In contrast, Hannibal suffered no dissention. Hannibal was noted to be cruel in an inhuman degree.[42] In modern parlance we educe Hannibal when we speak of "military discipline" and chant the orthodoxy that military duty demands unquestioning obedience.[43] The judgements at Nuremberg mean this thinking is insupportable. At Nuremberg generals were hanged since they behaved like postmen delivering legal yet unconscionable orders without a moral second thought.

Huntington gives voice to a commonly unsatisfactory response to the Nuremberg judgements. Huntington says – and I agree with him – the soldier is a morally autonomous individual who bears ultimate responsibility for the judgements he or she makes.[44] Yet, Huntington offers a conventional lip-service to broad-spectrum ideas of human goodness, character, virtue, or excellence. Huntington claims that soldiers should obey unconscionable *legal* orders since legal orders are explicit and precise in a way the dictates of conscience are not.[45] Huntington tows an orthodox line: "obedience [is] the highest virtue of military men."[46] In the rattle between conscience and obedience to legal unconscionable orders, obedience is expected to win. But, at Nuremberg generals were hanged since they behaved this way. In the twenty-first century it is perverse for law to prescribe the same morally unconcerned obedience.

There is no doubt that discipline and obedience have their place. Machiavelli makes this plain in *The Art of War* when he has Fabrizio say to Cosimo "without [good] discipline observed and practiced with utmost care and diligence, never was an army good."[47] But the case against military drill and rote is strong.

> It is time wasting, excruciatingly boring for those with more than the most mediocre intellect, and a poor substitute for thought. Since it aims to govern behaviour by a set of rules and defines a rigid programme for different occasions, it cannot meet the unanticipated event. This may have fatal consequences, such as the possibility of admirals standing stiffly to attention, hands at the salute, while their battleships sink slowly under them.[48]

In conditions of general, willing, and responsible obedience, practical flexibility is a prerequisite for military efficiency and national security. Automatic conformance is essential to some things; parades for one thing; immediate action drills for another. But for the most part, robotic conformance is uncalled-for and properly effective militaries work against machine automatism.[49] Beyond set-piece parade square choreography, efficient soldiers must think, and improvise, and make calculated decisions. Soldiers must decide right from wrong – if this were not the case, why would so many of the world's militaries invest in military ethics education? *A fortiori,* generals must be expected to think for themselves, and law must make provision for this sort of responsible independence. Some plausible scenarios show national security will not be compromised.

Taking it as granted that the general would not refuse to effect a war in defence of the nation, let us suppose the general refused direction to effect expeditionary operations which, by any objective standard, were horrible and unconscionable. The general is between a rock and a hard place. Caught, as Bernard Williams has it, between "intervening and letting things take their course,"[50] the general knows refusal – even resignation – is not going to make unconscionable direction go away. Political leaders have seldom had trouble finding people to fight their unjust wars.[51] Thus the general is reasonably assured that were he to refuse – or resign – the vice-chief (let us assume an officer uninhibited by scruple) will be a fervent implementer of the minister's awful direction. The utilitarian answer is: the general should do as the minister wants, since the general gets to implement ministerial direction with at least a degree of moral feeling, and national security is not compromised. But even were the general to reject the utilitarian ultimatum, national security is not endangered, since the vice-chief becomes the zealous engine of the minister's direction.

Offering the general a right in law to refuse does not endanger the state any more than the general's resignation. Bad things will happen no matter what the general does. Unless the minister recants, the minister's plan will come about. The general's deep moral commitments and projects are up against the circumstances, no matter what.[52] I cannot and do not answer for the general. I argue only that law should offer the general a choice.

The general operates in the sort of environment where reflexive obedience is not valuable; an environment where argument and questioning are practical, possible, and constructive. The general is not a "combatant" who must do as ordinary soldiers do. The general must resist injustice and political folly. In fact, there is no case in history where forcing a general made a state more secure. Admiral of the Fleet, Jackie Fisher offers something of an example. Serving as First Sea Lord, Fisher resigned rather than accept Churchill's plan for the Gallipoli campaign. The Prime Minister, Mr Asquith, persuaded Fisher to remain. When the War Cabinet met on 28 January 1915, Asquith backed Churchill's plan. Once again, Fisher decided to resign and again he was persuaded to stay. The Gallipoli plan proceeded, the amphibious landing taking place on 25 April 1915. On 14 May 1915, irrevocable difference surfaced between Fisher and Churchill during a meeting of the War Cabinet. Feeling he could no longer be responsible for the war at sea, Fisher resigned the next morning.[53]

Forcing Fisher, the government wasted lives and strategic opportunity. Had Fisher enjoyed the legal opportunity to refuse Churchill, civil-military relations at the Admiralty would have been strained – as in fact they were. Fisher might have been relieved. (His resignation had the same effect.) But the dreadful landing at Gallipoli, *might* have been avoided.

Fleet Admiral Leahy offers another, slightly different example. Serving as Chief of Staff to Presidents Roosevelt and Truman, Fleet Admiral Leahy occupied the office which has come to be known as Chairman of the Joint Chiefs of Staff. After the Second World War, reflecting on the use of the atomic bomb, Admiral Leahy wrote a memoir in which he expressed strong opposition to the bomb. Admiral Leahy said: "not even the fanatical followers of Hitler and Hirohito, who committed so many other unspeakable atrocities, dared use poison gas, for fear of retaliation. To me, the atomic bomb belongs in exactly the same category."[54] After the atomic bomb was tested successfully, President Truman faced a decision; to use it or not.

The President was persuaded that the nuclear weapon would shorten the war against Japan and save American lives. Fleet Admiral Leahy opposed the use of the atomic bomb. He thought it was barbarous, and unnecessary, since to his mind Japan had been defeated by an effective sea blockade and a conventional bombing campaign.[55]

On the account of his memoir, the Admiral found himself confronted by a utilitarian decision which affronted his deep moral commitments. The record of history tells us that the Admiral decided to stick it out, to exercise the most constructive moral influence he could in a situation he found uncomfortable. Even if we accept there is no solid evidence that any high-ranking American military leader, other than General George C. Marshall expressed moral objections to the use of the atomic bomb on Japanese cities,[56] Admiral Leahy's memoir shows that a general can resist a perceived injustice and not jeopardise the national security. National security must not be compromised. But offering the general rights in law to refuse unconscionable executive direction will not hazard the state. The proceedings at Nuremberg establish that more harm is likely to ensue when generals are – or feel they are – coerced by the law. Aggressive war was waged, gas chambers were built, death camps were guarded, and daily murder was possible on a massive scale because law compelled obedience and because people lacked the moral courage to refuse.

Of course, if not reserve, it might be hubris which leads people as Homer has it, "beyond their very destiny."[57] This was the fate of Patroklos who sought honour beyond his station before Homer has the gods and then Hektor strike him down. In Patroklos, we see the pretension and vaulting swagger that defaces high command. We see the same run-amok gasconade in the example of General Macarthur. On 25 June 1950, North Korea invaded South Korea, starting the Korean War. After the United Nations authorised forces to assist South Korea, President Truman placed General Douglas MacArthur in command. Two more opposite figures would be hard to find. One was plain-spoken and modest, the other a near-genius egomaniac.

By the time Truman became president in the spring of 1945, after serving 82 days as Roosevelt's vice president, MacArthur was already a legend. First in his class at West Point, where he scored higher than all but two former graduates in the military academy's history, MacArthur was appointed Supreme Commander of the Allied Powers in Japan. When North Korean troops swarmed across the 38th parallel to capture the South Korean capital of Seoul, President Truman appointed MacArthur to command the resistance. Truman euphemised the war as a "police action." MacArthur knew better. Indeed, the problem was that MacArthur knew better.[58] On 27 November 1950, four Communist Chinese Armies attacked United Nations forces and drove them back. General MacArthur protested orders not to attack Chinese Communist forces north of the Korean border. Five days later, on 6 December, President Truman directed General MacArthur to clear all press releases and statements through the Secretary of Defense. Disregarding this directive, General MacArthur published an insulting surrender demand on 24 March. He also sent a letter to Congressman Joe Martin, the House Minority Leader, which criticised the President's foreign policy. After this letter was read on the floor of the House of Representatives, MacArthur was relieved.[59]

MacArthur demonstrates the problem of a defiant, shameless, sinuous general. But he does not defeat my claim for law reform. First, MacArthur was not *the* general in supreme command, he was *a* general appointed to theatre command. But most importantly, MacArthur exceeded the constraints of my proposal. I propose merely that the general have a right in law to refuse unconscionable direction from politics. MacArthur wanted to go further than this. MacArthur was relieved by the President and, in accord with conventional process, the order for his relief was signed by General Bradley the Chairman of the Joint Chiefs. The state was never jeopardised by MacArthur's vanity or perversity.

I do not contemplate a contumacious general. Rather, my proposal contemplates politics which would seek to overturn justice. General Shinseki goes part of the way towards an example. Between 1999 and 2003, General Eric Shinseki served as Chief of Staff of the United States Army. General Shinseki's tenure was notable for an exchange with the Defence Secretary, Donald Rumsfeld, and Paul Wolfowitz, the Deputy Defence Secretary. The exchange concerned the costs of war with Iraq.

On 25 February 2003 (just before the invasion of Iraq, which began on 19 March), General Shinseki testified to the United States Senate Armed Services Committee that several hundred thousand soldiers would be required to secure post-war Iraq. General Shinseki's estimate was publicly disputed by Mr. Wolfowitz, and by Mr. Rumsfeld. The *New York Times* reported

> both men were clearly irritated at the general's suggestion that a post-war Iraq might require many more forces than the 100,000 American troops and the tens of thousands of allied forces that are also expected to join a reconstruction effort.[60]

General Shinseki was very senior, but he was not the general in supreme command. Moreover, and more to the point, General Shinseki did not initiate any dispute. He answered a question put to him by a Senate committee. He answered that question to the best of his ability, and with a mind to his considerable experience as the commander of peacekeeping forces in Bosnia. The general was contradicted by political figures in public, likely for reasons of political convenience. The dispute between General Shinseki is an imperfect example of my claim that the law should offer the general room to resist political injustice. The general does, however, demonstrate that dispute – even in public – between the military and politics does not endanger national security.

The question which provoked this book is illustrated most clearly and recently by the case of General Milley and the president, Donald Trump: what does the general do when politics threatens to direct the military to some unconscionable act?[61]

On the evening of 1 June 2020, General Milley, Chairman of the Joint Chiefs of Staff, walked across Lafayette Square in company with President Trump and a phalanx of presidential advisers. The president intended to pose for photographs in front of Ashburton House, the parish house of St. John's Church. Ashburton House had been damaged by protesters the night before.[62] Earlier, the president had clashed with General Milley, the Attorney General William Barr, and the Defence Secretary, Mark Esper. The president wanted to invoke the *Insurrection Act* of 1807. He wanted the 82nd Airborne called up, and he demanded General Milley take personal charge. When General Milley and the others said the National Guard would be sufficient, Trump shouted, "You are all losers! You are all fucking losers!" Turning to General Milley, Trump said, "Can't you just shoot them? Just shoot them in the legs or something?"[63]

We wonder how the general handled the national security threat posed by the Commander-in-Chief? The answer is in General Milley's common sense resolve to decline orders which would involve the United States in unjust expeditionary war, or in operations against the citizens of the United States.[64]

Yet General Milley's *prima facie* rationality is problematic. Critics will not say that the more dubious suggestions offered up by the president were ethical or legal. Following Justice Marshall in *Gillette v. United States*,[65] critics say the general is subordinate to politics and, for this reason, duty bound to obey political direction. Critics accept political direction might be morally wrong, but insist it is not the place of the general to make this determination.

I shape a different course. I accept the subordination of the military to politics, but I do not believe the general in supreme command can plead obedience and sweep the problem of unconscionable political direction under the rug. The general bears a special responsibility to resist unconscionable direction from politics, and law should offer the general a right to refuse so resignation or non-conformity with law are not the only morally acceptable courses of action.

Critics will say, despite *prima facie* common sense, General Milley contravened the convention that the military is totally subordinate to politics, and military juniors are entirely subordinate to military seniors.[66] By conventional lights, "if the statesman decides upon war which the soldier knows can only lead to national catastrophe, then the soldier, after presenting his opinion, must fall to and make the best of a bad situation."[67] On these terms, obedience is unquestioning. My argument is different. Like Pauline Shanks-Kaurin,[68] I place value on responsible obedience, and I argue for law to enable individually responsible decision. I see supremacy of civil authority, not in the general's servility, but in the civil authority's unqualified power to relieve the general.

Individual Responsibility

Arguing for an exception so the general might refuse in plain sight, I argue for reform of law and the collateral conventions that dissolve individual responsibility and make the general merely another pair of hands among the culpable multitude. I am against the notion that injustice is excused so long as injustice is legal, against the idea that law can define and prescribe each little thing and against any suggestion that compliance with law is a defence against war's evil. I am against institutional practices designed to cover up political corruption, against the conventions of political concealment which deny citizens the right to know about, and the right to resist, political evil done in their name.

The unsound 2002 September Dossier, the 2014 report of the United States Senate Select Committee on Intelligence, the Chilcot Report, and the Afghanistan Papers reveal political immorality, done and disguised in the plain brown wrapper of legal language and due process. These reports give the general a very good reason to doubt the integrity of political actors, and a very good reason to say no.

But the significance of these reports goes beyond the exposure of instances of political scoundrelism. These reports are deeply and profoundly significant since they are the tips of an iceberg. Whilst they might speak to the deliberate villainy of only a very few people, the reports gesture to commonplace, morally unconcerned legal rationalisations. This is the problem of many hands rendered in the anonymous hum of bureaucracy and in the paradox of sophisticated, cultured people who commit great evil.[69] The historian Laurence Rees offers an insight when he describes the Wansee Conference – a January 1942 meeting of senior Nazi officials held at the villa Wansee in Berlin to work out the so-called "Final Solution." Rees says:

> Those who attended were not mad. They were not deranged. They were all successful men, holding down tough and difficult jobs. Most were highly educated – out of fifteen who sat round the table at Wansee, eight held academic doctorates. They discussed the extermination of the Jews in elegant and convivial surroundings. The invitation that Heydrich sent out for the meeting mentioned that lunch would be provided, and during the discussions cognac was served. The building they sat in was a stylish villa, with a terrace overlooking the lake – one of the most beautiful and popular recreation spots for Berliners.[70]

In Australia, the politicians and civil service bureaucrats are successful, seeming civilised people; they are well-dressed and well-spoken. Judging by their rhetoric they are concerned with truth and justice. They are not like the Nazis who, despite their refinement, embodied and lived out the cruel injustice their politics forced upon innocents. In Australian democracy – in liberal democracies ordinarily – the politicians and the bureaucrats live conventional lives. They write briefing papers in ambiguous official Escher sentences. They watch cricket in summer, footy in winter. Nothing they do seems to have even a minor negative effect upon global justice. The pervading social reality is benign. Most people are not expressly and emphatically involved in the premeditated deception of parliaments and the cruelty wrought by governments on peoples – but some people are. Most people in politics are not involved in orchestrated falsehoods or calculated malpractice. Most people are not implicated in smirk and mirrors hypocrisy and pretext – but some are. Recalling Robert Kempner's interrogation of the truculent Wansee participants after the Second World War, some people "know the things you have to know."[71] Some people are deeply involved in the moral contraventions of politics.

Kempner provokes us to wonder how these people might be believed when they claim to have "never realised," to have "never questioned," to have been "out of the loop," in a state of comprehensive ignorance, uncurious and unaware. Kempner provokes us to wonder how people doing responsible jobs could be oblivious to the point of irresponsibility. When the September Dossier, the United States Senate Select Committee report, the Chilcot Report, and the Afghanistan Papers reveal that parliaments and peoples are deceived, that torture happens though it is denied, and that wars are planned and initiated despite the absence of clear aims or clear strategy, Kempner asks us to question law that makes the general in supreme command powerless, merely another pair of hands.

No Patent Medicine

My proposal does not jeopardise the state. Neither does my proposal promise the riddance of evil doings. Bad things will happen. But bad things will not happen *because* the general finds the right in law to *refuse* unconscionable executive direction.

Asking law to allow generals the liberty to refuse unconscionable political direction I look for a chance to forestall fundamentally unjust, avoidable, unnecessary, unwinnable war; the sort of war I call unconscionable. But I am realistic. No war is entirely just or entirely compliant with international laws which seek to minimise war's inevitable harms. The best we can hope for is that war is the lesser of two evils. There is no patent medicine that will make war wholly just, and no magic that will stop war. In the world as we know it, if people are to succeed, they must conform to entrenched and problematic conventions.

The point is generals are people. Sometimes they will do well in a crisis, at other times they will be like senior officers described by the British brigadier and Member of Parliament, Edward Spears; confused by great events they had brought about, made small, puzzled, bewildered, and inconsequent by circumstances.[72]

Like most who get to the top, the generals will have sharp elbows, they will want to do well, and they will lean in the direction which does not always make for the best judgement, moral or practical.[73] The record of history verifies this statement. Detailing the looming menace of the Great War, Christopher Clark[74] and Barbara Tuchman[75] relate the tragedy of senior people addicted to deference, unable to break away from prevalent modes, and unable to resist political imprudence. Prepared to destroy the world they knew, no-one stood for common sense, no-one sought to avert conflict, no-one criticised a ruinous strategy.

Most likely, the general will be psychologically unable to resist the sort of avoidable, unwinnable, fruitless war I want avoided. But there is a chance. There is a possibility the general might take advantage of reformed law to refuse political injustice, the sort of folly war which has tarnished our past and blackened our present. This is a chance we cannot afford to pass up.

Conclusion

We must expect the general to safeguard our democracy. We must expect the general to be obedient. But we must not reduce generals to the level of postmen, anticipating nothing more than that the general pass on political direction without a moral second thought. We must expect practically efficient militaries, but we must also be concerned by the undiscriminating overstatement of utilitarian claims that so-called "military efficiency" depends upon unreflective compliance by all and sundry.

I argue that the general should obey the minister, refusing only when ministerial direction is unconscionable. The generals should not do what they believe to be unconscionable, and law should not force them to infringe the deep registers of their conscience.

On my account, section 8 (2) of the *Defence Act* should be reformed to say something like: "the Chief of the Defence Force must comply with any directions of the Minister except when direction by the Minister is unconscionable, infringing the laws of humanity or the dictates of public conscience."

Notes

1 Jeremy Horder, *Excusing Crime* (Oxford: Oxford University Press, 2004), p. 200.
2 Joseph Raz, *The Morality of Freedom* (Oxford: Clarendon Press, 2009), p. 77.
3 Joseph Raz, *The Authority of Law: Essays on Law and Morality* (Oxford: Clarendon Press, 1979), pp. 30–31.
4 *Attorney General of the Government of Israel v. Eichmann*, Unreported Minutes of the opening address, Chapter 1, Attorney General's Opening Address, "The Accused" by Mr. Gideon Hausner, p. 4.
5 Massimo Renzo, "Political Authority and Unjust Wars," in *Philosophy and Phenomenological Research*, (2019) 99:2, pp. 336–357, 344–345.
6 Thomas Hobbes (ed.), C.B. Macpherson, *Leviathan* (England: Penguin, 1985), Chap. 18, p. 232.
7 Joseph Raz, *The Morality of Freedom* (Oxford: Clarendon Press, 2009), p. 76.
8 Joseph Raz, *The Morality of Freedom* (Oxford: Clarendon Press, 2009), pp. 47–48.
9 Lon Fuller, "Positivism and Fidelity to Law: A Reply to Professor Hart," in *Harvard Law Review*, (1958) 71:4, pp. 630–672, 645.
10 Joseph Raz, *Practical Reason and Norms* (Oxford: Oxford University Press, 1999), pp. 187, 213–214.
11 (1977) 139 CLR 54.
12 (1977) 139 CLR 54, 83 *per* Mason J.
13 (1977) 139 CLR 54, 83 *per* Mason J.
14 (1965) 113 CLR 177.
15 (1965) 113 CLR 177, 189 *per* Kitto J.
16 (2014) 249 CLR 332.
17 (2014) 249 CLR 332, 351 *per* French CJ.
18 (2014) 249 CLR 332, 351 *per* French CJ.
19 (2014) 249 CLR 332, 350 *per* French CJ.
20 (2014) 249 CLR 332, 352 *per* Hayne, Kiefel and Bell JJ.
21 (1945) 69 CLR 613.
22 (1945) 69 CLR 613, 629–630 *per* Dixon J.
23 Kimberley Brownlee, *Conscience and Conviction: The Case for Civil Disobedience* (Oxford: Oxford University Press, 2015), p. 112.
24 James Dubik, *Just War Reconsidered: Strategy, Ethics and Theory* (Kentucky: University Press of Kentucky, 2018), pp. 85–86, 157–158.
25 Bernard Williams, "Politics and Moral Character," in *Moral Luck* (Cambridge: Cambridge University Press, 1999), p. 57.
26 Kimberley Brownlee, *Conscience and Conviction: The Case for Civil Disobedience* (Oxford: Oxford University Press, 2015), p. 29.
27 James Dubik, *Just War Reconsidered: Strategy, Ethics and Theory* (Kentucky: University Press of Kentucky, 2018), p. 120.
28 Frances Kamm, *Intricate Ethics* (Oxford: Oxford University Press, 2007), p. 95.
29 Ronald Beiner, *Political Judgment* (Chicago: University of Chicago Press, 1983)

30 *Scott v Scott* [1913] AC 417.
31 Dennis F. Thompson, *Political Ethics and Public Office* (Cambridge, MA: Harvard University Press, 1987), p. 24.
32 Jeffrey E. Green, *The Eyes of the People: Democracy in an Age of Spectatorship* (Oxford: Oxford University Press, 2011), p. 128.
33 John Rawls, *A Theory of Justice* (Cambridge, MA: The Belknap Press of Harvard University Press, 1999), p. 115.
34 William Shakespeare, "Othello," Act 3, scene iii, in *The Works of William Shakespeare* (London: MacMillian and Co., 1866), p. 896.
35 Cited in Dennis F. Thompson, *Political Ethics and Public Office* (Cambridge, MA: Harvard University Press, 1987), pp. 116–117.
36 Richmond Lattimore (tr.), *The Iliad of Homer* (Chicago and London: University of Chicago Press, 1961), Book 9, Line 376, p. 208.
37 Richmond Lattimore (tr.), *The Iliad of Homer* (Chicago and London: University of Chicago Press, 1961), Book 9, Line 421, p. 209.
38 Richmond Lattimore (tr.), *The Iliad of Homer* (Chicago and London: University of Chicago Press, 1961), Book 1, Lines 280–281, p. 66.
39 Dennis F. Thompson, *Political Ethics and Public Office* (Cambridge, MA: Harvard University Press, 1987), p. 38.
40 Samuel P. Huntington, *The Soldier and the State: The Theory and Politics of Civil-Military Relations* (Cambridge, MA: Belknap Press of the Harvard University Press, 1981), p. 463.
41 Russell Price, "The Senses of *Virtu* in Machiavelli," in *European Studies Review*, (1973) 3:4, pp. 315–345. *passim*.
42 Nicolo Machiavelli, *The Prince* with an Introduction by Gary J. Nederman (London: Watkins, 2007), p. 125.
43 Samuel P. Huntington, *The Soldier and the State: The Theory and Politics of Civil-Military Relations* (Cambridge, MA: Belknap Press of the Harvard University Press, 1981), pp. 71, 72, 73, 231.
44 Samuel P. Huntington, *The Soldier and the State: The Theory and Politics of Civil-Military Relations* (Cambridge, MA: Belknap Press of the Harvard University Press, 1981), p. 78.
45 Samuel P. Huntington, *The Soldier and the State: The Theory and Politics of Civil-Military Relations* (Cambridge, MA: Belknap Press of the Harvard University Press, 1981), pp. 77, 78.
46 Samuel P. Huntington, *The Soldier and the State: The Theory and Politics of Civil-Military Relations* (Cambridge, MA: Belknap Press of the Harvard University Press, 1981), p. 79.
47 Nicolo Machiavelli, *The Art of War* (Chicago and London: University of Chicago Press, 2005) Bk. II:140–141, p. 46, II: 167, p. 48, II: 281, p. 58, VI:116, p. 127.
48 Norman Dixon, *On the Psychology of Military Incompetence* (London: Pimlico, 1994), p. 178.
49 Bruce Condell and David Zabecki, Editors' Introduction to *On the German Art of War: Truppenfuhrung - The German Army Manual for Unit Command in World War II* (Mechanicsburg, PA: Stackpole Books, 2011), pp. 3–4.
Jim Storr, "A Command Philosophy for the Information Age: The Continuing Relevance of Mission Command," in *Defence Studies*, (2003) 3:3, pp. 119, 121, 122.
Colonel Ardant Du Picq (tr.), J.N. Greely and R.C. Cotton, *Battle Studies: Ancient and Modern* (Milton Keynes: Bibliobazaar, 2006), p. 53.
Charles C. Krulak, "The Strategic Corporal: Leadership in the Three Block War," *The Marine Corps Gazette*, (1999) 83:1, pp. 18–22, 21.
50 Bernard Williams, "A Critique of Utilitarianism," in J.J.C. Smart and Bernard Williams (eds.), *Utilitarianism: For and Against* (Cambridge: Cambridge University Press, 2008), p. 109.

51 Jeff McMahan, *Killing in War* (Oxford: Clarendon Press, 2009), p. 3.
52 Bernard Williams, "A Critique of Utilitarianism," in J.J.C. Smart and Bernard Williams (eds.), *Utilitarianism: For and Against* (Cambridge: Cambridge University Press, 2008), p. 97. Williams offers the case of "George the chemist."
53 Andrew Lambert, "John Fisher," in *Admirals: The Naval Commanders who Made Britain Great* (London: Faber and Faber, 2008), pp. 327, 330, 331.
54 Fleet Admiral William D. Leahy, *I was There: The Personal Story of the Chief of Staff to Presidents Roosevelt and Wilson, Based on His Notes and Diaries Made at the Time* (London: Victor Gollancz Ltd., 1950), p. 513.
55 Fleet Admiral William D. Leahy, *I was There: The Personal Story of the Chief of Staff to Presidents Roosevelt and Wilson, Based on His Notes and Diaries Made at the Time* (London: Victor Gollancz Ltd., 1950), pp. 513–514.
56 Barton J. Bernstein, "Ike and Hiroshima: Did He Oppose It?" in *The Journal of Strategic Studies*, (1987) 10:3, pp. 377–389, 386.
57 Richmond Lattimore (tr.), *The Iliad of Homer* (Chicago and London: University of Chicago Press, 1961), Book 16, Line 780. p. 351.
58 Tom Moran, "Truman, MacArthur and Korea: Two Icons of the 20th Century and the Gulf that Separated Them," *Chicago Tribune*, October 09, 2016, p. 8.
59 *President Truman's Dismissal of General MacArthur: A Case Study in Bureaucratic Politics* (National War College, 300 5th Avenue, Fort Lesley J. McNair, Washington, DC: National Defense University, 1995), pp. 2–3.
60 Eric Schmitt, "Pentagon Contradicts General on Iraq Occupation Force's Size," in *New York Times*, New York, Feb. 28, 2003, p. 1.
61 Susan B. Glasser and Peter Baker, "Trump's Last General: How did the Pentagon Handle the National Security Threat Posed by its Own Commander-in-Chief?" in *The New Yorker*, 15 August 2022, pp. 36–47.
Jeffrey Goldberg, "The Patriot: What does a General do When the Commander in Chief Undermines the Constitution?" in *The Atlantic*, (November 2023) 332:4, pp. 14–32.
62 Protests, which had raged outside the White House, and across the country, were in response to the 25 May killing of George Floyd, a black man, by a white police officer, in Minneapolis.
63 Susan B. Glasser and Peter Baker, "Trump's Last General: How did the Pentagon Handle the National Security Threat Posed by its Own Commander-in-Chief?" in *The New Yorker*, August 15, 2022, pp. 36–47, 40.
Jeffrey Goldberg, "The Patriot: What does a General do When the Commander in Chief Undermines the Constitution?" in *The Atlantic*, (November 2023) 332:4, pp. 14–32, 25–26.
64 Susan B. Glasser and Peter Baker, "Trump's Last General: How did the Pentagon Handle the National Security Threat Posed by its Own Commander-in-Chief?" in *The New Yorker*, 15 August 2022, pp. 36–47, p. 42.
65 *Gillette v. United States*, 401 U.S. 437 (1971), pp. 441–448.
66 Samuel P. Huntington, *The Soldier and the State: The Theory and Politics of Civil-Military Relations* (Cambridge, MA: Belknap Press of the Harvard University Press, 1981), p. 73.
67 Samuel P. Huntington, *The Soldier and the State: The Theory and Politics of Civil-Military Relations* (Cambridge, MA: Belknap Press of the Harvard University Press, 1981), pp. 76–77.
68 Pauline Shanks-Kaurin, *On Obedience: Contrasting Philosophies for the Military, Citizenry, and Community* (Annapolis: Naval Institute Press, 2020).
69 Dennis F. Thompson, *Political Ethics and Public Office* (Cambridge, MA: Harvard University Press, 1987), p. 40.
70 Laurence Rees, *The Holocaust: A New History* (New York: Public Affairs, 2017), pp. 252–253.

71 Mark Roseman, *The Wansee Conference and the Final Solution: A Reconsideration* (London: Folio, 2012), p. 61.
72 Edward Spears, *Prelude to Victory 1917* (London: Jonathan Cape, 1940), p. 435.
73 Bernard Williams, "Politics and Moral Character," in *Moral Luck* (Cambridge: Cambridge University Press, 1999), p. 68.
74 Christopher Clark, *The Sleepwalkers: How Europe Went to War in 1914* (New York: HarperPerennial, 2014).
75 Barbara Tuchman, *The Guns of August* (New York: Random House, 2014), p. 213. Henry Kissinger, *Diplomacy* (New York: Simon and Schuster, 1994), p. 201.

References

Australian Cases

Ansett Transport Industries (Operations) Pty. Ltd. V Commonwealth (1977) 139 CLR 54.
Minister for Immigration and Citizenship v Li (2014) 249 CLR 217.
R v. Anderson ex parte Ipec Air Pty. Ltd (1965) 113 CLR 177.
Shrimpton v. The Commonwealth (1945) 69 CLR 613.

United Kingdom Cases

Scott v Scott [1913] AC 417.

United States Cases

Gillette v. United States 401 U.S. 437 (1971), pp. 441–448.

Unreported Case Minutes

Attorney General of the Government of Israel v. Eichmann, Unreported Minutes held in the Library of St. Antony's College, the University of Oxford.

Journal Articles

Bernstein, Barton J. "Ike and Hiroshima: Did he Oppose It?" in *The Journal of Strategic Studies*, (1987) 10:3, pp. 377–389.
Fuller, Lon. "Positivism and Fidelity to Law: A Reply to Professor Hart," in *Harvard Law Review*, (1958) 71:4, pp. 630–672.
Glasser, Susan B. and Baker, Peter. "Trump's Last General: How did the Pentagon Handle the National Security Threat Posed by its Own Commander-in-Chief?" in *The New Yorker*, August 15, 2022, pp. 36–47.
Goldberg, Jeffrey. "The Patriot: What does a General do When the Commander in Chief Undermines the Constitution?" in *The Atlantic*, (November 2023) 332:4, pp. 14–32.
Krulak, General Charles C. 'The Strategic Corporal: Leadership in the Three Block War,' in *The Marine Corps Gazette*, (1999) 83:1, pp. 18–22. Reprinted in *Leatherneck*, (1999) 82:1, pp. 14–17.
Price, Russell. "The Senses of *Virtu* in Machiavelli," in *European Studies Review*, (1973) 3:4, pp. 315–345.

Renzo, Massimo. "Political Authority and Unjust Wars," in *Philosophy and Phenomenological Research*, (2019) 99: 2, pp. 336–357.

Shanks-Kaurin, Pauline. *On Obedience: Contrasting Philosophies for the Military, Citizenry, and Community* (Annapolis: Naval Institute Press, 2020).

Storr, Jim. "A Command Philosophy for the Information Age: The Continuing Relevance of Mission Command," in *Defence Studies*, (2003) 3:3, pp. 119–129.

Books

Beiner, Ronald. *Political Judgment* (Chicago: University of Chicago Press, 1983).

Brownlee, Kimberley. *Conscience and Conviction: The Case for Civil Disobedience* (Oxford: Oxford University Press, 2015).

Clark, Christopher. *The Sleepwalkers: How Europe Went to War in 1914* (New York: HarperPerennial, 2014).

Condell, Bruce and Zabecki, David (tr. and ed.) *On the German Art of War: Truppenfuhrung - The German Army Manual for Unit Command in World War II* (Mechanicsburg, PA: Stackpole Books, 2011).

Dixon, Norman. *On the Psychology of Military Incompetence* (London: Pimlico, 1994).

Dubik, James. *Just War Reconsidered: Strategy, Ethics and Theory* (Kentucky: University Press of Kentucky, 2018).

Du Picq, Colonel Ardant (tr.) J.N. Greely and R.C. Cotton, *Battle Studies: Ancient and Modern* (Milton Keynes: Bibliobazaar, 2006).

Green J. Edward. *The Eyes of the People: Democracy in an Age of Spectatorship* (Oxford: Oxford University Press, 2011).

Hobbes, Thomas. (ed.) C.B. Macpherson, *Leviathan* (England: Penguin, 1985).

Horder, Jeremy. *Excusing Crime* (Oxford: Oxford University Press, 2004).

Huntington, Samuel P. *The Soldier and the State: The Theory and Politics of Civil-Military Relations* (Cambridge, MA: Belknap Press of the Harvard University Press, 1981).

Kamm, Frances. *Intricate Ethics* (Oxford: Oxford University Press, 2007).

Kant, Immanuel (tr.) E.B. Ashton, *On the Old Saw: That May be Right in Theory, but it Won't Work in Practice* (Philadelphia: University of Pennsylvania Press, 1974).

Kissinger, Henry. *Diplomacy* (New York: Simon and Schuster, 1994).

Lattimore Richmond (tr.) *The Iliad of Homer* (Chicago and London: University of Chicago Press, 1961).

Lambert, Andrew. *Admirals: The Naval Commanders who Made Britain Great* (London: Faber and Faber, 2008).

Leahy, Fleet Admiral William D. *I was There: The Personal Story of the Chief of Staff to Presidents Roosevelt and Wilson, Based on His Notes and Diaries Made at the Time* (London: Victor Gollancz Ltd., 1950).

Machiavelli, Nicolo (tr. and ed.) Christopher Lynch, *The Art of War* (Chicago and London: University of Chicago Press, 2005).

Machiavelli, Nicolo. *The Prince* with an Introduction by Gary J. Nederman (London: Watkins, 2007).

McMahan, Jeff. *Killing in War* (Oxford: Clarendon Press, 2009).

Rawls, John. *A Theory of Justice* (Cambridge, MA: The Belknap Press of Harvard University Press, 1999).

Raz, Joseph. *Practical Reason and Norms* (Oxford: Oxford University Press, 1999).

Raz, Joseph. *The Morality of Freedom* (Oxford: Clarendon Press, 2009).

Rees, Laurence. *The Holocaust: A New History* (New York: Public Affairs, 2017).
Roseman, Mark. *The Wansee Conference and the Final Solution: A Reconsideration* (London: Folio, 2012).
Shakespeare, William. "Othello," in George Clark and William A. Wright (eds.), *The Works of William Shakespeare* (London: MacMillian and Co., 1866).
Simmons, A. John. *Moral Principles and Political Obligations* (Princeton, NJ: Princeton University Press, 1979).
Smart, J.J.C. and Williams, Bernard. *Utilitarianism: For and Against* (Cambridge: Cambridge University Press, 2008).
Spears, Edward. *Prelude to Victory 1917* (London: Jonathan Cape, 1940).
Thompson, Dennis F. *Political Ethics and Public Office* (Cambridge, MA: Harvard University Press, 1987).
Tuchman, Barbara. *The Guns of August* (New York: Random House, 2014).
Williams, Bernard. *Ethics and the Limits of Philosophy* (Cambridge, MA: Harvard University Press, 1985).
Williams, Bernard. *Moral Luck* (Cambridge: Cambridge University Press, 1999).

United States Government Documents

President Truman's Dismissal of General MacArthur: A Case Study in Bureaucratic Politics (National War College, 300 5th Avenue, Fort Lesley J. McNair, Washington, DC: National Defense University, 1995).

Newspapers

Moran, Tom. "Truman, MacArthur and Korea: Two Icons of the 20th Century and the Gulf that Separated Them," *Chicago Tribune*, October 09, 2016. https://www.chicagotribune.com/entertainment/books/ct-books-general-vs-the-president-hw-brand-20161005-story.html
Schmitt, Eric. "Pentagon Contradicts General on Iraq Occupation Force's Size," in *New York Times*, Feb. 28, 2003, p. 1. https://www.nytimes.com/2003/02/28/us/threats-responses-military-spending-pentagon-contradicts-general-iraq-occupation.html

9 Conclusion

Generally, debate concerning soldiers and politics has not spoken to the special case of the supreme commander, the general – or admiral or air chief marshal – serving as Chief of the Defence Force. Offering the only connection between the military and politics, the officer in supreme command has unique opportunity to resist unconscionable direction from politics to launch unjust war or to conduct or expand war unjustly. For all other officers and for ordinary soldiers, remote from politics and much less influential than the general, the decision to fight can be made only *after* the decision to go to war, *after* the mechanisms of war have begun to act. Only the general might act in the calm before the storm.

Mindful of the special obligations of supreme command, I have disputed the terms of section 8 (2) of the Australian *Defence Act*, which says: "the Chief of the Defence Force *must* comply with *any* directions of the Minister."

I point to a problem which is front, centre, and universal. Political direction can be "lawful but awful;" tailored to avoid legal pitfalls, yet morally wrong. In such a case, the familiar maxim holds the general must either comply or resign. James Dubik, for example, says "everyone including senior political and military leaders, remains a moral agent responsible for his or her conscience."[1] For Dubik, resignation recognises a fundamental moral autonomy, enabling people to remain "moral agents, not mere instruments of a government."[2] But the fact the general might resign hardly establishes that the state respects the rights of citizens to their conscience, or the positional obligation of the citizen who serves as general.

I have argued that law, and conventions collateral to law, take up an exception so the general might refuse executive direction which, though legal, is unconscionable. On my account, a reasonably liberal, democratic society should take the moral convictions of citizens seriously and enable individuals to examine and to act upon deeply held beliefs. In the case of the supreme command, this claim is extended and elaborated by the general's positional duty to exercise especially careful moral judgement.

The practical importance of this book is in the failure of the general to resist political injustice and in the larger failure of the army. This failure has been abetted by law which has outspread to shape the conventions, the etiquettes, and the proprieties of military culture. As law prescribes unquestioning obedience for the general, so soldiers are trained, coercively, to obey without question. Acculturated

DOI: 10.4324/9781003527886-9

to *feel* that when they are obedient, they do the right thing,[3] men and women in uniform come to be heedlessly obedient to destructive authority.

The Failure of the Army

Describing the *Psychology of Military Incompetence*, Norman Dixon detailed an authoritarian culture; supposedly justified by the need to ensure "military efficiency." I have experience of this culture. When I gave a talk to the Australian Command and Staff Course at the Australian War College on Tuesday, 1 March 2022, my claim for common sense moral reasonableness was resisted by army officers who insisted on the orthodox discipline-and-obedience culture. These officers said they carried pistols so they might shoot soldiers who refused orders. They claimed this sort of discipline makes an army efficient – whatever that means – and they said these things to me in a quarrelsome way as if, since I was a Navy officer, I did not understand.

Yet following the shambolic and shameful withdrawal from Afghanistan, where Afghan forces built at breathtaking cost collapsed in days, and after the awful Brereton Report implicates the Australian Special Air Service Regiment in war crimes, we might doubt the brilliance of an army set on foundations of blind obedience, rather than moral right conduct. At least we might question the brilliance and moral courage of the army's leaders. The absence of moral feeling is seeming in failure by the Chief of the Defence Force, or the Chief of the Army or indeed any other officer to resign or to accept moral responsibility for events detailed in the Brereton Report,[4] and in the decision to halt investigations into officers implicated in war crimes.[5]

When the Australian Army pulled out of Afghanistan, unclear objectives – variously dismantling the opium trade, furthering the rights of women, defeating the Taliban, defeating extremism, extending democracy – were unmade. Yet officers who commanded the fiasco have routinely been promoted and decorated. The failure of our politicians has played its part. But the army has been responsible for its own calamity. This is not to deny the courage of soldiers, who bear the physical burden and psychological trauma. But the bravery of soldiers does not dim the failure of leaders. Greedy for promotion and too nervous to speak truth to power, the army's officers are to blame for the bad running of our futile wars.

But only one officer, the general in supreme command, bears responsibility for the inauguration of our failed, purposeless, unjust wars. Only the general might refuse to turn political folly into practical calamity.

On my account, law should make it easier for the general to meet this obligation. When law says the general *must* comply with *any* of the Minister's directions, law makes it difficult, if not infeasible, for the general to resist injustice. But the decay of politics makes this sort of moral withstanding critical.

> Never has our future been more unpredictable, never have we depended so much on political forces that cannot be trusted to follow the rules of common sense and self-interest – forces that look like sheer insanity, if judged by the standards of other centuries.[6]

Nations have become powerful, not wise. The failure of nations was made poignant when, on 4 April 1967, Martin Luther King Jr. spoke at the Riverside Church in Manhattan. In a talk resonant with insight and high-mindedness, King spoke of the "long, dark, and shameful corridors of time reserved for those who possess power without compassion, might without morality, and strength without sight."[7] Beyond the cold-blooded, uncharitable, unpitying miscalculation of politics, there is also a deep river of mendacity which makes it difficult for the general to place unquestioning confidence in politics, and offer a good reason for legislative reform.[8]

The Debacle of Politics

In recent years, Western politicians have failed to recognise war as a rarely justified,[9] totally consuming, brutal endeavour which must be an absolutely last resort, and which must be won. Gerry Simpson describes a modern "pagan ethos: one unconstrained by commitments to non-intervention, or law or morality or the predilections of the Security Council."[10] There is a false confidence in exaggerated intelligence estimates,[11] and the misbelief that force is the only way to pursue international order.

In a statement made on publication of the Report of the Iraq Inquiry, Sir John Chilcot noted the Prime Minister, Mr. Blair, presented purported evidence of Iraq's "weapons of mass destruction" with an unjustified certainty.[12] The Iraq War was not a last resort, the Security Council was not convinced peaceful options to disarm Iraq had been exhausted and that military action was justified.[13]

In 12 volumes, the Chilcot Report details political deceit and failure which has become ubiquitous and comprehensively barefaced. "The Afghanistan Papers"[14] published on 10 December 2019, by the *Washington Post* and subsequently in a book by Craig Whitlock, detail prevalent and deliberate political duplicity. Boiling commonplace political misanthropy and underhandedness down to the example of one man, Justice Bell found the Australian prime minister, Mr. Morrison, had acted bizarrely, in secret, with an artful lack of transparency, to undermine the parliamentary democracy.[15] In the *New Yorker* Liz Cheney described Donald Trump. He has been judged liable for sexual abuse. In courts from Georgia to New York and Washington, DC, he faces four criminal indictments and 91 felony charges. (Of course, Trump denies all charges.) He has suggested that General Milley, the former chairman of the Joint Chiefs deserves to be executed. He has promised to wage vengeful "retribution" on the press, the Justice Department, the FBI, the IRS, and a host of other federal agencies. His persistence, shamelessness, and Republican pre-eminence exemplify the knavery of modern politics and defy understanding.[16]

The inevitably lying character of political speech sets up a kind of cynicism, an absolute refusal to believe in the truth of anything. As we lose confidence in the distinction between truth and falsehood, so we cede advantage to political liars who say anything to secure power.[17] As Michael Oakeshott has it, contemporary politics is an unpleasing spectacle. "The obscurity, the muddle, the excess, the compromise, the indelible appearance of dishonesty, the counterfeit piety, the moralism and the immorality, the corruption, the intrigue, the negligence, the meddlesomeness, the vanity, the self-deception."[18] Risk is real, and stakes are high. The run-amok moral trespass of political leaders who have effected a deliberate deceit to wage war they knew – or should have known – to be unwinnable, reveals the pressing need for reform of the law.

Commanding United Kingdom Forces to operations in Iraq in 2003, Admiral Boyce sought explicit assurance of the Attorney General that invasion was properly legal, which he received.[19] But "legality" does not erase moral doubt. Narrowly designed, official legality was nothing more than politically convenient.[20] Perhaps, were he morally concerned, Admiral Boyce should have resigned. But that is beside the point. The point is: purposive government falseness means it is not reasonable for the general to place unquestioning confidence in executive direction.

What is at Stake

In her book, *Last Witnesses*, Svetlana Alexievich asks us to wonder that we allow the general to be coerced to prosecute politically convenient, morally impermissible war. Alexievich details the accounts of men and women who were children when the Nazis invaded the Soviet Union in 1941. There is no introduction. Instead of a preface there is a question from Dostoyevsky:

> Can we justify our world, our happiness, and even eternal harmony, if in its name, to strengthen its foundation, at least one little tear of an innocent child will be spilled? ... this tear will not justify any progress, any revolution. Any war. It will always outweigh them. Just one little tear...[21]

The voices of children – horrified, hesitant, desperate, bewildered, and raw with heartbreak – hallow the subsequent pages.

> I remember it. I was very little, but I remember everything.... The last thing I remember from the peaceful life was a fairy tale that mama read us at bedtime. My favourite one – about the Golden Fish.... Dear Golden Fish ... In the morning I woke up from fear. From some unfamiliar sounds.... Then I remember the black sky and the black plane. Our mama lies by the side of the road with her arms spread. We ask her to get up, but she doesn't. She doesn't rise. The soldiers wrapped mama in a tarpaulin and buried her in the sand, right there. We shouted and begged: "Don't put our mama in the ground. She'll get up and we'll go on.[22]

Alexievich captures the child's gaze and the child's incomprehension of things clear, and horrid and indelible: "The hanged people were so frozen that, when the wind swung them, they tinkled. Tinkled like frozen trees in the forest..."[23] The voices of Alexievich's children carry across decades, insufficient against the experience they narrate, but all that is left of unimaginable horror. The children ask us to have a feeling for the human cost and moral significance of war, a significance beyond the ken of law but evident in war's unceasing, futile, and cruel reiteration. The children ask us to wonder that law might make the general a dogsbody, unable to resist political folly which preindicates unjust war.

Implications for Modern Politics and Warfare

When the United States and its coalition partners invaded Iraq in 2003, global publics were persuaded to believe a flotsam of mass destruction weapons would bob to the surface. This did not happen. War in Iraq – and the related war in Afghanistan – have proven to be an extended global tragedy. Propelled by exaggerated intelligence estimates, and by the misbelief that force is the only way to pursue international order and justice, the Iraq and Afghanistan wars have corroded conventional Westphalian restraints.

Confronted by the prospect of war, anxiety and protest were ubiquitous, notable, and notably ineffective. A conspicuous example is in the "revolt of the generals" in which six retired general officers publicly criticised Secretary of Defence Donald Rumsfeld and revealed their doubts about, and their objections to, war in Iraq.[24]

Plausibly, the general in Australia harboured moral concerns about war in Iraq and Afghanistan. But in Australia, conscientious misgiving is inconsequent, since legislation forces the general to comply with direction from politics. Arguing for reform of this sort of illiberal legislation, I ask us to reassess the supreme command, the nature of liberalism, and the effect of liberalism on the world.

In the liberal democracy it is not enough to determine upon a utilitarian solution to problems of national security and public order, and then to move on to the rest of the agenda. This is not to make light of the categorical importance of security and political good order, which depend upon reasonable force. Law, social stability, civil cooperation, and the like depend upon the coercion and constraint of individuals. But there is no slippery slope. In-the-moment utilitarian calculation does not extinguish durable principles. Exigency in one moment does not set a precedent. Exigency in one moment does not open a floodgate to wash away moral ideas. Every decision must be anguished over. No moral decision can be forced. No moral decision can be unthinking, automatic, or simply the following of precedent, routine, or law. The state ought never be ignorant of, or disinterested in, human rights and dignities. In the liberal democracy, the problem of good order requires constant attention, and constant reform.[25] This is a far-reaching assertion. When law prohibits moral speaking and moral refusal, then moral withstanding comes to be impossible or at least improbable. The seriousness of this situation is aggravated when those who are fettered – like the general – bear a positional onus to exercise autonomous moral judgement. Proscribing moral speaking and independent decision, law censors the general and coerces obedience; in effect, making the general an accessory to political crime.[26]

Of course, trade-offs are part and parcel of political life, and military life. Generals will get their hands dirty in defence of the nation. Indeed, it would be wrong if, on occasion, they did not. But illiberal law deprives the general of critical independent agency and makes the general an instrument to be used. I ask the democracy to think seriously about the supreme command.

Generals owe their appointment to political figures, and they are expected to be obedient to political direction. Even so, the general stands for the citizens. The significance of this remark is in the nature of the democracy, where sovereignty is in the people, and the highest duty of public office is to the people. To be obvious: the general capacitates violence in the name of the citizens, and for the sake of the citizens. If the Tomb of the Unknown Soldier, countless cenotaphs, and war graves maintained at public expense stand as monuments to those who offered military service to the democracy, they also stand as a metaphor for the service of the general, and for expectations democracy holds of the general.

The general is expected to be considered and careful, to think seriously about decisions, and to make decisions. Generals are not expected to do merely as they are told. The general is not above and beyond moral and legal requirements that apply to ordinary people. The general is expected to exercise responsible autonomous judgement, and to resist injustice.[27] The general owes an appointment to politics. But the legitimacy of the general obtains in only the barest degree from political validity. To be wholly legitimate, the general must abide by moral expectations, which find canonical expression in the Martens Clause.

But the general is not fitted for the task. The general is conditioned to conformability by military training and military life. The philosopher and suffragist, Mary Wollstonecraft saw the moral abrasion of coercive military training which meant standing armies can never consist of resolute, robust men. The soldiers may be well-disciplined, but they will seldom be men of evident moral courage.[28] Coercive military training works to eradicate moral autonomy and instill the habits of unreflective obedience.[29] I have experience of this training. At the Australian Defence Force Academy, midshipmen and officer cadets swear oaths and undertake various initiation ceremonies. They spend the first months of their enlistment marching and chanting; "left, right, left, right." When a path curves, a command is bawled; "follow the path around." There is a rococo, caricatural emphasis on hierarchy and compliance. Nothing is done unless it is commanded, or unless permission is granted. Travestying obedience, the Australian Defence Force Academy, like many (most?) military academies, acculturates habits of consensus and inattentive repetition. The quintessential methods of the military academies work because people have no sense organ for detecting duty or responsibility. Our apprehension of these ideas takes shape and colour from the activities, routines, rewards and punishments to which the ideas are connected.[30] The dogmas and Weltanschauung normalised at the academies are perpetuated in the ordinary routines of military life. Uniforms are worn in accordance with standards published in manuals of dress, people fill out limitless forms, they assume a baroque dialect of acronyms, jargon, and mannerism, and they abide by the serpentine etiquettes which are part and parcel of the daily grind.

The fetish for discipline-and-obedience which soaks military life derives licence from the myth of military efficiency. The idea of efficiency is entirely made-up, it is a modern watchword, a shibboleth, it means whatever the user intends it to mean. Military efficiency is undefined, but latent presumptions about strictness and subordination, regulation and drill must be defrocked. Conventional confidence in discipline-and-obedience is unmasked by the failure of orderly, methodical modern western armies in Iraq and Afghanistan, and by the success of an essentially amateur Ukrainian resistance. The Houthi militia, continue to confound some of the world's most powerful militaries. They fire rockets at international shipping and seem undaunted by strikes against their bases. In 2021 the Taliban returned to power, reversing their ouster by western armies.

The west needs to re-think the approach it takes to supreme command, to military service, and to war. It will not be good enough to repeat mistakes of the recent past, or the distant past. It will not be good enough to keep the general in supreme command shackled to the illiberal myth of unreflective, compulsory obedience. It will be unreasonable to keep up the marching and shouting, whilst our enemies learn from the example and experience of the militia and insurgent forces which confound conventional armies.

Bad Things Will Happen

Reflecting upon the mistakes of war in Vietnam, Henry Kissinger puts our failure in a nutshell: "a nation should not send half a million of its young to a distant continent or stake its international standing and domestic cohesion unless its leaders can describe their political goals and offer a realistic strategy for achieving them."[31] But Western governments don't have an evident long-term strategy. Governments allegedly fighting to advance justice and to end inequality turn a blind eye to tax havens, which enable the globe's richest to hide trillions. Governments profess to safeguard human rights, whilst trading with repressive regimes. For example, a Royal Commission found the Australian Wheat Board undermined sanctions against Iraq, thus supporting the regime of Saddam Hussein, to "work a trickery on the United Nations."[32] Governments turn blind eyes as corporations trade arms with regimes known for systematic cruelties. The Australian government, for example, is reported to have approved and concealed the export of arms to countries accused of war crimes.[33]

Resorting to war with an insufficient grasp of the need for war to be a last resort, and with an insufficient grasp of the unqualified need to win, nations have forgotten Caspar Weinberger, who rejected the reckless squander of military power. In an address to the National Press Club in Washington, DC on 28 November 1984, Weinberger argued military force must be used only when military means were critical to well-defined and urgently important political objectives, only with a clear military strategy, and dedicated to winning.[34]

For all humanity, we must discard our hypocrisy and face our obligations. We must accept that the world is not more secure, more just or better since we wage ceaseless war. The knee-jerk resort to military means must be made obsolete. The democracies must safeguard their interests and defend human rights, but they must not approach the challenge of statecraft spontaneously as a military challenge. The democracies must avoid the sort of war which has left Afghanistan a ruin, spiralling towards humanitarian catastrophe. Democracies must abandon legislation which makes the military a slave to political corruption and ineptitude.

Bad things will happen. But bad things should not happen because law makes it illegal for the general to resist injustice.

Conclusion

In the Australian Senate, on Wednesday, 4 March 2015, Senator Ludlum recognised the wrong of Ministers sending the nation to war on the basis of mediaeval notions of Crown prerogative. Senator Ludlum said:

> Australia is one of the few remaining democracies that can legally deploy its defence forces into conflict zones without recourse to the Parliament: the decision is reserved to the executive alone. As kindred democracies around the world have enacted reforms to vest the so-called 'War Power' in elected Parliaments, Australia has remained anchored to a pre-democratic tradition founded in hereditary monarchies and feudal states.
>
> If this anachronism had served Australia well, it might be possible to mount an argument that 'if it isn't broken, it doesn't need fixing.'
>
> If the horror unfolding in Iraq does not comprehensively put this view to rest, it is difficult to imagine what would. On the basis of fabricated and wilfully misinterpreted intelligence, Prime Minister John Howard followed the United States and the United Kingdom into an illegal and open-ended war in Iraq. Our Parliament, and by extension the voting public of Australia, were cut out of the decision, despite the fact that hundreds of millions of people around the world organised and campaigned against the decision to go to war.
>
> There are few credible analysts left anywhere who do not regard the decision [to go to war] as one of the most grievous strategic disasters in modern history. The vast majority of Australians were right, and the executive authorities in the US, the UK and Australia, were wrong….[35]

Similarly critical of the political unilateralism that botched the Vietnam War, Vice Admiral James Stockdale said: "What a mess! High-handed entry into the war … mismanagement of the battle, squandering of the public trust … nothing to show for it … and we are asked to close the books?"[36] Since we have had countless chances to learn, our failure is flagrant. Now is not the time to close the books, to turn a blind eye to law which leaves the general unprotected against unconscionable direction from politics.

Notes

1 James Dubik, *Just War Reconsidered: Strategy, Ethics and Theory* (Kentucky: University Press of Kentucky, 2018), p. 158.
2 James Dubik, *Just War Reconsidered: Strategy, Ethics and Theory* (Kentucky: University Press of Kentucky, 2018), p. 157.
3 Jeff McMahan, *Killing in War* (Oxford: Clarendon Press, 2009), pp. 119, 120.
4 Ben Packham, "Defence Ducks Probe into War Crimes Accountability," in *The Australian Newspaper*, 13 September 2022, pp. 1–2. Packham argues the Australian Department

of Defence failed to hold senior commanders properly accountable for war crimes. He reports findings of the independent Afghanistan Inquiry Oversight Panel that Defence has failed to bear the weight of its "corporate responsibility" for the murders of Afghan civilians and prisoners identified in the Brereton report.

5 Letter: General Campbell, Chief of the Defence Force to Lt. General Burr, Chief of the Army, ref. BN32034912 dated 19 July 2021 on the Defence Freedom of Information Disclosure Log dated 08 April 2022 reference 349–351–353–2122.
Letter: The Hon Peter Dutton MP, Minister for Defence to General Campbell, Chief of the Defence Force copied to the Secretary of the Department of Defence Mr. Moriarty, no reference, dated 2 June 2021, on the Defence Freedom of Information Disclosure Log dated 08 April 2022 reference 349–351–353–2122.
Ben Packham, "Officers Escape Punishment For 'Commando' Crimes," in *The Australian Newspaper*, April 12, 2022, pp. 1, 2. Note, however, that the Commando Regiment was not implicated by the Brereton Report in alleged war crimes. The Brereton identified soldiers of the Special Air Service Regiment as likely culpable.

6 Hannah Arendt, *The Origins of Totalitarianism* (Orlando, Austin, New York, San Diego, London: Harvest, 1994), vii.

7 Martin L. King, *A Time to Break Silence* (Boston: Beacon, 1994), p. 96.

8 Rt. Hon. The Lord Nolan, Committee on Standards in Public Life, Chairman, Rt. Hon. The Lord Nolan, *First Report of the Committee on Standards in Public Life, presented to Parliament by the Prime Minister* (London: HMSO, 1995), pp. 15, 16.
Jeff McMahan, "Collectivist Defenses of the Moral Equality of Combatants," in *Journal of Military Ethics*, (2007) 6:1, pp. 50–59, 58.
Hannah Arendt, "Lying in Politics," in *Crises of the Republic* (San Diego, New York and London: Harcourt Bruce and Company, 1969), pp. 4, 7.
Bob Woodward, *The Last of the President's Men* (New York: Simon & Schuster, 2015), pp. 113, 114.
Neill Sheehan, *A Bright Shining Lie: John Paul Vann and America in Vietnam* (New York: Vintage Books, 1989) pp. 269–386.
Aldous Huxley, 'Brave New World Revisited,' in *Brave New World and Brave New World Revisited* (New York: HarperCollins, 2004), pp. 333–334.
George Orwell, *Politics and the English Language* (England: Penguin, 2013) p. 14.
Thomas Pogge, "Making War on Terrorists – Reflections on Harming the Innocent," in *The Journal of Political Philosophy*, (2008) 16:1, pp. 1–25, 11.

9 Jeff McMahan, "The Morality of War and the Law of War," in David Rodin and Henry Shue (eds.), *Just and Unjust Warriors: The Moral and Legal Status of Soldiers* (Oxford: Oxford University Press, 2013), p. 31.

10 Gerry Simpson, *Law War and Crime* (Cambridge: Polity, 2007), p. 154.

11 Richard J. Aldrich, Rory Cormac and Michael S. Goodman, *Spying on the World: The Declassified Documents of the Joint Intelligence Committee 1936–2013* (Edinburgh: Edinburgh University Press, 2014), p. 391. The authors describe the distortion and misuse of intelligence, which was a feature of the infamous 2002 September Dossier tabled by Prime Minister Blair in the Commons.
Kenneth M. Pollack, "Spies, Lies and Weapons That Went Wrong," in *The Atlantic Monthly* (2004) 293:1, pp. 78–92, 78–92, 92.

12 Statement by Sir John Chilcot, p. 5.

13 Statement by Sir John Chilcot, pp. 1, 4.

14 Concerned about the war in Afghanistan, the United States Congress created the Office of the Special Inspector General for Afghanistan Reconstruction (SIGAR). In the preparation of reports concerning the war, SIGAR conducted interviews with policymakers and senior military officers. These interviews were kept secret, until the *Washington Post* filed two federal lawsuits and gained access to transcripts through the Freedom of Information Act.

15 The Hon Virginia Bell AC, *Report of the Inquiry into the Appointment of the Former Prime Minister to Administer Multiple Departments* (25 November 2022), pp. 6, 9, 19, 44, 89, 92, 93, 95.

16 Liz Cheyney, "Sleepwalking," in *The New Yorker*, (Dec. 18, 2023) pp. 7–9.
17 Hannah Arendt, "Truth and Politics," in *The New Yorker*, (1967) Feb. 25, pp. 49–88, 50, 78.
18 Michael Oakeshott (ed.), Timothy Fuller, *The Politics of Faith and the Politics of Scepticism* (New Haven: Yale University Press, 1996), p. 19.
19 Chilcot Report, Section 5, paragraph 702, p. 282.
20 Chilcot Report, Section 5.
Philippe Sands "A Grand and Disastrous Deceit: The Report of the Inquiry by John Chilcot," in *London Review of Books*, (2016) 38:15, pp. 9–11.
Jonathan Bailey, "The Political Context: Why We Went to War and the Mismatch of Ends, Ways and Means," in Jonathan Bailey, Richard Iron and Hew Strachan (eds.), *British Generals in Blair's Wars*, (London: Ashgate, 2013), p. 8.
21 Svetlana Alexievich (tr.), Richard Pevear and Larissa Volokhonsky, *Last Witnesses: An Oral History of the Children of World War II* (New York: Random House, 2019), p. xiii.
22 Svetlana Alexievich (tr.), Richard Pevear and Larissa Volokhonsky, *Last Witnesses: An Oral History of the Children of World War II* (New York: Random House, 2019), pp. 3, 4.
23 Svetlana Alexievich (tr.), Richard Pevear and Larissa Volokhonsky, *Last Witnesses: An Oral History of the Children of World War II* (New York: Random House, 2019), pp. 54–55.
24 Martin L. Cook, "The Role of the Military in the Decision to use Armed Force" in James T. Johnson and Eric D. Patterson (eds.), *The Ashgate Research Companion to Military Ethics* (Ashgate: Surrey and Vermont, 2015), p. 54.
David S. Cloud, Eric Schmidt and Thom Shanker, "Rumsfeldt Faces Growing Revolt by Retired Generals," in *The New York Times Newspaper*, April 13, 2006.
25 Bernard Williams, "Realism and Moralism," in *In the Beginning was the Deed* (Princeton: Princeton University Press, 2005), p. 3.
26 Hannah Arendt, *The Origins of Totalitarianism* (Orlando, Austin, New York, San Diego, London: Harvest, 1994), p. 432.
27 Telford Taylor, *The Anatomy of the Nuremberg Trials: A Personal Memoir* (New York: Skyhorse, 2013), pp. 252–253.
Also: Ann Tusa and John Tusa, *The Nuremberg Trial* (New York: Skyhorse, 2010), p. 438.
28 Mary Wollstonecraft, *A Vindication of the Rights of Woman and the Wrongs of Woman, or Maria*, Anne K. Mellor and Noelle Chao (eds.) (New York, Boston and San Francisco: Pearson Longman, 2007), p. 41.
29 Jessica Wolfendale, *Torture and the Military Profession* (Hampshire: Palgrave MacMillan, 2007), p. 128
30 Hilary Putnam, *Pragmatism and Realism* (London and New York: Routledge, 2006), p. 20.
31 Henry Kissinger, *Diplomacy* (New York: Simon and Schuster, 1994), p. 659.
32 Terence R.H. Cole, *Report of the Inquiry into Certain Australian Companies in Relation to the UN Oil-for-Food Programme* (Five Volumes, Vol. 1), Commissioner the Honourable Terence R.H. Cole, AO, RFD, QC (Canberra: Commonwealth of Australia, November 2006), p. xi.
The Economist, "Rolling up the Culprits: The UN's Oil-for-Food Scandal," (2008) 386: 8571.
33 Ben Doherty and Christopher Knaus, "Australia urged to stop selling weapons to countries accused of war crimes" in *The Guardian*, 15 January 2020.
Ben Doherty and Christopher Knaus, "Blanket secrecy surrounds Australian weapons sales to countries accused of war crimes," in *The Guardian*, 14 January 2020.
Dylan Welch, "Fighting Yemen's Dirty War: An Arab Military is Buying a Weapons System Made in Canberra," *Australian Broadcasting Corporation*, published 25 July 2019. https://www.abc.net.au/news/2019-07-25/australian-company-sending-weapons-systems-directly-to-uae/11322974

For example: *SIPRI Yearbook 2016: Armaments, Disarmament and International Security*, (Stockholm International Peace Research Institute: Oxford University Press, 2016). The SIPRI website offers databases describing international arms transfers: https://www.sipri.org.

34 John Stone, *Military Strategy: The Politics and Technique of War* (London: Bloomsbury, 2013), pp. 132, 133.

35 Commonwealth of Australia, *Parliamentary Debates*, Senate, 4 March 2015, p. 1174 (Senator Scott Ludlam).

36 Vice Admiral James Bond Stockdale, *Thoughts of a Philosophical Fighter Pilot* (California: Hoover Institution Press, Stanford University, 1995), p. 98.

References

Journal Articles

Arendt, Hannah. "Truth and Politics," in *The New Yorker*, (Feb. 25, 1967), pp. 49–88.

Cheney, Liz. "Sleepwalking," in *The New Yorker*, (Dec. 18, 2023), pp. 7–8.

The Economist, "Rolling up the Culprits: The UN's Oil-for-Food Scandal," (2008) 386: 8571.

McMahan, Jeff. "Collectivist Defenses of the Moral Equality of Combatants," in *Journal of Military Ethics*, (2007) 6:1, pp. 50–59.

Pogge, Thomas. "Making War on Terrorists – Reflections on Harming the Innocent," in *The Journal of Political Philosophy*, (2008) 16:1, pp. 1–25.

Pollack, Kenneth M. "Spies, Lies and Weapons That Went Wrong," in *The Atlantic Monthly*, (2004) 293:1, pp. 78–92.

Sands, Philippe. "A Grand and Disastrous Deceit: The Report of the Inquiry by John Chilcot," in *London Review of Books*, (2016) 38: 15 pp. 9–11.

Books

Aldrich, Richard J., Cormac, Rory and Goodman, Michael S. *Spying on the World: The Declassified Documents of the Joint Intelligence Committee 1936–2013* (Edinburgh: Edinburgh University Press, 2014).

Alexievich, Svetlana (tr.) Richard Pevear and Larissa Volokhonsky, *Last Witnesses: An Oral History of the Children of World War II* (New York: Random House, 2019).

Arendt, Hannah. *Crises of the Republic* (San Diego, New York and London: Harcourt Bruce and Company, 1969).

Arendt, Hannah. *The Origins of Totalitarianism* (Orlando, Austin, New York, San Diego, London: Harvest, 1994).

Bailey, Jonathan, Iron, Richard and Strachan, Hew (eds.) *British Generals in Blair's Wars* (London: Ashgate, 2013).

Cook, Martin L. "The Role of the Military in the Decision to use Armed Force," in James Turner Johnson and Eric D. Patterson (eds.), *The Ashgate Research Companion to Military Ethics* (Surrey and Vermont: Ashgate, 2015).

Dubik, James. *Just War Reconsidered: Strategy, Ethics and Theory* (Kentucky: University Press of Kentucky, 2018).

Huxley, Aldous. *Brave New World and Brave New World Revisited* (New York: HarperCollins, 2004).

King, Martin L. *A Time to Break Silence* (Boston: Beacon, 1994).

Kissinger, Henry. *Diplomacy* (New York: Simon and Schuster, 1994).
McMahan, Jeff. *Killing in War* (Oxford: Clarendon Press, 2009).
Oakeshott, Michael (ed.) Timothy Fuller, *The Politics of Faith and the Politics of Scepticism* (New Haven: Yale University Press, 1996).
Orwell, George. *Politics and the English Language* (England: Penguin, 2013).
Putnam, Hilary. *Pragmatism and Realism* (London and New York: Routledge, 2006).
Rodin, David and Shue, Henry (eds.) *Just and Unjust Warriors: The Moral and Legal Status of Soldiers* (Oxford: Oxford University Press, 2013).
Sheehan, Neill. *A Bright Shining Lie: John Paul Vann and America in Vietnam* (New York: Vintage Books, 1989).
Simpson, Gerry. *Law War and Crime* (Cambridge: Polity, 2007).
Stockdale, Vice Admiral James Bond. *Thoughts of a Philosophical Fighter Pilot* (California: Hoover Institution Press, Stanford University, 1995).
Stone, John. *Military Strategy: The Politics and Technique of War* (London: Bloomsbury, 2013).
Taylor, Telford. *The Anatomy of the Nuremberg Trials: A Personal Memoir* (New York: Skyhorse, 2013).
Tusa, Ann and Tusa, John. *The Nuremberg Trial* (New York: Skyhorse, 2010).
Williams, Bernard. "Realism and Moralism," in *In the Beginning was the Deed* (Princeton: Princeton University Press, 2005).
Wolfendale, Jessica. *Torture and the Military Profession* (Hampshire: Palgrave MacMillan, 2007).
Wollstonecraft, Mary. *A Vindication of the Rights of Woman and the Wrongs of Woman, or Maria*, Anne K. Mellor and Noelle Chao (eds.) (New York, Boston and San Francisco: Pearson Longman, 2007).
Woodward, Bob. *The Last of the President's Men* (New York: Simon & Schuster, 2015).
Zimbardo, Philip. *The Lucifer Effect: Understanding How Good People Turn Evil* (New York: Random House, 2007).

Commonwealth of Australia Parliamentary Debates

Commonwealth of Australia, *Parliamentary Debates*, Senate, 4 March 2015, p. 1174 (Senator Scott Ludlam).

Australian Government Documents

Bell, Justice the Hon Virginia, AC. *Report of the Inquiry into the Appointment of the Former Prime Minister to Administer Multiple Departments* (25 November 2022).
Campbell, General Angus, Chief of the Defence Force. Letter to Lt. General Burr, Chief of the Army, ref. BN32034912 dated 19 July 2021 on the Defence Freedom of Information Disclosure Log dated 08 April 2022 reference 349–351–353–2122.
Cole, Commissioner the Rt. Hon. Terence R.H., AO, RFD, QC. *Report of the Inquiry into Certain Australian Companies in Relation to the UN oil-for-Food Programme* (Five Volumes, Vol. 1) (Commonwealth of Australia: Canberra, November 2006).
Dutton, the Hon Peter MP, Minister for Defence. Letter to General Campbell, Chief of the Defence Force copied to the Secretary of the Department of Defence Mr. Moriarty, no reference, dated 02 June 2021, on the Defence Freedom of Information Disclosure Log dated 08 April 2022 reference 349–351–353–2122.

United Kingdom Government Documents

Chilcot, Sir John. (Chairman) Report of the Iraq Inquiry: *Report of a Committee of Privy Counsellors* (Twelve Volumes) (London: HMSO, 2016). https://webarchive.nationalarchives.gov.uk/20171123122743/https://www.iraqinquiry.org.uk/the-report/

Nolan, Michael, Lord the Rt. Hon. *First Report of the Committee on Standards in Public Life, Presented to Parliament by the Prime Minister* Committee on Standards in Public Life, Chairman (London: HMSO, 1995).

Newspapers

David S. Cloud, Eric Schmidt and Thom Shanker. "Rumsfeldt Faces Growing Revolt by Retired Generals," in *The New York Times*, April 13, 2006. https://www.nytimes.com/2006/04/13/washington/rumsfeld-faces-growing-revolt-by-retired-generals.html

Doherty, Ben. and Knaus, Christopher. "Blanket secrecy surrounds Australian weapons sales to countries accused of war crimes," in *The Guardian*, January 14, 2020. https://www.theguardian.com/world/2020/jan/14/blanket-secrecy-surrounds-australian-weapons-sales-to-countries-accused-of-war-crimes

Doherty, Ben. and Knaus, Christopher. "Australia urged to stop selling weapons to countries accused of war crimes," in *The Guardian*, January 15, 2020. https://www.theguardian.com/australia-news/2020/jan/15/australia-urged-to-stop-selling-weapons-to-countries-accused-of-war-crimes

Packham, Ben. "Officers Escape Punishment For 'Commando' Crimes," in *The Australian*, April 12, 2022, pp. 1, 2.

Packham, Ben. "Defence Ducks Probe into War Crimes Accountability," in *The Australian*, September 13, 2022, pp. 1, 2.

Public Statements

Chilcot, Sir John. Statement on the Release of the *Chilcot Report*. https://webarchive.nationalarchives.gov.uk/20171123123237/https://www.iraqinquiry.org.uk/

Internet Material

Stockholm International Peace Research Institute. https://www.sipri.org

Welch, Dylan, "Fighting Yemen's Dirty War: An Arab Military is Buying a Weapons System Made in Canberra," in *Australian Broadcasting Corporation*, published 25 July 2019. https://www.abc.net.au/news/2019-07-25/australian-company-sending-weapons-systems-directly-to-uae/11322974

Index

Note: Page numbers followed by "n" denote endnotes.

For Product Safety Concerns and Information please contact our EU representative GPSR@taylorandfrancis.com
Taylor & Francis Verlag GmbH, Kaufingerstraße 24, 80331 München, Germany

www.ingramcontent.com/pod-product-compliance
Ingram Content Group UK Ltd.
Pitfield, Milton Keynes, MK11 3LW, UK
UKHW022042061126
477531UK00009B/486
* 9 7 8 1 0 3 2 8 6 5 2 3 2 *